Growing
Vegetables

GROWING VEGETABLES

Series Concept: Robert J. Dolezal
Encyclopedia Concept: Barbara K. Dolezal
Managing Editor: Victoria Cebalo Irwin
Photography Editor: John M. Rickard
Designer: Jerry Simon
Layout Artist: Barbara K. Dolezal
Photoshop Artist: Gerald A. Bates
Horticulturist: Peggy Henry
Index: Dolezal & Associates

President/CEO: Michael Eleftheriou
Vice President/Editorial: Linda Ball
Vice President/Retail Sales & Marketing: Kevin Haas

Home Improvement/Gardening
Executive Editor: Bryan Trandem
Editorial Director: Jerri Farris
Creative Director: Tim Himsel

Created by: Dolezal & Associates,
in partnership with Creative Publishing international, Inc.,
in cooperation with Black & Decker.
BLACK&DECKER. is a trademark of the Black & Decker
Corporation and is used under license.

Library of Congress
Cataloging-in-Publication Data

Dolezal, Robert J.
  Growing vegetables : a basic guide to vegetable gardening /
author, Robert J. Dolezal ; photographer, John M. Rickard.
    p. cm. – (Black & Decker outdoor home)
  ISBN 1-58923-056-6 (soft cover)
  1. Vegetable gardening. 2. Vegetables. I. Title. II. Series.
S SB321 .D653 2002
635–dc21

                                        2002031397

PHOTOGRAPHY & ILLUSTRATION

PRINCIPAL PHOTOGRAPHY:

JOHN M. RICKARD: All photographs except where otherwise noted.

OTHER PHOTOGRAPHY AND ILLUSTRATION:

TIM BUTLER: pgs. iv (top), 3 (top), 5 (bot), 11 (top & bot), 28 (mid), 34 (mid), 54 (top), 60 (bot), 70 (mid), 107 (bot).

KYLE CHESSER: pgs vii, 66 (bot R), 68 (bot R), 76 (mid R).

CREATIVE PUBLISHING INTERNATIONAL: pg. 62 (bot).

DOUG DEALEY: pg. 4 (bot).

ROBERT J. DOLEZAL: pgs. 4 (top), 6, 36 (bot), 64 (bot), 68 (mid), 83 (top), 100 (bot), 110 (bot), 114 (bot).

THOMAS E. ELTZROTH: pgs: 105 (bot), 110 (top), 113 (top).

FLORA GRAPHICS: pgs. 100 (top), 104 (bot).

IMAGE POINT: pgs. v (3rd from top), 7, 22 (bot), 37, 58 (bot), 59 (step B), 66 (2nd from top), 76 (top, bot L & R), 102 (bot).

DONNA KRISCHAN: pgs: 66 (bot L), 70 (top).

SANDI MEHLER: pg. viii.

JERRY PAVIA: pgs: 3 (bot., GARDEN DESIGN: Freeland & Sabrina Tanner), 5 (top), 91 (bot), 111 (top).

PAM PEIRCE: pgs. 82 (bot), 104 (top).

CHARLES SLAY: pgs. 90, 101 (bot), 109 (top).

ILLUSTRATIONS AND CARTOGRAPHY: HILDEBRAND DESIGN

ACKNOWLEDGEMENTS

The editors acknowledge with gratitude the following for their assistance while preparing this book: Michelle Cunha and Beverly Shannon of Mt. Shasta, California, and Flora and Roger Smith of McCloud, California.

Growing
Vegetables

Author
Robert J. Dolezal

Photographer
John M. Rickard

Series Concept
Robert J. Dolezal

A Basic Guide to Vegetable Gardening

CREATIVE
PUBLISHING
international

CHANHASSEN, MINNESOTA

www.creativepub.com

C O N T E N T S

PRETTY, PRODUCTIVE VEGETABLE GARDENS

Page 1

THE GUIDE TO PRODUCTIVE GARDENS

Page 9

PREPARING FOR PLANTING

Page 21

Vegetable gardeners are a special breed. As a hobby, growing produce, fruit, and berries appeals to all generations, young and old. Anyone can participate, from a youngster helping to water rows of peas to an octogenarian tending an herb garden or a window box filled with chives.

In this book, the world of gardening will come alive as you discover it has special allure, heritage, and the appeal that has kept it at the forefront of hobby interest for many centuries.

I live and garden in a charmed setting—a warm, inland valley of California tempered by the moderating influences of the nearby Pacific—where gardening is a sport that begins in February or March and continues until November. Within 100 miles or so, every climate zone can be found, from freezing alpine to subtropical, each with its own seasons and rhythms. My son lives in the southern Cascades, where warm-season vegetables such as tomatoes and squash must wait until May for planting, and my hometown is a fog-bathed stretch of the coastal northwest, so mild that melons seldom ripen there.

I have vegetable gardening in my genes, and I have passed on my love for growing table produce to family and friends. My grandparents were vegetable gardeners, as were my parents, and the links of past generations are strong.

*"I have a garden
of my own.*

*Shining with every hue,
I loved it dearly while alone.*

*But I shall love it more
with you."*

THOMAS MOORE

Sharing first plantings with my wife and grandchildren marks for me the true beginning of the year in a way that the New Year's holiday fails to inspire. Even while what passes in these parts for winter winds still are blowing, spring seems just around the corner as I tuck the first tomato, summer squash, or pepper seed into a tray, wrap it loosely in plastic, and set it in the warmth of a sunny window to germinate.

And what of the bounty that results when it comes time to harvest? Does any heart fail to flutter as English peas warm from the vine are shucked and steamed? Does corn from the market ever rise to the wholesome richness of ears plunged into ice water right after picking, wrapped in foil, and seared on the grill? Can the delight children feel as they pick and eat ripe strawberries be compared to any other experience?

As a bonus, the garden is a place of respite and refuge from the cares of the world. Time spent hoeing and raking, pinching and picking, or hefting the weight of a ripening gourd amid the smells of sun-warmed foliage and flowers restores one's calm and perspective.

For those filled with the urge to try their hand at vegetable gardening for the first time, this book will satisfy their curiosity and answer their questions. For others who face challenges in an established garden, clear and concise explanations coupled with detail-filled photographs will shed new light on bed preparation, planting, culture, and the bounty of harvest, or help them choose a new vegetable for their garden.

Gardening is a pastime and an avocation to enjoy for a lifetime, one that will allow you to discover the satisfaction that comes from learning how to successfully grow vegetables, from choosing a site for your garden, through planning your beds, to storing and preserving your harvest.

Catching your eye as you glance over a neighbor's fence or drive along a suburban street or country lane—even as you gaze down from a city skyscraper—attractive vegetable gardens claim your attention. Side yards may be filled with tall rows of corn and beans, borders might sport lush plants with a bounty of tomatoes, and rooftops may be adorned with containers overflowing with produce that is interspersed with pots of colorful flowers.

Growing vegetables is a quiet, peaceful pastime with many rewards. It's a hobby that demands little in terms of specialized needs and equipment beyond a measure of your time, hands, and attention. From the earth, plants grow to yield succulent fruits, crisp greens, and other crunchy, flavorful produce. Their taste and texture remind us that homegrown is a far cry from store bought, and their beauty gives us a satisfaction that extends beyond mere nutrition. We are drawn by the very idea of nuturing plants, sowing and reaping, and we are inspired by the great gardens we see.

Vegetable gardens thrive in every locale, in every region. Whether a collection of pots on a patio or deck, a spread planted in neat rows, or a precisely planned layout of raised beds and terraces linked by inviting paths and bounded by rustic stone walls, a well-tended vegetable garden reflects its owner's care and pride of craft and is a linkage to gardeners everywhere and in every time.

Vegetable gardening is an ancient art, and for some of us its appeal may lie in ancestral memories held deep within us. For others, it's simply a retreat from the pressures of career and responsibility. Whatever may be our reasons for taking to the land, the desire to garden lies nascent within each of us. How we respond to this shared cultural calling is a celebration of both the hobby of gardening and a recognition of our mutual past. As the hustle and bustle of modern life weigh down our collective soul, we turn back to the soil as a place of refuge. In our gardens, we are released from stress, freed to enjoy the touch of sunshine on our faces, and contented as we see and hear nature's creatures and feel the textures and smell the scents of growing things around us.

Whether you garden in a large plot or a container, you can savor the delights of fresh, crisp, and tasty produce throughout the gardening season

Pretty, Productive Vegetable Gardens

Vegetable gardens easily blend both productivity and beauty, as this fine example demonstrates. It has raised-bed plantings that include perennial table grapes grown on trellises and broad-leaved rhubarb, annuals such as corn, leafy greens for use in salads, and various root vegetables, with tall sunflowers for their added charm, beauty, and heads filled with tasty seed.

CONTAINER VEGETABLE GARDENS

(Right) Tomatoes love the warmth of sheltered patios and decks.

(Below, left to right) Container plantings mix pepper, eggplant, cucumber, and marigold; fragrant and flavorful mint; and tomatillo and endive.

How better to try your hand at vegetable gardening than by growing pots of old-time favorites such as strawberries, tomatoes, or herbs on a sunny balcony, deck, or path? Container vegetable gardens bring a bounty of fresh, good-tasting produce within the grasp of city dwellers, gardeners with limited space, and those seeking a healthier alternative to market vegetables of doubtful age or origin.

You'll receive a big payoff when you garden in containers even as you conserve your time and resources. The amount of space you will need is small, suitable pots are economical, and soil can be obtained by the bag at your local garden center or nursery. With nursery starts, many vegetables mature in as little as 6–10 weeks from planting, and you'll have your first crop of leafy greens in a month.

Pots used to grow vegetables should be deep and tall rather than shallow and wide. If they are large, set them in their final location before you fill them with soil; after they're filled, they'll be quite heavy. Install them on so-called pot feet or other risers to allow them to drain properly.

Choose locations for your container vegetables that receive full sun for at least 6 hours per day—but remember that even shady locations also are suitable for some vegetables such as cabbage and spinach. Pick a position for your plants that also is protected from wind, which can cause stems to break or foliage to tear.

Begin your container vegetable garden with a strawberry pot or a mixed herb garden. Strawberry pots have numerous openings in their sides, each accommodating a plant that will produce two or three berries at a time, then repeat for several months. A small pot with 12 plants will yield a cereal bowl full of ripe strawberries several times a week throughout most of the summer. For a seasoning garden, plant kitchen herbs such as chives, oregano, parsley, rosemary, sage, tarragon, and thyme. Allow at least 6–8 sq. in. (39–52 cm²) for each plant in a mixed container, and harvest when the plants become well-established, usually in 6–8 weeks. Fresh herbs are more flavorful than those that have been dried, so add a bit to your culinary creations, take a taste, then pick and add more if needed.

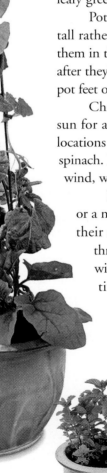

Gardeners also can experiment with salad greens such as amaranth, celtuce and Malabar spinach as well as root vegetables, including leeks, radishes, shallots, and salsify. Try planting Yukon gold potatoes in a half barrel, or grow tasty and unusually colored heritage tomatoes. You'll experience unsurpassed taste and pride as you pick produce directly from your containers.

SMALL-SPACE VEGETABLE GARDENS

Gardening in small spaces has become an increasingly popular activity as more of us live in city dwellings with limited green space or in homes with smaller yards. While it is true that those who would garden in downscaled plots should adjust their expectations and put away their tillers and forks, they still can have a large yield of flavorful, nutritious, vine-fresh produce and experience the feel of soil in their fingers.

Many homeowners plan compact vegetable gardens as an alternative to traditional landscaping around decks and patios. Often, small-space gardens are a combination of container plantings and in-ground beds, capitalizing on the benefits of both [see Container Vegetable Gardens, previous pg.]. While pots are movable, beds allow deep roots to form and increase the yield from the garden and the flavor of the vegetables.

Any space can be right for a vegetable garden. The two elements that truly are important—full sun and fertile soil—can be found in gardens of every dimension and scale. By using French intensive methods—spacing plantings closely together in enriched beds—gardeners can produce large harvests from a few plants. Plan your garden 1 sq. ft. (0.09 m^2) at a time, choosing those vegetables that you most enjoy growing and eating.

Consider planting a mixture of vegetables and flowering plants to increase the appeal of your vegetable garden. Some companions that attractively mix include green beans and scarlet runner beans, sweetpeas and English peas, and marigolds and red lettuce. Add to the size of your garden by using walls and hanging containers to fill otherwise vacant space. Trailing plants —mint, nasturtium, and rosemary—look best cascading down from overhead. Layer your garden using plants at your feet, others that grow on an arbor or are hung overhead, with still more that climb on supporting trellises.

A small-space vegetable garden is a treasure to both the eye and the soul. Soil, sunshine, and a strip of land will bring fulfillment to your life.

(Left) Sunny spots found on urban rooftops and balconies are good locations for containers and small beds of vegetables.

(Below) Freeland and Sabrina Tanner designed this attractive stone wall bordering a garden path as a niche for arugula, lettuce, and parsley, along with an espaliered pear tree, tulips, and viola.

RAISED BEDS AND FRENCH INTENSIVE GARDENS

(Right) These strawberry plants are planted in French intensive mounded rows of rich compost, then mulched with black plastic. The plastic warms their soil and helps conserve moisture.

(Below) Radishes.

(Bottom) The neat appearance of a raised-bed garden complements the diverse, heavy-bearing plants it contains. Such gardens have many convenient paths, making their plants easy to access and maintain.

Building planter boxes may seem like extra effort when your soil is right at hand, but a quick glance at the photograph below will reveal the special appeal such gardens hold, both functionally and aesthetically.

In Europe, such gardens were first developed in those countries where the space for cultivation always has been at a premium. French, Spanish, Belgian, and Italian gardeners, among others, soon found that planting in such beds reduced the amount of labor required to sustain their gardens and increased the yield from their plots.

Similar approaches to gardening also were practiced in Asia, where Chinese and Japanese gardeners used intensive methods to produce bountiful harvests despite the limits of space and soil. Their familiar rice paddies are really submerged intensive plots.

From both regions, raised-bed cultivation spread throughout the world, and today, this gardening technique is positively regarded for its neat and orderly appearance as well as for the outstanding results it provides.

Installing a raised-bed garden allows you to overcome the challenges posed by rocky, clay-filled, or boggy soil by replacing it in the limited areas used to grow your vegetables. The beds raise the soil surface, limiting the need for bending and stooping during care, and they add visual interest to the landscape.

Planting in raised beds also dramatically increases the yield of the garden because soil conditions within them can be made ideal for rearing plants and the beds tend to warm up earlier in the spring, extending the growing season.

If you presently rear vegetables in containers, you may wish to try microgardening, a more intensive gardening technique that calls for sowing individual plants in areas as small as 1 sq. ft. (0.09 m²). You can use this approach to grow exotic vegetables or special varietals. When only a small space is used, bell jars, cold frames, and applying specialty fertilizers become practical.

In a later chapter, you'll learn how to build raised beds in your own garden [see Preparing a Raised Bed, pg. 29]. They'll make your landscape more attractive even as they increase the yield of vegetables.

HILLSIDE TERRACE GARDENS

In landscapes where there are hillsides, retaining wall terraces and planters made of structural timbers, stone, and masonry can create fertile planting spots that restrain erosion and provide flat surfaces for planting. By creating a series of steps that are walled on the downside slope and filled with rich garden soil, you can increase dramatically your area for growing vegetables.

The retaining walls hold the soil in place, preventing erosion during periods of rain. They also allow you to add amendments to the planting soil that improve its texture or alter its acid-alkaline balance. Besides being efficient and practical, terraced hillsides often are among the most attractive and interesting of vegetable gardens.

When planning a terraced garden on a steep slope, it's important to recognize the substantial weight and structural forces that affect it. A gallon (3.8 l) of rain water weighs about 8 ⅓ lbs. (3.8 kg), and a single sustained downpour may add significant weight to the soil behind your retaining walls unless the water can pass through weep holes or other drains in them. In general, it's a good idea for garden walls taller than 2 ft. (60 cm) to be designed and built following the recommendations of an engineering professional and using materials that are specified for your terracing project and particular site.

(Left) Terraces built on steep slopes sometimes are narrow and closely spaced. They make excellent spots for planting paired rows of beans, lettuce, and peas.

(Below) This formerly vacant hill is lush with both vegetable and flower plantings. Galvanized pipes secured to posts are a safety aid used to ascend or descend steeply pitched steps linking the terraces.

Gentle slopes often are ideal sites for building dry-stacked field-stone walls. In addition to giving your garden the benefit of interesting texture and adding value, these walls allow water to drain easily through spaces between the stones. They step backward, leaning into the hillside, as they rise in height, granting them great stability. Many such walls also have ample room for built-in niches and ledges suitable for containers of flowering plants or trailing vines, even statuary and fountains, to add visual appeal to your landscape.

A major advantage of many wall-and-terrace gardens is the ease of their care. You can stand at the foot of a terrace and cultivate, hoe, weed, or water the plants in the tier above with less bending.

A hillside terrace garden has all of the benefits of a French intensive garden, plus the added beauty that a lush and productive vegetable garden can add to your home's backyard.

ROW GARDENS

Row gardens are the classic vegetable gardens most often pictured in the mind's eye. Where space permits, crops planted in long lines from north to south take advantage of both morning and afternoon sun, each plant receiving its fair share. Space between the rows permits easy access for maintenance tasks such as cultivation and irrigation. Row gardens are spacious, attractive, and neat.

Before you create a row garden, bear a few considerations in mind. First, any sod or turf either must be cut and removed or turned, allowed to decompose, and tilled. Once that's done, you can establish a perimeter. Often, row gardens exist without formal boundaries, but the most attractive ones have borders of tidy stone, brick, timber, fencing, or flowers. A border serves a practical purpose, too. Establishing a clear, well-defined edge eases mowing or sowing of nearby areas. Furthermore, borders often act as barriers to nuisance animal pests.

Row gardens have other practical advantages. Because a single vegetable species is planted in each furrow, successions of crops can be planted over time to provide for a sustained harvest. It's easy to imagine such planning in use—think of corn plants of varying heights or young peas planted next to more mature vines, two common plant successions. Harvest can proceed along the row, guaranteeing a steady production of tender, fresh vegetables as the season progresses.

Irrigating a row garden is easy. A trench beside each row provides an even flow of water to the base of every plant, and use of soaker hoses and special irrigation appliances is a simple matter of straight-line runs [see Laying Drip and Soaker Hose Irrigation, pg. 35]. Watering tends to be more consistent for rows than would be the case for other vegetable garden layouts, since the water penetrates equally to all plants along the row.

Another benefit of these gardens is that they tend to be healthy. The free circulation of air around the rows of plants allows them to dry quickly in the morning sun after a dewy night or a morning irrigation, limiting the potential for fungus and mildew infections. Also, tall plantings such as corn shelter lower-growing rows from the effects of wind.

Consider a row garden if your site's space permits and the idea of a neat and orderly, usually rectangular-shaped layout appeals to you. If the area previously was used as a garden, so much the better. Otherwise, prepare the site for planting by giving it a good tilling, removing all rocks and debris, amending the soil to a depth of at least 18 in. (45 cm), and raising the rows [see Preparing Beds, Hills, and Rows, pg. 31].

If the size of the garden is limited, you can save space within each row by offsetting every other plant to double your yield over planting in a straight line. Take advantage of vertical space, too, growing vines on trellises, fences, and supports.

Large or small, a row garden will always draw favorable comment from passersby.

(Opposite pg.) Row gardens often are a good choice for growing your vegetables in flat, regular plots. Linear rows, spaced for the needs of both the plants and gardener, permit easy cultivating, watering, and harvesting of their produce.

(Below) Scarlet runner beans on poles, each supporting six plants, make a striking addition to both garden and table. Their tasty pods are filled with richly creamy and flavorful beans. Like all the other plants in this row garden, they are arranged in long, neat lines.

The Guide to Productive Gardens

Make your garden all that it should be, matching it to your climate and site, while planting it with an eye to your needs and future

The requirements of a vegetable gardener are quite different from those of a landscape or flower gardener. While each is striving for beauty in the yard, one with vegetables first in mind usually is seeking a bounty of flavors and tastes in addition to a visual treat.

Great vegetable gardens begin with an appreciation for the benefits of fresh, homegrown produce. They are valued for their scent, flavor, and crisp or succulent textures, which appeal to your senses; their wholesome goodness as measured by the vitamins and minerals they contain; and their addition to the pantry, a bonus for your household budget.

To achieve a bounty of vegetables, you first must know the factors that influence their growth and production of fruit or leafy greens. Besides your climate, the most important of these elements are your garden site, the lay of the land, and the presence—or absence of—sunlight and good air circulation. Knowing your climate and site will help you make important decisions about your vegetable garden, including the basic layout of its beds, hills, and rows.

Both novice gardeners and experienced hands with several seasons under their belts will appreciate the wisdom of choosing their plantings by following some simple rules of space planning. Whether bound by the size of your garden or by the quantity of vegetables you wish to harvest, using a grid system to space your plantings is an excellent idea. After you consult the supplied diagrams with suggested space allocations for many common vegetables, you'll soon be filling your beds with the plants you prefer and enjoy.

What other helpful hints are there for creating a productive garden? In the following pages, you will find information to help you choose quality tools, which will ease the tasks associated with caring for your vegetables, reduce the amount of effort they will require, and save you time. You also will become familiar with materials that are time-proven standards for growing vegetables, from mulches to fertilizers and soil amendments.

Finally, an array of helpful advice, ranging from the electronic answer to the spoken word, is available to you should you experience a challenge in your vegetable garden.

Vegetable gardens that overflow with bountiful produce all season long are created by their caretakers through careful acts of planning as they design their beds, select and plant healthy vegetables from seed or seedlings, and tend and nurture them as they grow. The results of these efforts are apparent to all.

FRESH AND NUTRITIOUS VEGETABLES

What is the appeal of homegrown vegetables? For many of us, it is love at first bite—the luscious rush of flavors that fill our mouths. It's as though our ancestral memories have come alive, stirring from deep within. "Ahh," we say to ourselves, "so that's how corn is supposed to taste!"

The simple truth is, homegrown vegetables bear little resemblance to truck farm or grocery store produce. While we welcome the commercial growers' ability to put fresh berries and grapes on store shelves in midwinter, something always is missing when it comes to their product's flavor and texture. Part of the reason stems from the practical needs of the growers. They rear vegetable plants that produce harvestable, shippable produce. Too often, the result is flavorless, woody, hard fruit and limp greens—and sometimes the illusion of wholesome freshness is just that.

(Above) Fresh-picked squash, corn, tomatoes, peppers, and parsley exemplify the bounty available in your produce garden. Each day allows you to harvest something new, choosing between the many vegetables that can be grown at home during the garden season.

(Below) A tossed salad made from curly-leaved lettuce, sweet bell peppers, cucumber, carrots, and tomatoes, topped with tangy feta cheese and cured calamata olives brings the tastes found in a seaside Greek taverna right to your own kitchen table.

Those red-ripe tomatoes found in your local supermarket likely were picked hard and green, trucked many miles, and treated en route with ethylene gas to turn them red prior to your purchase. Their appearance might fool the inexperienced eye, but the test they're sure to fail rests in your taste buds. Commercially grown tomatoes—selected genetically for their ability to endure mechanical picking without bruising or spoilage—lack the essential sugars and fully developed texture of vine-ripened fruit.

Homegrown vegetables, by comparison, are nature-packed with flavor to spare and hold a complete complement of nutrients. Grown with your loving care, they have time to fully develop, are loaded with wholesome sugars and other carbohydrates, and have a bonus of healthy vitamins. They travel from garden to table in minutes or hours rather than days or weeks, sparing them the inevitable conversion of their sugars into tasteless starches. Organic and pure, they deliver on every promise made to your sight, scent, and touch—both at harvest and on your table.

Productive vegetable gardens exist in harmony with their surroundings, climate, and site. When it comes to growing vegetables, location, elevation, prevailing winds, sunlight, and a host of other factors affect your success.

The U.S. Department of Agriculture (USDA) has divided the world into 10 hardiness zones, based on the average lowest temperatures they experience during winter [see USDA Plant Hardiness Around the World, pgs. 116–117]. Take a few minutes to determine your hardiness zone by consulting the USDA maps. Knowing your zone will help you predict which plants will survive in your yard. Because the zones relate indirectly to the length of the growing season, they also are helpful guides to which vegetables you'll be able to grow.

In addition to hardiness zones, microclimates—localized climatic variations—can affect your plants' performance. These temperature fluctuations result from the effects caused by surrounding foliage, structures, and the lay of the land. Low areas may trap cool air and influence the growth of your plants; in a similar fashion, a slope facing the sun will be warmer and drier than other areas. Take note of conditions near walls, fences, trees, and structures such as sheds and fences in the area you intend to garden, as well as the amount of sunlight your garden will receive during each season, and how exposed it is to prevailing winds. The best gardens are full-sunlight areas free of strong winds. While many vegetables will grow in locations with as little as 4–6 hours of sunlight daily, only a few will thrive with less. Drying winds reduce their numbers even more.

It's possible that the area you plan to garden is shaded by surrounding trees or structures. Pruning foliage and limbs will permit sunlight to penetrate through many deciduous trees, increasing the amount of light your vegetables will receive. Painting walls and fences white reflects sun back into shady areas of the garden, also making a real difference in the plants' ability to grow and produce.

Gardens of the deep south and the desert southwestern United States may experience high temperatures that limit the plants that will grow in summer to heat-loving vegetables. They still are suited for planting cool-season vegetables during the winter months, and are called "reverse-season" gardens. Regions with mild-winter conditions such as southern California, Florida, and Hawaii also may be suited to autumn or winter plantings because frosts are rare and daytime conditions are warm and sunny.

Choose your site with care and foresight. The right location is likely the most important factor in successful gardening. Once you have determined the proper site, you can plan your garden's layout.

CLIMATE AND EXPOSURE

(Left) Early frost may be in your garden, but hardy crops such as pumpkin, winter squash, and root and cole vegetables will add rich flavors to family meals long into the winter season.

(Below) Even, regular watering, whether from natural sources such as rain or from irrigation, is an essential element of growing good garden vegetables.

(Bottom) Most vegetables prefer full-sun locations. Ensure all your plants receive their fair share by planting beds in north-south rows.

GARDEN OPTIONS AND DECISIONS

One of the most enjoyable aspects of vegetable gardening is the planning you'll do in the weeks and months before it's time to plant. You should start this process by choosing the best location for your garden [see Climate and Exposure, previous pg.]. Next, you'll determine its size by weighing two factors: your needs and your available space.

Most vegetable gardens are limited in their scope by the area available to plant. If your garden has room to sprawl, you'll only have to consider which vegetables to plant and how many are necessary to satisfy your needs. If instead your garden must match the scale of an area within a smaller yard—or is limited still further to containers or small-space beds—you'll want to use so-called intensive methods to yield as much produce as is possible from the space you have available.

(Right) In a few weeks, you'll be choosing healthy young plants for your garden. Now is the time to plan which vegetables you wish to grow. Use information found on plant care tags to help in your selection, or get all the necessary information on specific cultivars by consulting the catalogs sent by growers or seed packages.

(Below) Planning your plantings helps you to visualize your garden, and it records your start-of-season decisions for reference if a plant does exceptionally well or succumbs to disease or pests.

The decision to grow vegetables intensively is a matter of choosing the plants that most interest you and dividing your space to accommodate them. A few vegetables require a number of plants to yield quality produce. Corn, for instance, needs cross-pollination, which is achieved best by close group plantings. Most other vegetables, however, can be grown successfully either solo or in isolated beds comprising just a few plants. Separating plantings also helps prevent pests and diseases.

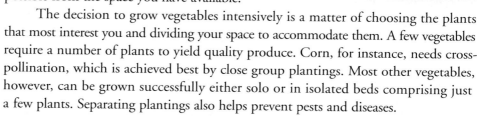

Start by listing the vegetables you want to grow. The most popular vegetables include beans, carrots, peas, peppers, pumpkins, salad greens such as lettuce and spinach, and tomatoes. Your choices might extend to okra, southern peas, potatoes, swiss chard, and watermelon, or you may want to try growing unusual vegetables such as gourds, peanuts, or popcorn.

Once you have made your initial selections, consult the plants in the back of the book [see Vegetable Encyclopedia, pgs. 79–115]. You'll find recommendations for yields and spacing. As you choose vegetables for your beds, decide on the number of vegetables to plant and note the space that they'll require.

Finally, sketch out your planting areas. One popular method for arranging vegetable plantings is to use a grid based on square-foot (0.09-m^2) units. Example bed layouts can be found on the following pages; use graph paper and colored pencils to plan sections of your beds and design your own garden. The diagrams allow for use of vertical space as well as the soil area, and some plants such as peppers and bush and pole beans have two options for spacing. Armed with your vegetable list and plot sketches, you'll be ready to prepare your garden for planting.

BUILDING GARDENS IN SMALL UNITS

Using a grid system is an easy way to visualize your vegetable garden, especially if you choose to have successions of crops grown in the same space at different times throughout the gardening season. Succession plantings allow you to reap harvests from more than one vegetable in a limited amount of space, increasing your garden's yield. Examples of successions include carrots, beets, and peppers; radishes, corn, and winter squash; chard, canteloupes, and endive; and spinach, green onion, and cucumber.

Try to think of your garden beds as a series of equal squares, each 1 ft. (30 cm) to a side. You can fill either an individual square or several combined squares with a vegetable planting, according to your garden's size and your needs. Because most beds are rectangular, the examples on the pages that follow show rectangular and square gardens with plant allocations based on the needs of a single household member. Circular and triangular plans also are shown, to aid you in fitting plants into irregular beds. If your household has more than one member, or if a vegetable is particularly popular with one or more of you, simply multiply the squares needed to fit your needs.

It's best to draw a scale diagram of your own garden on graph paper, using a scale of ¼ in.=1 ft. (6 mm=30 cm). Then, using colored pencils, shade the squares to show your plantings by counting the number of squares used for each vegetable in the example garden diagrams and transferring an equal number of squares—or multiple if you have several family members—to your garden diagram. Keep an eraser handy, and try to visualize how the garden will look as it grows. Substitute other vegetables by consulting the plant lists given for each grid planting diagram.

As you fill in your grid, keep your garden's climatic conditions in mind. Avoid planting tall vegetables to the sunny side of the garden; it's best to have the plants increase in height as you move away from the sun. If your garden is subject to prevailing wind, plant your tall crops to that side so that they will shield the rest of your plants from it. Areas that receive light from the sun as well as by reflection from a light-colored fence or a structure's walls are best for warm-season vegetables that grow best with lots of heat—examples include eggplants, melons, peppers, and tomatoes—especially if they are protected from wind. Open areas with a few hours of shade will be the right spots for cool-season vegetables, such as broccoli, cauliflower, radish, spinach, and Swiss chard.

An important consideration for corn is planting a sufficient number of plants in close proximity so that they cross-pollinate; the diagrams for corn allow for this need. Assist pollination by shaking each plant as its tassels ripen with pollen. For other plants, dividing the plantings among several areas has multiple benefits. It will make your garden more attractive, limit the spread between plants of any pest infestations and diseases, and allow you to grow other vegetables after the plantings mature.

Remember that each garden is unique while the recommendations given are general in nature. Let your growing experience be your guide. It's better to allow a bit more space for each vegetable than you need, but keep in mind that too many zucchinis are often produced by a single vine.

Trace bed layouts using the grid diagrams and bed layouts shown on the pages that follow, or use graph paper to draw a diagram of your garden's unique design. Either method can be helpful as you choose which vegetables you'll plant and allocate spaces for them in your garden.

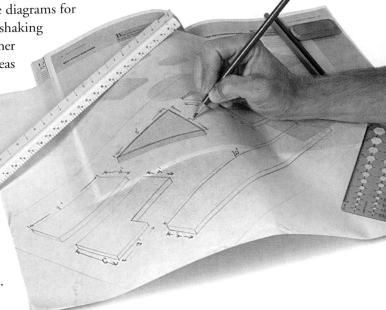

GRID-PLANTING DIAGRAMS

Placing plants in your garden beds is easy when you use a grid system. Each diagram shows how to plant the seed or seedlings of one or more vegetable species. Plant adjacent areas using the same or different grids, and mix different vegetable species in your beds to vary your harvest.

Some diagrams allow multiple plants in a single square; visually divide the area as shown into the orange dashed units and place the number of plants required. Other diagrams use two, three, four, or nine base squares; divide the area according to the orange dashed lines, and place a seedling at the center of each area or as shown in the diagram.

For best results, make small, separated plantings of each vegetable rather than a single, massed planting. Dividing your plantings will reduce disease or pest damage.

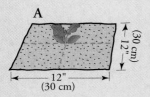

A
Broccoli
Cauliflower and
   Broccoflower
Collards
Corn (Late)
Horseradish
Husk Tomato and
   Tomatillo
Melon, Summer
Melon, Winter
Peanut
Popcorn
Potato
Strawberry
Sunflower
Sweet Potato and
   Yam
Tomato (Vine)

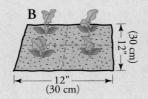

B
Amaranth
Beans: Dried, Fava,
   and Lima (Pole)
Endive and Escarole
Lettuce: Butterhead,
   Celtuce, Crisphead,
   Leaf, and Romaine
Rutabaga
Shallot
Spinach (New Zealand)
Swiss Chard

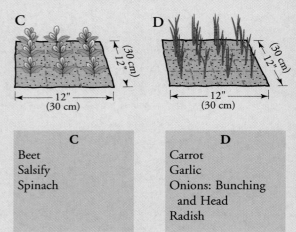

C
Beet
Salsify
Spinach

D
Carrot
Garlic
Onions: Bunching
   and Head
Radish

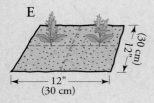

E
Celery and Celeriac
Chinese Cabbage
Kohlrabi
Leeks
(on vertical supports)
Beans: Lima (Bush)
Chicory, Belgian
   Endive, and
   Radicchio
Cucumbers

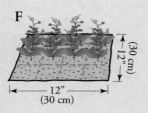

F
(on vertical supports)
Chickpeas or
   Garbanzo Beans
Beans: Snap, Wax,
   and Romano (Bush
   or Pole)
Peas: Garden and
   Sugar (Bush or Pole)

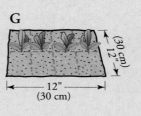
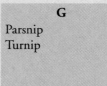

G
Parsnip
Turnip

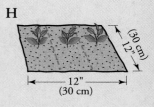

H
Eggplant
Jerusalem Artichoke
   or Sunchoke
Peas: Southern and
   Black-eyed

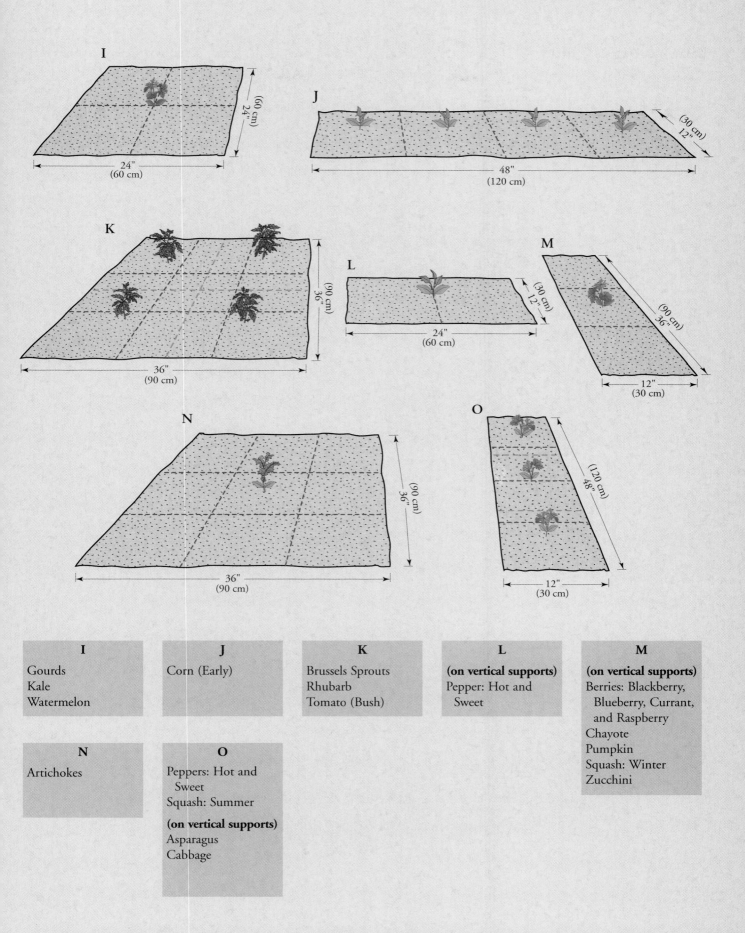

I
24"
(60 cm)
(60 cm)
24"

J
48"
(120 cm)
(30 cm)
12"

K
36"
(90 cm)
(90 cm)
36"

L
24"
(60 cm)
(30 cm)
12"

M
12"
(30 cm)
(90 cm)
36"

N
36"
(90 cm)
(90 cm)
36"

O
12"
(30 cm)
(120 cm)
48"

I	J	K	L	M

Gourds
Kale
Watermelon
	Corn (Early)	Brussels Sprouts
		Rhubarb
		Tomato (Bush)
			(on vertical supports)
			Pepper: Hot and
			Sweet
				(on vertical supports)
				Berries: Blackberry,
				  Blueberry, Currant,
				  and Raspberry
				Chayote
				Pumpkin
				Squash: Winter
				Zucchini

N	O
Artichokes	Peppers: Hot and Sweet Squash: Summer **(on vertical supports)** Asparagus Cabbage

BED LAYOUT DIAGRAMS

Beds may be square, round, rectangular, or triangular, as shown in the examples below, or irregular in shape.

Combine the beds shown to fill larger areas, create L- or T-shaped layouts, or long, narrow rows. For example, square 4-ft. (1.2-m) beds can be combined to make a rectangle 4 × 8 ft. (1.2 × 2.4 m).

Each bed has been divided into roughly equal areas for ease of use with spacing diagrams [see Grid-Planting Diagrams, pg. 14].

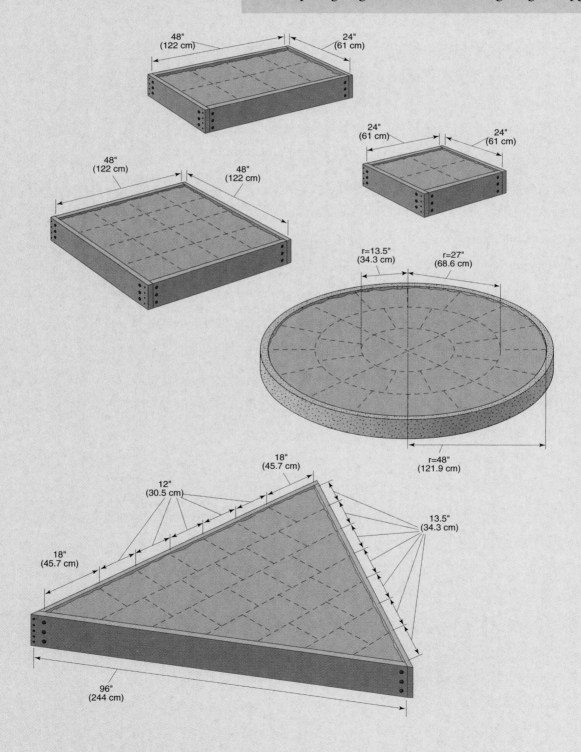

PLANTING SUCCESSION DIAGRAMS

Succession planting can allow you to grow and harvest several different vegetables in the same bed during a single season. For convenience, an example bed is shown below at three different times during the season.

Many different successions are possible. Typically, start the year with plantings of fast-maturing, cool-season vegetables. As they are harvested, plant warm-season species to replace some or all of them.

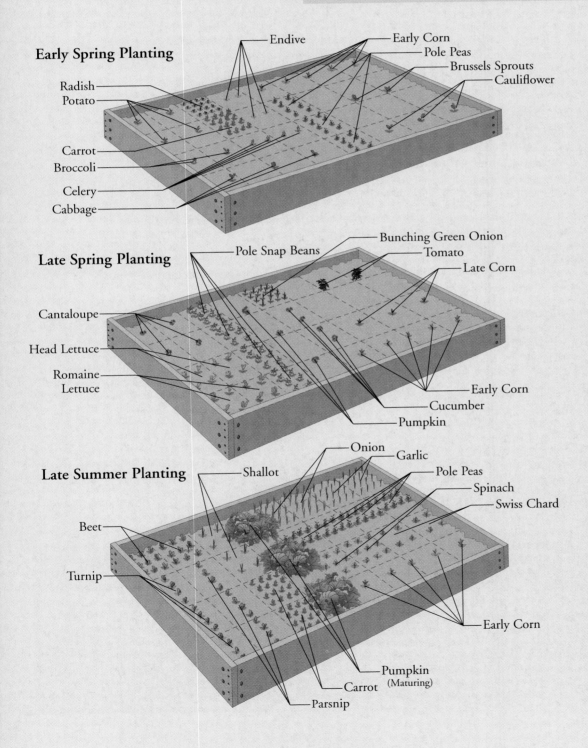

Early Spring Planting

Endive — Early Corn — Pole Peas — Brussels Sprouts — Cauliflower

Radish — Potato — Carrot — Broccoli — Celery — Cabbage

Late Spring Planting

Pole Snap Beans — Bunching Green Onion — Tomato — Late Corn

Cantaloupe — Head Lettuce — Romaine Lettuce — Early Corn — Cucumber — Pumpkin

Late Summer Planting

Shallot — Onion — Garlic — Pole Peas — Spinach — Swiss Chard

Beet — Turnip — Parsnip — Carrot — Pumpkin (Maturing) — Early Corn

TOOLS, EQUIPMENT, AND MATERIALS

While there are scores of unique and enticing tools that can assist your efforts as you prepare your soil or plant and care for your vegetable garden, the number of essential tools is limited to a basic set found in most households.

Those who garden in containers and small-scale beds should have a good set of hand tools—trowel, hand fork, and cultivator—plus a watering can and a pair of bypass pruners. If you wish, a small shovel and a plastic spray bottle complete the set of tools you'll need to succeed in vegetable gardening.

For those with a somewhat larger garden of raised beds or terraces, or for small row gardens, add a shovel, a rake, a hoe, and a garden cart or wheelbarrow to the collection of hand tools described above. You'll also need a garden hose and a hose-end spray nozzle. Many folks also add a dibber to aid them in planting onion and garlic bulbs, and a kneeling pad of soft foam rubber to ease the task of weeding.

Large-scale gardeners probably will also need a garden tiller, waterproof boots or clogs, a garden fork, a cultivating tool, a hose-end or pump-pressure sprayer for applying garden chemicals, a bucket, plus soaker hoses, drip irrigation tubing, and emitters or fittings that they will require to water their vegetables.

Besides the tools listed, an outdoor potting table is considered essential by many gardeners. Stout waterproof or leather gloves will protect skin from abrasions and blisters. Those wishing to have an early start will likely need a cold frame, several cloches or hot caps, or a floating row cover to protect their plants from frost. Stakes, trellises, and garden string will help support your plants, and you should lay in a good supply of organic fertilizer, soil amendments, potting soil, and mulch before the season begins so they will be handy once you begin to plant.

(Right) A hand fork, used for cultivating in containers and beds, is also handy for mixing fertilizer into the soil after it is applied.

(Below) Well-equipped vegetable gardeners will have a variety of tools, materials, and implements to aid them, such as the many items shown here. A potting table is a helpful addition for gardeners to consider, since it gives them a weatherproof work surface at a convenient height.

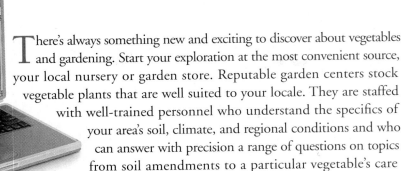

SOURCES AND RESOURCES

There's always something new and exciting to discover about vegetables and gardening. Start your exploration at the most convenient source, your local nursery or garden store. Reputable garden centers stock vegetable plants that are well suited to your locale. They are staffed with well-trained personnel who understand the specifics of your area's soil, climate, and regional conditions and who can answer with precision a range of questions on topics from soil amendments to a particular vegetable's care needs. They'll be happy to guide your choice of new vegetable cultivars and recommend disease-resistant plants.

Another valuable resource is your local USDA, Agriculture Canada, or university extension. Regional offices of the Cooperative Extension Service produce many pamphlets dealing with gardening issues in your area, while extension agents familiar with the latest scientific research are available to answer gardening questions, identify pests, or recommend treatments for disease conditions. Some offices use trained volunteer Master Gardeners to assist or advise home gardeners on how to construct their gardens or care for their plants.

(Left) Electronic information sources have useful, timely data that can help you research, choose, plant, and care for vegetables.

(Below) When personal attention is best due to a complex question or need for specific advice, consult the knowledgeable staff of your local nursery or garden center for help.

Since education is an important goal of most botanical gardens and university arboretums, a trip to one allows you to see a variety of plants and gather ideas that you can apply to your own yard. In addition, you can sign up for classes, use the facility's library or bookstore, or ask questions of one of the staff horticulturists during your visit. Many community colleges and adult-education programs also offer gardening courses.

With a computer, information is at your fingertips [see On-line, pg. 118]. Among the many useful electronic information sources are growers, gardening clubs, and individual hobbyists. Electronic retailers also offer special equipment, plants, and tools direct to consumers.

Print and electronic media are good resources as well. Many city and suburban newspapers feature weekly columns about gardening. Radio and television programming is filled with shows on the subject, some with call-in hosts answering the public's gardening questions. To find such programs, check your regional listings.

Learn the essentials of preparing your garden by testing and improving soil, building raised beds, adding an irrigation system or aids, and installing supports

Preparing for Planting

Now that you have planned your vegetable garden, it's time to turn to your site. Before you can plant, you'll need to prepare your soil to ensure your vegetables the optimum environment for their growth.

For a garden planted in newly turned earth, it's wise to check the drainage, fertility, and acid-alkaline balance of your soil by testing it and making necessary changes before planting your vegetables. Most garden soils can be improved by adding ample organic material—to loosen dense clays and help retain water in sandy soils, to provide a balanced mix of macronutrients, micronutrients, trace elements, and living soil organisms, and to buffer too-alkaline or too-acidic soils.

In special situations, amend your soil by adding garden lime to sweeten it, or sulfur to make it more acidic. Gypsum is another additive that can help drainage and porosity if your soil is too dense. Apply a fertilizer of well-rotted manure or decomposed plant waste to increase fertility, and consider enzyme-rich kelp extract to promote strong plants and quick growth.

For container and raised-bed gardens, some different preparations are necessary. Pots should be sterilized prior to use to avoid infecting plants with fungal diseases that might be present. You'll also need to be sure your containers have large drain holes to prevent water from standing in the pots, making them susceptible to suffocation, softened roots, and fungal infection.

Where garden soil conditions are too challenging or the site slopes, consider building raised beds or terraces and filling them with fertile soil. Raised beds lined with porous landscape fabric are simple to build and assure a successful garden.

There are several other preparatory steps that you should consider before you plant your vegetables. Besides preparing your beds, rows, and hills, you may need to protect your garden from animal pests. To use vertical space, you may wish to install trellises and other supports before sowing seed, and you'll certainly want to organize your irrigation regardless of your site and garden type.

With these facts in mind, you'll be ready to plant your cold frame with cool-season vegetables and have transplants ready for the garden soon after frost hazard has passed.

There is a lot to consider before your plants can go into the ground: testing and amending your soil, preparing containers and building beds for planting, installing plant supports, arranging for a watering system, and getting a head start on the season.

SITE AND SOIL

Soil condition is of the essence of success when growing vegetables. Many garden experts suggest that you focus on maintaining the health of your soil even as you nuture your plants, and there's lots of scientific data supporting their position.

Healthy soil is composed of many organic, mineral, and even living elements, microbes that digest and break down decaying plant matter into its components, making the food that growing vegetables need to thrive and prosper. The top 6 in. (15 cm) of soil contain 80 percent of its microorganisms.

The three most common nutrients found in garden soil are nitrogen (N), phosphorus (P), and potassium (K). Nitrogen is the only one of the three that's water soluble and is necessary for foliage growth. Too little nitrogen stunts growth, while too much causes lush foliage growth at the expense of flowers, fruit, and seed. Phosphorus, a common element found naturally in abundance in many soils, affects plant vitality and aids flower, fruit, and seed formation. Too much phosphorus limits the uptake of copper, iron, and zinc by plants, stunting their growth. Potassium influences the growth of both stems and roots by influencing efficient protein and carbohydrate synthesis inside plant cells. Your soil needs all three nutrients. The amounts of these nutrients found in your soil depend on the minerals contained in the bedrock underlying your site. It may have taken 100 years or more for mother nature to produce each inch (25 mm) of the topsoil found in your garden.

Macronutrients—as nitrogen, phosphorus, and potassium are called—are just part of the story. More than 30 micronutrients and dozens of trace elements are found in most soils. Their presence or absence depends mostly on two factors: the quantity of decomposed organic material that the soil contains, and the maintenance of a proper acid-alkaline balance to break the ionic bonds of these compounds and free them for use by your plants. The best vegetable garden soil is loose, fertile loam with equal parts mineral clay, silt, and sand mixed with ample decomposed organic material. It has an acid-alkaline balance measuring 6.0–6.8 on the pH scale, a reading that is slightly acidic.

(Below) Good garden loam consists of equal parts of sand, silt, and clay mixed with abundant quantities of decayed organic matter. Such soil drains easily and retains ample air while it avoids compacting.

(Bottom) Select a site for your garden that is in full sun, has protection from wind, and is as level as possible. The radiated heat and reflected light from nearby slopes or walls can help your warm-season vegetables to ripen.

PERCOLATION TEST

This test evaluates the texture of your soil and the amount of organic matter it contains to determine how quickly it will drain. Good drainage—neither too fast nor too slow—is important on the one hand to avoid having your plants stand in water, and on the other hand to prevent their roots from drying out too quickly.

To perrform a percolation test, dig several holes in your planting beds, 2 ft. (60 cm) deep, and fill them with water. After the water drains, refill the holes with water and note how long it takes for them to empty.

The level in a typical, well-drained garden soil should drop 1–2 in. (25–50 mm) per hour. Soil that drains near such rates will be ideal for growing vegetables, while those that drain slower or faster require amendments.

Drainage rates that are slower reveal that the soil is too heavy with clay or that other conditions might be a cause. Investigate to see if a layer of hardpan or impermeable rock beneath the planting bed might be the cause of the slow drainage.

If the soil drains much more quickly, it is likely that it is porous because it contains too much sand. Drainage rates faster than 1–2 in. (25–50 mm) in 15 minutes or less require correction.

Correct either drainage condition by incorporating 2–4 in. (50–100 mm) of organic compost into the top 1 ft. (30 cm) of the soil.

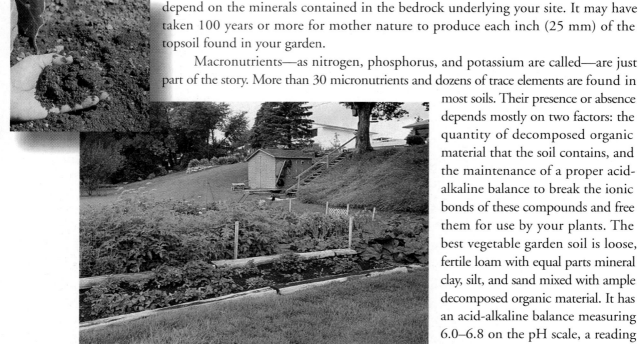

TESTING SOIL

You can perform soil tests for texture, nutrients, and pH. Many nurseries and garden centers provide testing services to assess soil and recommend necessary amendments as well as offer reliable home test kits. If you use a laboratory, follow its staff's instructions to gather your soil sample. **To perform soil tests at home, follow these easy steps:**

1 Dig a hole at the planting site. Using a clean container, collect a small amount of soil from the hole's side, 3–4 in. (75–100 mm) below the surface. For large gardens, thoroughly mix soil from different locations or evaluate each area separately.

2 Using part of the sample of moist soil, squeeze it in your fist, then open your hand. If it feels gritty and falls apart when poked with a finger, the soil contains excess sand. If it holds together, roll it between your forefinger and thumb to produce a cylinder-shaped rope of soil. If it breaks before reaching ½ in. (12 mm) long, the soil has ample silt or loam. If the soil reaches 1 in. (25 mm) or more before breaking, the soil contains excess clay.

3 Measure relative amounts of three soil nutrients—nitrogen, phosphorus, and potassium—using a home soil test kit. Follow package instructions, which vary according to the specific kit. Always use distilled water when testing soil.

5 Electronic meters check soil pH, too. Verify accuracy by testing cow's milk—it's 6.5–7.0 pH. Thoroughly clean the probe before you test your soil sample.

4 Determine your soil's acid-alkaline balance using a pH test kit. Use distilled water and follow all the package instructions for best results.

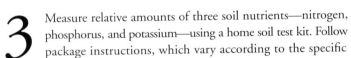

AMENDING SOIL

Each time that you till your garden soil you incorporate large amounts of air into it, fueling a population explosion in the microorganisms it contains. It's always important to add compost or well-rotted manure whenever you till in order to give these microbes an ample food supply.

Remember that your garden soil consists of layers that extend from the surface to deep within the earth. The top foot (30 cm), which is most important to your plants, is the most biologically active layer. Beneath the topsoil is a layer of subsurface soil that, while rich in mineral nutrients, is mostly devoid of life. When you till, it's important to loosen each layer independently, but avoid mixing them together.

As you work your soil, it's a good idea to go beyond adding organic matter, especially if it drains too quickly or slowly [see Percolation Test, pg. 22]. A loosening agent, such as the mineral gypsum, may help prevent clay particles from sticking together. You may need to add garden lime or sulfur to raise or lower the pH, making your soil more alkaline or acidic. Soils that are too sandy will benefit from having clay and silt added to them them, while those that are too heavy will profit from additions of sand.

The process of amending soil with a mechanical tiller is shown in detail [see Incorporating Fertilizers and Amendments, opposite pg]. Garden tillers typically mix the topsoil layer, seldom reaching more than 8–10 in. (20–25 cm) deep into the earth. To loosen the subsurface layer, it is necessary to double dig the bed using a shovel. While the process is simple, it requires substantial effort if a large area is to be prepared. Most gardeners tackle part of the task in the autumn, part in the spring. Double digging in autumn has the added benefit of allowing fresh manure incorporated into the beds to decompose naturally during the winter months.

To double dig your beds, start by digging a trench 1 ft. (30 cm) deep across the width of your bed. Place the soil from the trench into a wheelbarrow or garden cart, reserving it for later in the process. Next, loosen the soil at the bottom of the trench and remove any rocks or debris, working an additional 9–12 in. (23–30 cm) deep.

Starting a second trench parallel to the first, turn the topsoil layer into the first trench, filling it with the soil from the second row. Then loosen the subsurface layer found at the bottom of the second trench. Continue in this fashion across the bed until a final trench remains, its subsurface layer turned and loosened. Fill the trench with the topsoil reserved from the first row.

When the entire bed has been double dug, spread your amendments, compost, and fertilizer in uniform layers on top of the soil, then mix it into the previously loosened top layer with a shovel, working down the length of the bed at right angles to the original trenches.

(Above) Soil test meters are used to measure pH, nutrient levels, or both soil properties. They make it easy to evaluate your soil.

(Right) A small garden tiller is a useful tool to use for working the top 8–10 in. (20–25 cm) of soil in large vegetable gardens.

(Below) Soil amendments and fertilizers have different purposes. Choose amendments to help loosen dense soils, correct its acid-alkaline balance, and add ample amounts of well-rotted manure or other organic fertilizers to enrich the soil.

INCORPORATING FERTILIZERS AND AMENDMENTS

1 Begin by clearing all weeds and plants you plan to remove. Kill weeds organically by covering the bed with clear plastic for about 2 weeks before you intend to work the soil.

Amend and fertilize your soil before planting. Most additives improve soil texture, adding air, retaining moisture, and hastening drainage. Fertilizers add the nutrients that vegetables need to grow. Test your soil to determine what fertilizers and amendments you'll need [see Testing Soil, pg. 23]. Then gather rakes, a shovel or a spading fork, a tarp, a tiller, a wheelbarrow or garden cart, amendments, and fertilizer, then follow these steps:

2 Dig a trench 9–12 in. (23–30 cm) deep and one shovel width wide along an edge of the bed, placing the removed soil on a tarp. Loosen the next 9–12 in. (23–30 cm) of soil within the trench. Remove all rocks and debris.

3 Widen the trench a second shovel width, placing the top 9–12 in. (23–30 cm) of its soil into the first trench. Progress across the area until all the soil has been dug. Fill the last trench with soil from the first. Use a tiller to thoroughly mix the topsoil.

4 Cover your area with a 4-in. (10-cm) layer of organic soil amendment, as needed. Add organic fertilizer, as needed, following package instructions.

5 Turn the soil amendments into the top 9–12 in. (23–30 cm) of soil using a shovel or fork.

6 Rake the top of the bed smooth. It will be high and fluffy with amendments and air. Water the bed with a sprinkler and allow it to settle for 3–5 days. When the soil firms, your plot is ready to plant with vegetables.

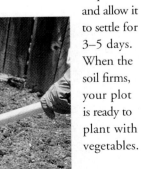

GARDENING IN CONTAINERS

Vegetables grown in containers are every bit as nutritious and delicious as those from garden soil. Paying heed to a few special requirements, you can grow most of the popular vegetables in containers on your deck, balcony, patio, or walkway.

First, choose a container large enough for the plants you wish to grow. Many vegetables grown in garden soil are deep rooted—sweet corn roots extend 3 ft. (90 cm) or more, tomatoes as deep as 4 ft. (1.2 m), and the lowly beet often extends its roots into the soil 10 ft. (3 m) or more—though they can grow in much shallower soil as long as it is kept rich with nutrients and drains properly. For most vegetables, choose pots that are at least 18 in. (45 cm) deep and sufficiently wide to accommodate stakes or other supports if they are tall or vining plants.

Select containers with adequate drain holes. Many pots are available with only a single hole that is just ¼ in. (6 mm) wide or smaller. In that case, you should enlarge it or add more drains prior to planting [see Choosing and Preparing Containers for Vegetables, next pg.]. Before you plant, protect the drain holes from clogging by lining the pot with porous landscape fabric or covering the holes with plastic mesh or broken pottery shards, then adding 1 in. (25 mm) of pea gravel. Such measures help prevent loose potting soil from washing down into the drains while still allowing the water to pass through their openings.

Vegetable gardening is a hobby that everyone can enjoy using containers, pots, and planters. Any sunny site—a balcony, deck, pathway, or patio—is suitable for growing produce. Here, gold tomatoes ripen in a pot filled with chives, Italian parsley, and other herbs.

Containers come in a variety of materials, including concrete, glazed clay pottery, stone, unglazed terra cotta, and wood, as well as plastic and various other synthetic materials. Concrete and stone planters are durable, offer insulation from overheating, and are porous, but salts leaching from concrete and such stones as limestone or marble can alter soil chemistry. Because they are heavy, they're best used as ground-level containers. Plastic pots are lightweight and economical, though they vary in durability, porosity, and ability to insulate the soil within. Avoid those with built-in watering reservoirs. Unglazed terra cotta pots are popular because they are moderate in weight, insulate well, are very porous, and are economical; they are subject to drying due to evaporation unless they are treated with waterproof sealant. Glazed clay pottery is light, waterproof, and quite durable if handled with care; it is subject to breakage and often is less econonmical than other materials. Wood is natural, offers good insulation, and is porous; seal wood containers to protect them from fungal rot.

Always use so-called pot feet, bricks, or other risers placed under the pots to keep them raised above the soil or installation surface.

CHOOSING AND PREPARING CONTAINERS FOR VEGETABLES

T he choice of a container starts with your selection of vegetables. Each species requires a different depth to accommodate its roots— a good rule of thumb is half to two-thirds as deep as the plant's height—and has specific soil needs. The container also must have several open drain holes to keep the plant's roots from standing in water. Choose and prepare your containers for planting by following these steps:

1 Select containers that are made of insulating materials to keep them from overheating. Best are ceramic, insulated composite plastic, terra cotta, and wood.

2 Add more drain holes, enlarge any that are too small, or drill your own, using a battery or electric hand drill fitted with a ⅜-in. (9-mm) masonry bit.

3 If you reuse containers, sterilize them in a solution of 1 part household bleach to 9 parts of water. Wear protective clothing and gloves. Dry pots overnight before planting.

Warning

Household bleach is made with sodium hypochlorite, a powerful skin and eye irritant. Avoid any hazard by wearing gloves and protective clothing whenever you handle bleach solution.

4 Reduce deposited mineral salts on porous pots such as those of terra cotta by painting the interior of the pots with a breathable latex sealant. Dry the sealant overnight before planting, and soak the terra-cotta pots in water before use.

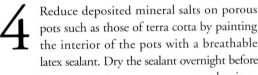

RAISED BEDS AND TERRACES

Using framed beds and terraces to create level planting areas is a practice that dates back to antiquity. In sites where conditions are less than ideal, raised beds allow you to concentrate nutrient-rich soil to increase the yield of the garden. They also make taking care of plants easier by raising them above the ground, so you can avoid stooping and bending as you cultivate, fertilize, and harvest them. On hillside slopes, terraces perform much the same function as raised beds, providing level planting locations filled with rich soil that is held in place with retaining walls.

Such beds are easy to build using landscape timbers [see Preparing a Raised Bed, opposite pg.]. With simple woodworking skills and common tools, you can achieve a good-looking, functional bed in a few hours. Terraces, especially those built on steep slopes, require greater planning and careful construction, especially if they are to be 3 ft. (90 cm) high or taller. Besides considering structural issues, allowing for drainage is essential. Terraces act as natural dams, trapping water in the soil on their uphill side. Unless weep holes, drains, or other options for draining this water are included during construction, the walls may collapse.

Keep the width of beds and terraces narrow enough to allow easy access to the plants growing within their walls; for most beds, doubling the length of your arm is the right choice. The beds may be made as long as you think is appropriate. Many beds are built 20 in. (50 cm) high, providing a natural seat for when you weed your garden.

Keep maintenance to a minimum by lining the inside of your bed or terrace with permeable landscape fabric that allows water to pass through but holds the soil of the bed in place.

(Top) Stout retaining walls made of discarded railroad ties lined with impermeable plastic fabric create a level terrace for planting.

(Above) Expand available space by using raised beds in flat areas and terraces on hillside slopes.

(Right) Gardens can be compact and productive. Here, 400 sq. ft. (37 m²) arranged in attractive, radiating raised beds will produce ample vegetables for the couple who plant and tend it. A raised terrace provides more space for beds of raspberries and strawberries.

PREPARING A RAISED BED

Building a simple raised bed of wood timbers is a project that's easy to accomplish in an afternoon. Filling the finished bed with a mixture of rich topsoil, humus, and compost will allow you to grow vegetables regardless of your soil's texture, composition, and fertility. Gather your tools, 4 x 4 (89 x 89-mm) timbers, 6-in. (15-cm) spikes, woven landscape fabric, and waterproof sealant, then build your raised bed following these steps:

1 Remove all existing turf and any weeds at the site to their roots to prevent them from growing in the bed or blocking the flow of water through the bed's base. Trench along the outside perimeter of the bed.

2 Divide 360° by the number of sides in your bed to calculate the end angles of your timbers, typically 90°, 60°, or 45° for beds with 4, 6, or 8 sides. Cut the timbers to fit. Paint the ends of each timber with clear sealant to waterproof its end-grain cuts.

3 Lay a first course of timbers in the trench, using a carpenter's level to align them evenly. Add or remove soil until the course is level and all joints are snug and match evenly.

4 Lay the timbers of the second and third courses, lapping them log-cabin fashion and driving a spike into each overlap to create strong joints able to withstand outward pressures caused when you fill the bed with soil.

5 If the subsoil is mostly clay, drill ½-in. (12-mm) weep holes at regular intervals along the base of the bottom course.

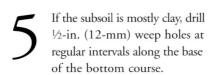

6 Line the inside of the bed with permeable landscape fabric, lapping and stapling it into the joints between the top two courses of timbers. If treated lumber is used, place solid barrier fabric between the timbers and the landscape fabric, extending it at least 6 in. (15 cm) below the bed's bottom timber.

PLOTS FOR PLANTING

Row gardens are among the most common vegetable plantings. In sites where good, rich soil is found naturally on a level site with good sun exposure and shelter from wind, your garden may be dug directly into the soil. You should add edge boards around the perimeter to block grasses or weeds from growing into the garden, using galvanized wire mesh barriers buried beneath the soil to prevent burrowing animals from eating your plants if they are common in your region [see Fences and Animal Pests, right].

If you are preparing a vegetable garden plot in soil that formerly was used to grow turfgrass lawn or landscape plants, you'll need to remove all of the turf and plant roots, then loosen the soil at least 18 in. (45 cm) deep [see Amending Soil, pg. 24]. Many vegetable plants have root systems that send down shoots even deeper than that, but the majority of all beneficial soil microbes are found in the topsoil layer, where they have abundant air as well as organic matter upon which they feed. Their digestion releases minerals that your vegetables need to grow and thrive, and by loosening the soil you will greatly increase both their numbers and activity.

Vegetables benefit when they have sufficient room to grow. Leaving room between plants, rows, and beds has several advantages. First, air circulation allows foliage to dry quickly. Second, allowing space between plantings helps prevent pests and diseases from becoming established. Third, maintenance and care are easier when plants can be accessed easily with garden carts and tools.

FENCES AND ANIMAL PESTS

Rodents, burrowing animals, birds, and even deer will view the tender plants and ripening fruit in your vegetable garden with envy unless you take steps to deny them access to it by erecting barriers and fences.

Stop gophers, moles, and other burrowing animals by burying galvenized wire mesh fabric along each edge of your garden plot, at least 18 in. (45 cm) down into the soil, or fit the mesh to the bottom of your raised beds before you fill them with soil.

Prevent birds, rabbits, and other browsers from feeding on your tender seedlings by covering the planting with a V-shaped arch of wire fabric, as shown below. The plants will grow right through the fabric, or you can remove the arch once the plants become established.

Large mammals, such as deer, can empty a garden of its plants in an evening. Block their access by erecting a tall fence at least 10 ft. (3 m) high around the garden's edge, or by building paired parallel, shorter fences, each 6 ft. (1.8 m) tall and 4–6 ft. (1.2–1.8 m) apart. Such fences may be built from many materials, including wire mesh, vinyl or wooden pickets, woven willow, or bamboo canes.

Take the time to lay out your beds using careful measurements. While free-form beds can be attractive, rectangular beds are neat and orderly. To ensure the sides are equal and parallel, measure and make the corner diagonals equal. Allow ample space between plots for access paths; temporary access can be made easier by laying planks alongside your rows, while all the permanent paths should be large enough to provide easy passage for wagons, wheelbarrows, or garden carts. Pave paths with non-skid materials such as wood chips, bark, or pea gravel.

When it's time for planting, use stakes and string to mark neat, even rows in your plots. As the sprouts emerge, they will line up in even ranks like soldiers, making it easy to identify your vegetables from any weed sprouts.

PREPARING BEDS, HILLS, AND ROWS

Areas in Beds

1 Plant carrots, leafy greens, and radishes in flat areas. Loosen the soil with a spade, breaking any clods and removing all debris.

Prepare for planting by raising hills or rows or by making flat areas to sow scattered seed. Your soil should be thoroughly loosened, with all your amendments and fertilizers added before beginning this step [see Incorporating Fertilizers and Amendments, pg. 25]. Use a spade, a hoe, and a rake to prepare your soil for seeding, following these easy steps:

2 Work the bed's soil thoroughly with a hoe, then smooth and level the bed using the back of a garden rake, working at right angles to the original direction.

Hills

1 Plant vine plants in hills. Loosen the soil using a spade, breaking up any clods and removing rocks and debris.

2 Use a hoe to raise a hill 1 ft. (30 cm) higher than the level of the surrounding soil and 12–14 in. (30–36 cm) wide, surrounded by a moat to serve as a watering basin for the plants.

Rows

1 Plant vegetables such as bush peas or beans in rows. Loosen the soil using a shovel or spade, breaking any clods and removing rocks and debris.

2 Use a hoe to raise a row 3–4 in. (75–100 mm) higher than the surrounding soil and 4–6 in. (10–15 cm) wide, then dig parallel watering furrows on both sides of the row.

SUPPORTING PLANTS

It's wise to install large stakes, trellises, tepees, and other sturdy supports at the time your beds are prepared for planting to accommodate climbing vines, including peas and beans and heavy-fruited vegetables such as melons, pumpkins, and squash. Lightweight supports—those built of stakes and string, for instance—can be installed after planting.

Depending on the materials used, vertical supports can make attractive additions to your garden. Common organic materials include bamboo, braided willow branches, and peeled logs. For a contemporary look, choose wrought iron, lathe, or dimensioned lumber. Simple carpentry skills and lashings made of garden twine are all it takes to add eye-catching, supports for your crops [see Installing Supports, opposite pg.].

Part of the appeal of climbing vines is that they are easier to harvest, eliminating the strain of bending to pick pea or bean pods, cucumbers, tomatoes, or eggplants. Besides this practical advantage, they also make the garden more interesting by varying the height of your plants. In small-space gardens, supports can reduce the footprint of sprawling vegetables such as pumpkin, watermelon, and winter squash. Gardeners with very limited space should prune and train vines onto supports once the plants begin to grow [see Staking and Supporting, pg. 54]. Directing growth and limiting the vine to a central shoot will cause the plants to produce fewer numbers of usually larger fruit.

(Right) Climbing vines require stout, sturdy supports if they are planted to grow vertically. Using such aids helps to conserve space. Here, cucumber vines are grown onto a wooden trellis.

(Below) Pole cultivars of peas and beans naturally like to climb. A central pole—metal, as used here, or wood—with staked strings form a vertical pyramid when the vines mature. Pole cultivars tend to yield more produce than bush varieties.

Plants that require support can be divided into two groups: natural climbers with tendrils or holdfasts, and plants that require tying. Pole cultivars of many beans and peas will follow a string or pole naturally as they grow, while other vines will need your direction and assistance. Soon after planting, these plants will send out dominant shoots. Gently lift them and redirect them onto your supports. As they grow, use stretchy plastic plant tape or twist ties to tie them to the supports.

Most heavy fruit will hang naturally from supported vines; their stems are fibrous, tough, and strong. In a few cases, you may need slings or other aids to support large melons or giant varieties of pumpkin.

Place your supports to avoid shading any nearby low-growing crops by keeping them on the side of the garden opposite its sun exposure. Keep in mind that some plants can grow 12 ft. (3.7 m) tall or higher and may grow together to form dense masses of foliage. Because of their growth habits, they are useful for sheltering other plants in the garden when they are planted on its upwind side.

INSTALLING SUPPORTS

Some vine and bush vegetables such as beans, peas, peppers, and tomatoes require string supports to help bear the weight of their branches and fruit. For best results, plant them in rows and install a string trellis along each side, or make a tepee of wood stakes for them to climb. Gather wooden stakes, a mallet, a marker, garden twine, a staple gun, and a pair of scissors, then follow the steps shown for each option before or after planting:

Installing String Trellises

1 Drive 2 parallel rows of wood stakes 42–60 in. (1.1–1.5 m) long into the soil 10 in. (25 cm) to each side of the center of the planting furrow and spaced 4 ft. (1.2 m) apart.

2 Mark points along each stake at 6-in. (15-cm) intervals from the soil to their tops. Stretch twine tautly between the marked points, fastening it to the stakes with a hand staple gun or tying it securely to each stake.

3 Repeat until the stakes have several tiers of string, making a fencelike structure to support the growing plants.

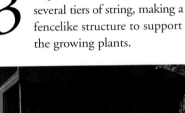

Installing Tepees

1 Use 3 poles, 8 ft. (2.4 m) long, to make a tepee for pole beans and peas. Lay 2 poles parallel to each other, with a third pole between them and overlapping their ends 16 in. (40 cm).

2 Using twine, loosely lash the poles together where they intersect, making 3–4 loops around each pole. Then tie the twine at both intersections with the poles.

3 Erect the tepee by folding the poles toward one another to make a tripod centered on the planting area.

PLANNING FOR IRRIGATION

With your plots prepared and your supports in place, next it's good to plan for your plant's water needs. Even if you live in a region with regular precipitation throughout the growing season, natural rains may be sporadic and can require you to take up the slack by irrigating your drought-prone plants. Gardeners in areas that experience long periods without rain must provide water in order to have success with vegetables.

The simplest watering system, applicable to most level sites with row or hill crops, is to furrow watering channels beside the plants and build circular moats around each hill. Using a garden hose, you can fill these irrigation channels with water that is allowed to slowly be absorbed into the soil around the growing plants' roots [see Watering Techniques, pg. 59]. If desired, such furrows should be installed at the time of planting.

Two other commonly used methods of irrigating crops are drip irrigation and watering with weeping soaker hoses [see Laying Drip and Soaker Hose Irrigation, opposite pg.]. Because both methods may be automated using economical components, they are a boon to labor-saving for those with limited time, and they provide your vegetables reliable, regular waterings in your absence.

Drip systems usually are connected to existing waterlines using a timer-controlled valve and delivery hose system that strings through your plantings. At each plant, a short spur terminates in an emitter that applies water to the plant's roots. As many as 32 plants may be served by a single watering circuit. Drip systems have the advantage of limiting the growth of weeds to the watered area and, when used with a covering of mulch, generally will eliminate the need to cultivate. Soaker hoses are ideal for providing water to rows of vegetables, and since they are flexible, they can be looped around hills or large perennial plants. Choose hoses that weep water, limiting spray that wets the plants' foliage.

After installation of drip or soaker hose irrigation, run the system for a timed period in order to gauge how much water reaches each plant.

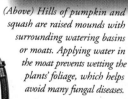

(Above) Hills of pumpkin and squash are raised mounds with surrounding watering basins or moats. Applying water in the moat prevents wetting the plants' foliage, which helps avoid many fungal diseases.

(Right) Row plantings with parallel furrows on a flat site can be watered easily. Apply water to either end of the row, and allow the water to spread down the furrow, irrigating your plants.

LAYING DRIP AND SOAKER-HOSE IRRIGATION

Drip irrigation and soaker hoses are both good options for vegetable gardens because they release water slowly at the plants' roots and avoid erosion and runoff. With an automatic timer, they assure your garden receives water regularly. Gather the materials shown, and follow the steps for each option:

Easy Drip Irrigation

1 Choose drip irrigation to spot-apply water to plants. Acquire and attach a battery-operated automatic timer and a valve assembly at a hose bib near your vegetable garden.

2 Connect a ½-in. (12-mm) feed line to the valve unit with a hose clamp. To serve 2 areas, place a Y-fitting between the valve and each feed line.

3 Attach several ¼-in. (6-mm) lateral lines to the drip feed line using couplers, each leading to a group of vegetables. Serve up to 4 plants with T-connectors.

4 A variety of drip irrigation emitters offer spray, bubbler, and drip options. Choose the emitter that best suits your plants, noting their flow rates.

Soaker Hoses

1 Use soaker hoses to apply water slowly to row and hill plantings. Acquire and attach a battery-operated automatic timer and valve assembly at the hose bib.

2 Attach a standard garden hose feed line to the valve, running it to the start of the soaker run.

3 Couple the soaker hose to the feed line, laying it at the base of your vegetables.

PREPARING FOR THE GARDEN SEASONS

*S*eed catalogs often beckon while the trees outside your windows are about to burst into bud, yet a few more weeks are needed before you finally can plant your garden. There are two vital measures of the time to plant: absence of frost in the evening and soil warmth, which takes sustained days of warm air temperatures to obtain.

The date of last spring frost varies according to your plant hardiness zone and local conditions that can moderate temperatures, including large bodies of water. In the warmest zones, it may occur before March 1, while in the cold areas, it may be June or even later before hazard of frost is past. Use the time between thaw and last frost to plan and prepare your beds and install supports and watering systems. Get an early start on weed control by turning the soil to prevent weed seed from germinating.

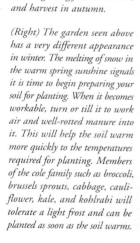

(Above) Most often, we think of vegetable gardens as they look during the gardening season, as shown here. All gardens actually are a continuum that begins with fallow land in winter, sprouting seed and transplants in spring, a bounty of growth, flowering, and burgeoning fruit in summer, and harvest in autumn.

(Right) The garden seen above has a very different appearance in winter. The melting of snow in the warm spring sunshine signals it is time to begin preparing your soil for planting. When it becomes workable, turn or till it to work air and well-rotted manure into it. This will help the soil warm more quickly to the temperatures required for planting. Members of the cole family such as broccoli, brussels sprouts, cabbage, cauliflower, kale, and kohlrabi will tolerate a light frost and can be planted as soon as the soil warms.

While a few vegetable plants reliably germinate and grow in soil with temperatures of 40–50°F (4–10°C), all do best when soil temperatures are above 60°F (16°C). Planting in warm soil avoids risk of fungal diseases that can rot seed or cause seedlings to fail soon after germination. Using a cold frame installed over a base of fresh manure and covered with a deep layer of topsoil will allow you to plant outdoors earlier [see Building a Cold Frame, opposite pg.]. As the manure decomposes, it will warm the soil above it, while the transluscent top of the cold frame will capture heat from sunlight and protect the plants within from cool nighttime temperatures. Vegetables that require even more protection and warmth—melons, peppers, squash, sunflowers, and sweet potatoes—may be started indoors or reared within a greenhouse [see Starting Plants Indoors, pg. 47].

(Bottom) The hinged transparent covers of these raised beds in Sooke Harbor, British Columbia, are closed to protect seedlings from cool overnight temperatures but remain open during the day when the weather begins to warm. By using such season-extending aids you can add 2 or more months to the growing time available in cold-winter regions.

BUILDING A COLD FRAME

1 Cut component pieces from plywood, then assemble the box by fastening the side, front, and back panels to the front and back corner braces with wood screws.

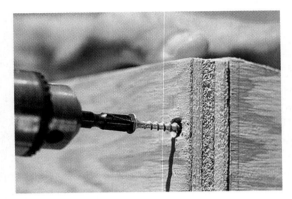

Y ou can give all of your warmth-loving vegetables head starts by planting them in a cold frame buried deeply in the soil.

With the use of a cold frame, you'll plant seed 6–8 weeks earlier in the season than would be possible for in-soil plantings. Make your cold frame of ACX plywood and a corrugated fiberglass panel, fastening it with galvanized hinges, screws, and washers. Gather the materials listed, and follow these steps:

2 Cut ¾-in. (19-mm) kerfs into each horizontal cover frame. Fit the fiberglass panel into the kerfs and fasten it with wood screws. Overlap the vertical and horizontal cover frame pieces and fasten each corner with 3 wood screws.

Fasten the fiberglass panel to the vertical frames with screws and washers.

Required Materials:

Raw Materials:

1	4 x 8-ft. (1.2 x 2.4-m) ¾-in. (19-mm) ACX plywood panel
1	26 x 36-in. (66 x 90-cm) corrugated fiberglass panel
1	96 x 2 x 2-in. (244 x 3.8 x 3.8-cm) dimensioned lumber

Cut Components:

1	26 x 36-in. (66 x 90-cm) back panel
1	22 x 36-in. (56 x 90-cm) front panel
2	22 x 26 x 28½-in. (56 x 66 x 72.4-cm) side panels
2	5½ x 30-in. (14 x 76-cm) vertical cover frames
2	4 x 36-in. (10 x 90-cm) horizontal cover frames
2	26 x 2 x 2-in. (66 x 3.8 x 3.8-cm) back corner braces
2	22 x 2 x 2-in. (56 x 3.8 x 3.8-cm) front corner braces

Hardware:

36	¼ x 1¼-in. (6 x 32-mm) Phillips galvanized wood screws
24	⅛ x ⅝-in. (3 x 16-mm) Phillips galvanized wood screws
12	½ x ⅛-in. (12 x 3-mm) galvanized washers
2	2-in. (50-mm) galvanized butt hinges and mounting hardware

3 Fit the 2 butt hinges 1 ft. (30 cm) from each corner of the back panel, fastening them with supplied hardware. Fasten them to the underside of the cold frame cover.

4 In a sunny, protected spot, dig a rectangular hole 36 x 42 x 24 in. (90 x 107 x 60 cm) deep. Line it with plastic, fitting the cold frame into the hole. Backfill around the cold frame.

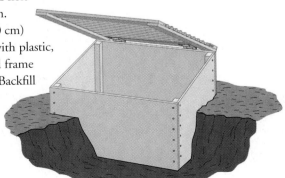

Choosing and Planting Vegetables

Discover various vegetables, make choices, and plant them from seed or nursery starts to get your garden up and growing

Vegetables that germinate quickly and tolerate cool soils and early-spring conditions are called cool-season vegetables. They include such popular plants as asparagus, beets, cabbage and its many close relatives, carrots, celery, many lettuce varieties, leeks, mustard, onions, peas, potatoes, and spinach, among others. Some cool-season vegetables are very cold hardy and tolerate even hard frosts once they become established. Others can take brief periods of cool temperatures or light frosts but need protection to prevent their foliage from freezing.

Those edible plants with large, starchy seeds that take a week or more to germinate and which prefer warm soils and mild to warm air temperatures are termed warm-season vegetables. They include amaranth, various beans, corn, cucumber, eggplant, gourds, melons, peppers, squash, and tomato. Planted in too-cool soil, they will fail because of fungal diseases or will struggle to become established.

These traits allow you to plant a succession of crops in your garden, beginning with cool-season vegetables planted soon after the soil has become workable and frost hazard has passed, then sowing a second or third planting after the early vegetables have been harvested.

Use the charts and tips found in this chapter to choose vegetables for your garden, then give the cool-season vegetables an extra-early start by sowing them indoors in bedding trays or individual pots. Repeat the process for your warm-season vegetables about 3–4 weeks before air temperatures rise above 60°F (16°C) and consistently stay there through the evening hours.

In the pages that follow, you'll find complete descriptions of how to sow seed, how to harden your tender seedlings, the best ways to transplant your sprouts and nursery starts into the garden, and techniques for caring for newly planted vegetables. You'll also learn how to install stakes and supports, and the best methods to train and tie vines or heavy-fruited vegetables to them.

Getting your plantings off to a good start is the best way to assure large, tasty harvests later in the season. Every gardener will find useful the charts in these pages with recommended planting times for most of the popular vegetables in each plant hardiness zone.

Sharing a gardening heritage with young children is a fine way to introduce them to a lifelong hobby, and it will give them the practical experience of caring for living things. The best vegetables for children are those with big paybacks: peanuts, popcorn, pumpkins, strawberries, and sunflowers.

SELECTING VEGETABLES

Several factors weigh in importance as you select vegetables for your garden. First among these, of course, are the species that you wish to grow. Your next consideration should be whether to plant seed or nursery starts. While both methods will yield good results, a wider choice of plants generally is available as seed, including those with characteristics that make them especially desirable. These include natural disease resistance, varied fruit color, size, or vigor and growth habit.

On the other hand, tender care and good growing conditions from germination until transplanting mark high among the benefits of planting seedlings from commercial vegetable growers that are offered by your garden center. Among the seedlings available each spring are popular varieties that your garden store's staff know will perform well in the local conditions found in your region.

Make your selections based on the next factor, the timing of plantings. The widest range of nursery starts often are available for about 6–8 weeks from the time that the soil becomes workable. Thereafter, the selection becomes limited; by the time that the season has become advanced, there may be few vegetable seedlings from which to choose. If you want to plant in succession or plant before or after your garden store offers stock, sowing seed may be your only choice. Note the length of time required for the seedling to grow to maturity and set fruit; a quick reference is the seed package or plant stake, but you also can check the information found later in this book [see Encyclopedia of Vegetable Plants, pg. 79].

For seed, choose from varieties offered by major growers, avoiding generic- or house-branded seed. From nursery starts, choose vigorous, immature, healthy seedlings free of damaged foliage or broken stems. Gently slip each plant out of its planter to inspect its roots, avoiding those that are rootbound, and skip over plants that already have begun to flower; most such seedlings will remain stunted after transplanting and generally will produce less fruit.

(Top) Nursery starts are a good choice for small-area plantings. Selected by growers for your local area, they are generally healthy when they arrive at your garden retailer and are ready to plant.

(Above) Depending on the species and cultivar, plants can differ considerably in needs, growth habits, and the time they need to mature. Note the differences before you plant by reading the seed package carefully.

(Right) Every spring, nurseries and garden centers have display racks that are filled with many choices of seed, offering a wider selection of rare cultivars than is true for nursery-started seedlings.

PLANNING VEGETABLE SUCCESSIONS

Progressive Plantings

1 For a continuous harvest, divide your bed into quarters, then seed the first area, leaving the other zones fallow.

Succession plantings are used to produce a sustained harvest of quick-maturing vegetables, such as carrots, lettuce and other greens, and radishes. Successions also allow you to harvest both cool-season vegetables and warm-season vegetables from the same plot. Follow the options shown to increase the yield of your vegetable garden as the season progresses:

2 Note the length of time the vegetable requires to mature, dividing it by 4. When that amount of time elapses, plant each zone in turn.

3 Begin to harvest when the first zone matures, then turn its soil and reseed as the next zone matures. You'll have a steady supply of fresh vegetables.

Successions of Vegetables

1 Start the succession in spring by planting an area with a cool-season, quick-maturing vegetable such as carrots, radishes, or spinach.

2 When the first planting fades, replant the area with another quick-maturing vegetable such as lettuce or green onions.

3 When the second planting fades, replant the area with a warm-season vegetable, such as beets, peppers, or turnips.

COOL-SEASON AND WARM-SEASON VEGETABLES

There's more to the story of cool- and warm-season vegetables than their category names may suggest. Only a few vegetables perform well if planted in soils cooler than 40°F (4°C)—temperatures commonly found inside a household refrigerator. They include endive, lettuce, onion, parsnip, and spinach, and it might be said that they are the cool-season champs. In a similar manner, there are only a few heat-loving species that germinate best in very warm soil of 75–95°F (24–35°C). Among them are amaranth, cantaloupe, eggplant, southern pea, pepper, sweet potato, watermelon, and New Zealand spinach.

While all the cool-season vegetables can germinate when the soil is 40–65°F (4–18°C), most of the remainder will germinate seed when the soil warms above 60°F (16°C). That said, nearly all vegetables grow when soil temperatures range from 70–80°F (21–27°)—a level that can be judged roughly as equal to the point when it is possible to sit comfortably on the ground for an extended period of time without becoming cold.

The second aspect of cool- versus warm-season vegetables pertains to the plant's requirement for an air temperature range necessary to flower and set fruit. If the temperature falls outside that range for many hours, these vegetables will drop their blossoms, fail to successfully pollinate, and will be fruitless. Some plants that need warmth to flower but must avoid excessive heat to set fruit are eggplant, melon, pumpkin, squash, and tomato. In very hot climates such as those found in tropical or desert regions you may find it necessary to partially shade these plants to reduce the temperature of their surroundings in order to grow fruit, and those in mild coastal or high mountain regions with generally low summer temperatures may wish for crops of melons and other produce that require warmth to set fruit.

In addition to germination and fruit-setting temperature ranges, a number of vegetables also are susceptible to a condition called "bolting" that occurs when the sunlight hours become long as the season progresses. Crops such as cabbage, lettuce, and spinach will prematurely form seed stalks and flower when the days lengthen. There is little that can be done to prevent bolting except for blanching—wrapping them with porous paper to block sunlight. You should plant leaf vegetables early in the season so that they can be harvested before they bolt, place them in shady areas of your garden to reduce the amount of light they receive, or cover them with shade fabric when days lengthen in summer.

Keeping these facts in mind will help you grow both cool-season and warm-season vegetables in your garden.

(Above) Plants such as radishes, brussels sprouts, carrots, cabbage, loosehead lettuce, cauliflower, and broccoli that need temperatures of 35–55°F (2–13°C) to plant are cool-season vegetables.

(Bottom) Warm-season vegetables such as eggplant, tomato, summer squash, snap beans, sweet peppers, summer melon, and winter squash require soil temperatures above 60°F (16°C) for planting.

PLANTING AND HARVEST PLANNER

USDA Zones 3 and 4
April Plantings
Vegetable—Harvest

Asparagus Spring of 3rd season
Beets* 45–60 days
Rhubarb 2–4 years

USDA Zones 3 and 4
May Plantings
Vegetable—Harvest

Artichoke Spring of 2nd season
Beets* 45–60 days
Broccoli 70–100 days
Brussels Sprouts 100–110 days
Cabbage* 50–60 days
Carrots* 50–75 days
Cauliflower 70–120 days
Endive, Curly 85–100 days
Garlic 90–100 days
Kale* 55–75 days
Kohlrabi* 45–60 days
Lettuce, Head* 65–90 days
Lettuce, Leaf* 40–50 days
Onion/Leeks/Shallots* 80–170 days
Parsnips 100–130 days
Peas, Garden* 55–70 days
Potatoes 90–140 days
Radishes* 22–70 days
Spinach* 40–50 days
Sunflowers 70–80 days
Sweet Potatoes 110–150 days
Swiss Chard* 45–55 days
Turnips* 30–60 days

USDA Zones 3 and 4
June Plantings
Vegetable—Harvest

Beans, Broad* 80–100 days
Beans, Lima* 65–95 days
Beans, Snap* 45–85 days
Beets* 45–60 days
Broccoli 70–100 days
Carrots* 50–75 days
Chinese Cabbage* 50–85 days
Collards* 60–90 days
Corn* 60–100 days
Cucumbers 55–65 days
Eggplants 100–140 days
Gourds 85–100 days
Kohlrabi* 45–60 days
Lettuce, Head* 65–90 days
Lettuce, Leaf* 40–50 days
Melons, Summer 70–100 days
Melons, Winter 110 days
Okra 55–65 days
Onion/Leeks/Shallots* 80–170 days

Parsnips* 100–130 days
Peas, Garden* 55–70 days
Peas, Southern* 60–70 days
Peppers* 60–95 days
Pumpkins 90–120 days
Radishes* 22–70 days
Rutabagas* 60–90 days
Spinach, New Zealand 50–75 days
Squash, Summer 50–65 days
Squash, Winter 60–110 days
Sunflowers 70–80 days
Sweet Potatoes 110–150 days
Tomatoes† 50–90 days
Turnips* 30–60 days

USDA Zones 3 and 4
July Plantings
Vegetable—Harvest

Beets* 45–60 days
Cabbage* 50–60 days
Kale* 55–75 days
Onion/Leeks/Shallots* 80–170 days

USDA Zones 5 and 6
March Plantings
Vegetable—Harvest

Artichoke Spring of 2nd season
Asparagus Spring of 3rd season
Beets* 45–60 days
Onion/Leeks/Shallots* 80–170 days
Radishes* 22–70 days
Rhubarb 2–4 years

USDA Zones 5 and 6
April Plantings
Vegetable—Harvest

Beets* 45–60 days
Broccoli 70–100 days
Brussels Sprouts 100–110 days
Cabbage* 50–60 days
Carrots* 50–75 days
Cauliflower 70–120 days
Celery 100–120 days
Chinese Cabbage* 50–85 days
Collards* 60–90 days
Cucumbers 55–65 days
Eggplants 100–140 days
Endive* 85–100 days
Gourds 85–100 days
Kale* 55–75 days
Lettuce, Head* 65–90 days
Lettuce, Leaf* 40–50 days
Melons, Summer 70–100 days
Melons, Winter 110 days
Okra 55–65 days
Parsnips* 100–130 days
Peas, Garden* 55–70 days

Potatoes 90–140 days
Radishes* 22–70 days
Rutabagas* 60–90 days
Spinach* 40–50 days
Sweet Potatoes 110–150 days
Swiss Chard* 45–55 days
Turnips* 30–60 days

USDA Zones 5 and 6
May Plantings
Vegetable—Harvest

Beans, Broad* 80–100 days
Beans, Lima* 65–95 days
Beans, Snap* 45–85 days
Beets* 45–60 days
Broccoli 70–100 days
Brussels Sprouts 100–110 days
Cabbage* 50–60 days
Carrots* 50–75 days
Cauliflower 70–120 days
Chinese Cabbage* 50–85 days
Collards* 60–90 days
Corn* 60–100 days
Cucumbers 55–65 days
Eggplants 100–140 days
Endive* 85–100 days
Garlic 90–100 days
Gourds 85–100 days
Kale* 55–75 days
Kohlrabi* 45–60 days
Lettuce, Head* 65–90 days
Melons, Summer 70–100 days
Melons, Winter 110 days
Okra 55–65 days
Onion/Leeks/Shallots* 80–170 days
Parsnips* 100–130 days
Peas, Garden* 55–70 days
Peas, Southern* 60–70 days
Potatoes 90–140 days
Pumpkins 90–120 days
Radishes* 22–70 days
Rutabagas* 60–90 days
Spinach, New Zealand 50–75 days
Squash, Summer 50–65 days
Squash, Winter 60–110 days
Sunflowers 70–80 days
Sweet Potatoes 110–150 days
Swiss Chard* 45–55 days
Tomatoes† 50–90 days
Turnips* 30–60 days

USDA Zones 5 and 6
June Plantings
Vegetable—Harvest

Beans, Broad* 80–100 days
Beans, Lima* 65–95 days
Beans, Snap* 45–85 days
Beets* 45–60 days
Carrots* 50–75 days

Corn* 60–100 days
Cucumbers 55–65 days
Eggplants 100–140 days
Gourds 85–100 days
Kohlrabi* 45–60 days
Lettuce, Head* 65–90 days
Melons, Summer 70–100 days
Melons, Winter 110 days
Okra 55–65 days
Parsnips* 100–130 days
Peas, Southern* 60–70 days
Peppers* 60–95 days
Potatoes 90–140 days
Pumpkins 90–120 days
Radishes* 22–70 days
Rutabagas* 60–90 days
Spinach, New Zealand 50–75 days
Squash, Summer 50–65 days
Squash, Winter 60–110 days
Sunflowers 70–80 days
Sweet Potatoes 110–150 days
Tomatoes† 50–90 days
Turnips* 30–60 days

USDA Zones 5 and 6
July Plantings
Vegetable—Harvest

Beets* 45–60 days
Garlic 90–100 days
Kale* 55–75 days
Kohlrabi* 45–60 days
Onion/Leeks/Shallots* 80–170 days
Radishes* 22–70 days
Sweet Potatoes 110–150 days

USDA Zones 5 and 6
August Plantings
Vegetable—Harvest

Beets* 45–60 days
Radishes* 22–70 days
Spinach* 40–50 days
Swiss Chard* 45–55 days

USDA Zones 7, 8, and 9
January Plantings
Vegetable—Harvest

Rhubarb 2–4 years
Turnips* 30–60 days

USDA Zones 7, 8, and 9
February Plantings
Vegetable—Harvest

Artichoke Spring of 2nd season
Asparagus Spring of 3rd season
Beets* 45–60 days

*Plant successions at recommended intervals for species. †Plant successions of determinate cultivars only.   (Chart continued on following page)

PLANTING AND HARVEST PLANNER

Broccoli 70–100 days
Brussels Sprouts 100–110 days
Cabbage* 50–60 days
Carrots* 50–75 days
Cauliflower 70–120 days
Collards* 60–90 days
Kale* 55–75 days
Kohlrabi* 45–60 days
Lettuce, Head* 65–90 days
Lettuce, Leaf* 40–50 days
Onion/Leeks/Shallots* 80–170 days
Parsnips* 100–130 days
Peas, Garden* 55–70 days
Potatoes 90–140 days
Radishes* 22–70 days
Spinach* 40–50 days
Swiss Chard* 45–55 days
Turnips* 30–60 days

USDA Zones 7, 8, and 9
March Plantings
Vegetable—Harvest

Beets* 45–60 days
Broccoli 70–100 days
Brussels Sprouts 100–110 days
Cabbage* 50–60 days
Carrots* 50–75 days
Cauliflower 70–120 days
Celery 100–120 days
Chinese Cabbage* 50–85 days
Collards* 60–90 days
Corn* 60–100 days
Eggplants 100–140 days
Garlic 90–100 days
Gourds 85–100 days
Kale* 55–75 days
Kohlrabi* 45–60 days
Lettuce, Head* 65–90 days
Lettuce, Leaf* 40–50 days
Onion/Leeks/Shallots* 80–170 days
Parsnips* 100–130 days
Peas, Garden* 55–70 days
Peppers* 60–95 days
Potatoes 90–140 days
Radishes* 22–70 days
Spinach* 40–50 days
Sunflowers 70–80 days
Swiss Chard* 45–55 days
Tomatoes† 50–90 days
Turnips* 30–60 days

USDA Zones 7, 8, and 9
April Plantings
Vegetable—Harvest

Asparagus Spring of 3rd season
Beans, Broad* 80–100 days
Beans, Lima* 65–95 days
Beans, Snap* 45–85 days

Beets* 45–60 days
Broccoli 70–100 days
Brussels Sprouts 100–110 days
Cabbage* 50–60 days
Celery 100–120 days
Chinese Cabbage* 50–85 days
Collards* 60–90 days
Corn* 60–100 days
Cucumbers 55–65 days
Eggplants 100–140 days
Garlic 90–100 days
Gourds 85–100 days
Kohlrabi* 45–60 days
Lettuce, Head* 65–90 days
Lettuce, Leaf* 40–50 days
Melons, Summer 70–100 days
Melons, Winter 110 days
Okra 55–65 days
Onion/Leeks/Shallots* 80–170 days
Parsnips* 100–130 days
Peas, Garden* 55–70 days
Peas, Southern* 60–70 days
Peppers* 60–95 days
Potatoes 90–140 days
Pumpkins 90–120 days
Radishes* 22–70 days
Spinach, New Zealand 50–75 days
Squash, Summer 50–65 days
Squash, Winter 60–110 days
Sunflowers 70–80 days
Sweet Potatoes 110–150 days
Swiss Chard* 45–55 days
Turnips* 30–60 days

USDA Zones 7, 8, and 9
May Plantings
Vegetable—Harvest

Beans, Broad* 80–100 days
Beans, Lima* 65–95 days
Beans, Snap* 45–85 days
Beets* 45–60 days
Collards* 60–90 days
Corn* 60–100 days
Cucumbers 55–65 days
Gourds 85–100 days
Kohlrabi* 45–60 days
Lettuce, Head* 65–90 days
Lettuce, Leaf* 40–50 days
Melons, Summer 70–100 days
Melons, Winter 110 days
Okra 55–65 days
Parsnips* 100–130 days
Peas, Southern* 60–70 days
Potatoes 90–140 days
Pumpkins 90–120 days
Spinach, New Zealand 50–75 days
Squash, Summer 50–65 days
Squash, Winter 60–110 days
Sunflowers 70–80 days
Sweet Potatoes 110–150 days
Turnips* 30–60 days

USDA Zones 7, 8, and 9
June Plantings
Vegetable—Harvest

Beans, Broad* 80–100 days
Beans, Lima* 65–95 days
Beets* 45–60 days
Collards* 60–90 days
Corn* 60–100 days
Cucumbers 55–65 days
Garlic 90–100 days
Gourds 85–100 days
Kohlrabi* 45–60 days
Lettuce, Leaf* 40–50 days
Melons, Summer 70–100 days
Melons, Winter 110 days
Okra 55–65 days
Parsnips* 100–130 days
Peas, Southern* 60–70 days
Pumpkins 90–120 days
Spinach, New Zealand 50–75 days
Squash, Summer 50–65 days
Squash, Winter 60–110 days
Sunflowers 70–80 days
Sweet Potatoes 110–150 days

USDA Zones 7, 8, and 9
July Plantings
Vegetable—Harvest

Beets* 45–60 days
Collards* 60–90 days
Garlic 90–100 days
Kohlrabi* 45–60 days
Lettuce, Head* 65–90 days
Sweet Potatoes 110–150 days

USDA Zones 7, 8, and 9
August Plantings
Vegetable—Harvest

Beets* 45–60 days
Collards* 60–90 days
Kohlrabi* 45–60 days
Lettuce, Head* 65–90 days
Radishes* 22–70 days
Rutabagas* 60–90 days
Turnips* 30–60 days

USDA Zones 7, 8, and 9
September Plantings
Vegetable—Harvest

Artichoke Spring of 2nd season
Beets* 45–60 days
Endive* 85–100 days
Kohlrabi* 45–60 days
Lettuce, Head* 65–90 days

Lettuce, Leaf* 40–50 days
Peas, Garden* 55–70 days
Radishes* 22–70 days
Rhubarb 2–4 years
Spinach* 40–50 days
Swiss Chard* 45–55 days
Turnips* 30–60 days

USDA Zones 7, 8, and 9
October Plantings
Vegetable—Harvest

Artichoke Spring of 2nd season
Beets* 45–60 days
Lettuce, Head* 65–90 days
Lettuce, Leaf* 40–50 days
Radishes* 22–70 days
Rhubarb 2–4 years
Spinach* 40–50 days
Turnips* 30–60 days

USDA Zone 10
January Plantings
Vegetable—Harvest

Artichoke Spring of 2nd season
Asparagus Spring of 3rd season
Beets* 45–60 days
Cabbage* 50–60 days
Carrots* 50–75 days
Chinese Cabbage* 50–85 days
Garlic 90–100 days
Kale* 55–75 days
Kohlrabi* 45–60 days
Lettuce, Head* 65–90 days
Lettuce, Leaf* 40–50 days
Onion/Leeks/Shallots* 80–170 days
Peas, Garden* 55–70 days
Potatoes 90–140 days
Radishes* 22–70 days
Rhubarb 2–4 years
Spinach* 40–50 days
Swiss Chard* 45–55 days
Turnips* 30–60 days

USDA Zone 10
February Plantings
Vegetable—Harvest

Artichoke Spring of 2nd season
Asparagus Spring of 3rd season
Beets* 45–60 days
Cabbage* 50–60 days
Carrots* 50–75 days
Chinese Cabbage* 50–85 days
Collards* 60–90 days
Garlic 90–100 days
Gourds 85–100 days
Kale* 55–75 days
Kohlrabi* 45–60 days

*Plant successions at recommended intervals for species. †Plant successions of determinate cultivars only.

PLANTING AND HARVEST PLANNER

Lettuce, Head* 65–90 days
Lettuce, Leaf* 40–50 days
Onion/Leeks/Shallots* 80–170 days
Peas, Garden* 55–70 days
Potatoes 90–140 days
Radishes* 22–70 days
Rhubarb 2–4 years
Spinach* 40–50 days
Sweet Potatoes 110–150 days
Swiss Chard* 45–55 days
Turnips* 30–60 days

USDA Zone 10
March Plantings
Vegetable—Harvest

Asparagus Spring of 3rd season
Beans, Broad* 80–100 days
Beans, Lima* 65–95 days
Beans, Snap* 45–85 days
Beets* 45–60 days
Carrots* 50–75 days
Collards* 60–90 days
Eggplants 100–140 days
Garlic 90–100 days
Gourds 85–100 days
Kale* 55–75 days
Kohlrabi* 45–60 days
Lettuce, Head* 65–90 days
Lettuce, Leaf* 40–50 days
Onion/Leeks/Shallots* 80–170 days
Parsnips* 100–130 days
Peas, Garden* 55–70 days
Peas, Southern* 60–70 days
Peppers* 60–95 days
Radishes* 22–70 days
Sunflowers 70–80 days
Sweet Potatoes 110–150 days
Swiss Chard* 45–55 days
Tomatoes† 50–90 days
Turnips* 30–60 days

USDA Zone 10
April Plantings
Vegetable—Harvest

Beans, Broad* 80–100 days
Beans, Lima* 65–95 days
Beans, Snap* 45–85 days
Beets* 45–60 days
Carrots* 50–75 days
Collards* 60–90 days
Corn* 60–100 days
Cucumbers 55–65 days
Gourds 85–100 days
Kale* 55–75 days
Kohlrabi* 45–60 days
Lettuce, Head* 65–90 days
Lettuce, Leaf* 40–50 days
Melons, Summer 70–100 days
Melons, Winter 110 days

Okra 55–65 days
Onion/Leeks/Shallots* 80–170 days
Parsnips* 100–130 days
Peas, Southern* 60–70 days
Peppers* 60–95 days
Pumpkins 90–120 days
Radishes* 22–70 days
Squash, Summer 50–65 days
Squash, Winter 60–110 days
Sunflowers 70–80 days
Sweet Potatoes 110–150 days
Turnips* 30–60 days

USDA Zone 10
May Plantings
Vegetable—Harvest

Beans, Broad* 80–100 days
Beans, Lima* 65–95 days
Beans, Snap* 45–85 days
Collards* 60–90 days
Corn* 60–100 days
Cucumbers 55–65 days
Gourds 85–100 days
Lettuce, Head* 65–90 days
Melons, Summer 70–100 days
Melons, Winter 110 days
Okra 55–65 days
Parsnips* 100–130 days
Peas, Southern* 60–70 days
Pumpkins 90–120 days
Spinach, New Zealand 50–75 days
Squash, Summer 50–65 days
Squash, Winter 60–110 days
Sunflowers 70–80 days
Sweet Potatoes 110–150 days
Turnips* 30–60 days

USDA Zone 10
June Plantings
Vegetable—Harvest

Beans, Broad* 80–100 days
Beans, Lima* 65–95 days
Beets* 45–60 days
Collards* 60–90 days
Corn* 60–100 days
Cucumbers 55–65 days
Gourds 85–100 days
Kohlrabi* 45–60 days
Melons, Summer 70–100 days
Melons, Winter 110 days
Okra 55–65 days
Parsnips* 100–130 days
Peas, Southern* 60–70 days
Pumpkins 90–120 days
Spinach, New Zealand 50–75 days
Squash, Summer 50–65 days
Squash, Winter 60–110 days
Sunflowers 70–80 days
Sweet Potatoes 110–150 days

USDA Zone 10
July Plantings
Vegetable—Harvest

Cauliflower 70–120 days
Collards* 60–90 days
Kohlrabi* 45–60 days
Peas, Southern* 60–70 days
Spinach, New Zealand 50–75 days
Squash, Summer 50–65 days
Squash, Winter 60–110 days
Sunflowers 70–80 days
Tomatoes† 50–90 days

USDA Zone 10
August Plantings
Vegetable—Harvest

Beans, Broad* 80–100 days
Beans, Lima* 65–95 days
Beets* 45–60 days
Cauliflower 70–120 days
Celery 100–120 days
Collards* 60–90 days
Peas, Southern* 60–70 days

USDA Zone 10
September Plantings
Vegetable—Harvest

Beets* 45–60 days
Broccoli 70–100 days
Brussels Sprouts 100–110 days
Cabbage* 50–60 days
Cauliflower 70–120 days
Celery 100–120 days
Chinese Cabbage* 50–85 days
Endive* 85–100 days
Garlic 90–100 days
Kale* 55–75 days
Kohlrabi* 45–60 days
Lettuce, Head* 65–90 days
Lettuce, Leaf* 40–50 days
Onion/Leeks/Shallots* 80–170 days
Rhubarb 2–4 years
Rutabagas* 60–90 days
Spinach* 40–50 days
Sweet Potatoes 110–150 days
Swiss Chard* 45–55 days
Turnips* 30–60 days

USDA Zone 10
October Plantings
Vegetable—Harvest

Artichoke Spring of 2nd season
Beets* 45–60 days
Broccoli 70–100 days

Brussels Sprouts 100–110 days
Cabbage* 50–60 days
Carrots* 50–75 days
Cauliflower 70–120 days
Celery 100–120 days
Chinese Cabbage* 50–85 days
Garlic 90–100 days
Kale* 55–75 days
Kohlrabi* 45–60 days
Lettuce, Head* 65–90 days
Lettuce, Leaf* 40–50 days
Onion/Leeks/Shallots* 80–170 days
Potatoes 90–140 days
Radishes* 22–70 days
Rhubarb 2–4 years
Spinach* 40–50 days
Sweet Potatoes 110–150 days
Swiss Chard* 45–55 days
Turnips* 30–60 days

USDA Zone 10
November Plantings
Vegetable—Harvest

Beets* 45–60 days
Cabbage* 50–60 days
Carrots* 50–75 days
Garlic 90–100 days
Kale* 55–75 days
Kohlrabi* 45–60 days
Lettuce, Head* 65–90 days
Lettuce, Leaf* 40–50 days
Onion/Leeks/Shallots* 80–170 days
Potatoes 90–140 days
Radishes* 22–70 days
Rhubarb 2–4 years
Spinach* 40–50 days
Swiss Chard* 45–55 days
Turnips* 30–60 days

USDA Zone 10
December Plantings
Vegetable—Harvest

Artichoke Spring of 2nd season
Asparagus Spring of 3rd season
Beets* 45–60 days
Cabbage* 50–60 days
Carrots* 50–75 days
Garlic 90–100 days
Kale* 55–75 days
Kohlrabi* 45–60 days
Lettuce, Head* 65–90 days
Lettuce, Leaf* 40–50 days
Onion/Leeks/Shallots* 80–170 days
Potatoes 90–140 days
Radishes* 22–70 days
Rhubarb 2–4 years
Spinach* 40–50 days
Swiss Chard* 45–55 days
Turnips* 30–60 days

*Plant successions at recommended intervals for species. †Plant successions of determinate cultivars only.

EARLY STARTS FOR VEGETABLES

(Top right) Start plants indoors to get a jump on the season. Use peat pots, as shown here, or plant in flats or divided-cell trays. Once your seedlings emerge, place them in a warm, well-lit spot out of direct sunlight.

(Middle right) Early spring days frequently are marked with cold spells or frost. Protect plants by installing tomato cages wrapped in sheet plastic, while leaving 1 in. (25 mm) of space between the bottom of the plastic and the soil.

(Below) Greenhouses trap radiant heat from sunlight to keep tender seedlings warm. Ventilate the space by opening the doors, vents, and windows on warm, sunny days.

While chilly winds still blow in the spring and frost remains a hazard, it still is possible to begin planting by using various early-start techniques. The simplest of these is planting indoors, where shirtsleeve temperatures are common [see Starting Plants Indoors, opposite pg]. Outdoors, a greenhouse or a cold frame will trap the sun's heat and keep frost from harming tender seedlings. Both greenhouses and cold frames have panels of glass or plastic to efficiently permit both visible light and infrared rays to pass through to the plants and soil within, where the light is absorbed. Glass is opaque to the longer wavelengths of radiated heat energy, so the temperature inside either type of structure will rise quickly whenever light falls on it. Cold frames are better insulated than greenhouses, because they are open-bottomed boxes that are buried deeply within the soil, sometimes within a layer of straw that helps hold their heat. Oftentimes, they are placed over a bed of green manure, which generates warmth as it decomposes.

When temperatures outdoors have moderated but frost is still probable, protection offered by cloches, hot caps, floating row covers, or other coverings that are made of clear glass, waxed paper,

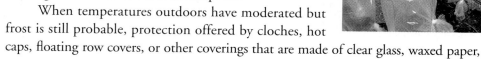

or sheet plastic film can protect your tender seedlings. Working on much the same principles as those for a greenhouse, these keep both air and soil warm for the growing plants, retaining moisture as a bonus. Those made of waterproof film or glass should be installed high enough to keep their sides from contact with the foliage; the air gap insulates and separates the covering from contact with the foliage, preventing water from condensing on the leaves and causing conditions that can result in fungal disease infections.

Using early-start techniques can add more than 6 weeks to the growing season in climates where long winters and cool springs and autumns are the norm. Combined with protection for your vegetables in autumn by use of covers during frosty evenings, these methods can extend the growing season 2 months or more. The difference can add enough time to allow you to plant slow-to-mature vegetables.

STARTING PLANTS INDOORS

Planting indoor starts is a good way to extend the season in cold-winter climates and allows earlier harvests than planting outdoors in the soil. Choose those vegetables suited to transplanting and sow them 3–6 weeks ahead of expected planting time in the garden. Because tender seedlings are protected from frost, pests, and fungal disease while they are young, they have a greater success rate in the garden after transplanting. Gather your bedding trays, potting soil, tools, and seed, then follow these steps:

1 Note the planting depth for the vegetable variety, then fill your bedding tray with potting soil, allowing ample room to add soil after the seed is sown.

2 Gently compact the potting soil by pressing down on it with a flat board or by using your open palms. Add more soil as needed to fill to the proper depth.

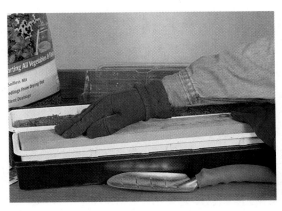

3 To assure room for transplanting and good germination, sow seed pairs about 3 in. (75 mm) apart. Some trays are subdivided to facilitate spacing.

4 Sift soil over the seed, covering to the depth that is recommended on the seed package. Firm the soil to assure good soil-to-seed contact.

5 Use a misting sprayer to apply water to the bedding tray until damp. Loosely cover the tray with clear plastic, then allow the seed to germinate in a warm spot with indirect sunlight.

6 In a few days, seedlings will emerge. Keep them evenly moist, then remove the cover. When each plant grows 2 true leaves, thin the weakest of each pair of seedlings with a pair of scissors.

GROWING VEGETABLES FROM SEED

(Right) Keep seed fresh by sealing the unopened packages in a zip-top plastic bag and storing it in the vegetable keeper of a household refrigerator until it is time to plant.

Growing vegetables from seed is among the most common method used for planting large gardens, raising unique or unusual vegetables, or ensuring that only pest- or disease-resistant strains well adapted to local conditions are selected. Planting seed is economical and makes starting new plants easy regardless of the stage of the season—a vital aid if you want to have successions of vegetables in your garden.

Choose quality seed dated for planting in the current year. Make your decisions of the plant varieties that you wish to grow while choices are plentiful, then store your seed in sealable, moisture-proof plastic bags, and place them in the vegetable keeper of your household refrigerator. The low temperature found there will keep the seed dormant until it warms and is planted, for as long as a year or more, depending on the vegetable variety.

You've already seen how to start seed in containers [see Starting Seed Indoors, previous pg.]. When the hazard of frost has passed and the soil has warmed sufficiently for planting, follow the instructions shown for planting seed in your garden [see Planting Seed in Gardens, opposite pg.].

It's important to plant seed correctly, referring to the packet directions or grower recommendations to determine the proper depth and spacing you'll use. Because germination is uncertain, avoid gaps in your plantings by sowing two or three seeds in each location, then thin the seedlings as needed. For vegetables with tiny seed such as carrot, lettuce, and radish, the depth of planting may be ¼ in. (6 mm)

(Above) Seed such as pumpkin will sprout in 8–10 days from the time of planting, producing two "seed leaves."

or less. Cover such seed with fine sandy loam or sandy soil by sifting it over the seed, then firm the area surrounding the planting to assure that the soil is in close contact with the seed. Large, starchy-seeded vegetables such as pea, pumpkin, or sunflower can be planted more deeply, either in a furrow or in holes made with a dibber, a hoe handle, or your finger. Again, firm the soil over the seed after planting.

Complete your planting by gently misting the surface of the soil over the seed with a fine spray, either with an adjustable nozzle on a garden hose or by using a watering can fitted with a diffusing rose on its spout. Be careful to avoid washing the newly planted seed from the soil, and keep the area evenly moist until the seed germinates and send up sprouts.

THINNING

When seed sprout, they usually will have two so-called seed leaves that can resemble weeds or other plants. Wait to thin until the plants have developed two or more true leaves; you can recognize them by referring to the diagrams commonly found on their seed packages.

Shallow-rooted plants such as carrots and radishes can be thinned by hand; for larger plants such as corn and squash, it may be easier to use a pair of scissors or small bypass pruning shears to cut the stems off at the soil line. Whichever method you use, consult the seed package to determine the optimum spacing for the species.

Thinning ensures that your plants will avoid crowding, prevents them from having to compete for moisture and nutrients, and enables them to form complete, deep root systems that makes them tolerant of brief periods of drought. For tall species such as corn or sunflowers, thinning prevents shading of nearby plants and allows air to circulate between them, hastening drying of dew and avoiding infections by fungal diseases common in moist conditions.

To interleave succession plantings, plant and thin to twice the specified distance for the species, then plant the intervals again 3–4 weeks after the first planting. The result will be an extended harvest.

PLANTING SEED IN GARDENS

Sowing vegetable seed directly in garden soil should be done once the soil warms in spring and all hazard of frost is over or, in mild-winter climates, when the heat of summer has ended. Most vegetables are planted as seeded areas, in raised hills, or as rows. Gather your seed, and follow these steps:

Seeding Areas in Beds

1 Plant leafy greens such as lettuce and radishes and carrots in areas. Scatter the seed evenly on the bed with your open palm, tossing the seed with a flinging motion of your wrist.

2 Sift topsoil or loose compost onto the bed to cover the seed to its recommended depth, firm the soil, then mist with water until the area is saturated.

Seeding Hills

1 Plant squash and pumpkin in hills. With your fingers, press 4 seed the recommended depth into the top of the hill, then cover with additional soil.

2 Firm the soil over the seed, then mist with water. Keep evenly moist until seedlings emerge, then apply water in the basin.

Seeding Rows

1 Plant bush peas and beans in rows. Press each seed into the soil to its recommended depth and spacing. Sift more soil over the seed until they are covered.

2 Firm the soil over the seed, then mist with water. Keep evenly moist until seedlings emerge, then water by filling the furrows beside the seedlings.

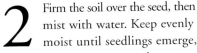

TRANSPLANTING TO GARDEN SOIL

Unless you sow seed directly in garden soil, you are likely to use the technique of transplanting for starts you grow yourself or obtain from a nursery or garden center. The best time to transplant is while the seedling is young, usually after it has formed several true leaves and, if a branching plant, after it has begun to develop its characteristic shape. The other consideration in transplanting is the weather. You should wait to transplant until the soil outdoors has warmed adequately to sustain continued growth of the young plants and the air temperatures at night stay above freezing. Even then, you should harden your plants—gradually expose tender seedlings to outdoor conditions—when you transplant your greenhouse or indoor starts outdoors [see Hardening Transplants, this pg.].

It's important to protect the roots of your seedlings as you transplant them, though an exception should be made for starts that have become rootbound. Inspect the root systems of plants grown in nursery containers. Remove them from the pot by inverting them in your palm and gently tapping the bottom of the container; the rootball should slide into your waiting hand. Rootbound plants have large, encircling roots that spiral around the edge of the rootball and which should be carefully unwound or cut prior to transplanting.

Follow the directions shown to transplant plants grown in nursery containers [see Planting Individual Plants, opposite pg.]. Loosen the garden soil several days before transplanting so the soil has time to settle and the new roots can grow into the nearby soil. Water immediately after transplanting to eliminate air pockets around the new plants.

Transplanting seedlings you have reared and those plants obtained from your garden center is easiest when you have the right tools. You will need both foliar and granular organic fertilizer, a hand fork, a pair of garden gloves, a trowel, a sharp pair of bypass pruners, as well as a watering can.

HARDENING TRANSPLANTS

Seedlings grown indoors or in a greenhouse or cold frame require a period of adjustment to help them acclimatize to outdoor conditions prior to planting. This process is called "hardening" the young plants.

Starting 7–10 days before the intended date of planting, move the seedlings outdoors during the days to a protected, shady area with plenty of indirect light. Too much direct sunlight will burn their foliage, while too little will slow their growth. For the first 2–3 days, bring the seedlings back indoors during cool evenings, or return them to the cold frame and close its top.

As the plants begin to adjust, you can leave them outside during the evening, covering them loosely with breathable fabric supported above the plants on stakes or a wooden frame. Avoid leaving plastic or other coverings in contact with the foliage of the plants; condensation that stands on the leaves can promote fungal disease. The covering should be left in place on cold days or whenever rain, hail, or sleet occur but should be lifted early in the morning during all warm, sunny days.

After a few more days, move the plants into a sunlit spot protected from wind, and limit the period they are covered to cold-night protection. They quickly will adjust to the outdoor conditions similar to those found in your garden.

As a final step during the last 2 days prior to planting, position the vegetables in the garden itself. They still may need nighttime protection, a precaution that could continue even several weeks after transplanting. Featherweight fabric row covers are ideal for that purpose.

PLANTING INDIVIDUAL PLANTS

Young vegetable plants are available in spring at garden retailers as individuals in plastic and peat pots, as well as in divided trays called 6-packs. Choose healthy plants free of broken leaves and stems, avoiding those that are yellowed, already bear flowers or fruit, or appear rootbound. Gather a trowel, a watering can, and your plants, and follow these steps:

Plants in Peat Pots

1 For plants in peat pots, tear away the top of the pot below the soil line to prevent water from wicking after planting.

2 Dig a planting hole 1–2 in. (25–50 mm) deeper than the distance from the top of the soil in the pot to its bottom. Sprinkle about 1 tsp. (5 ml) of granular 5–5–5 fertilizer in the hole, mixing it into the soil.

3 Backfill the hole with enough soil to make its depth equal to the soil in the peat pot. Set the plant in the hole, backfilling around it with soil. Water.

Plants in 6-Packs

1 For plants in 6-packs, carefully invert the pack and gently press in on the bottom of each cell to release the seedlings. Avoid pulling on the plants' stems.

2 Dig planting holes that are 1 in. (25 mm) deeper than the rootball's height. Sprinkle about ¼–½ tsp. (1–2 ml) of granular 5–5–5 fertilizer in each hole, adding soil to cover it.

3 Set plants in their hole with the soil around their rootballs level with the surrounding soil. Firm the soil and water.

EARLY CARE OF NEWLY PLANTED VEGETABLES

The only thing certain about spring weather is that it is filled with uncertainty. Warm, balmy days intermingle with periods of rain, wind, and cold. Frosts occur even weeks into the gardening season in many areas, so you will want to protect your new plantings whenever conditions turn unpredictable. Two methods can help you in this regard: covering and mulching.

Coverings made of translucent waxed paper, plastic, glass, or woven fabric insulate tender seedlings by isolating the air around them and preventing cold dew from forming on their foliage. Sunlight passing through the covers, while necessary to keep photosynthesis active, has an added benefit of warming the soil and air within the covering. Such coverings also help keep humidity levels high and reduce the need to water. Take care, however, on too-warm, sunny days; remove or partially lift your plant coverings to allow some solar heat to escape or tender shoots on your plants could be damaged. Remove the coverings entirely when the plants have become hardened and the hazard of frost has passed completely.

Used either alone or in conjunction with coverings, mulching around young plants will conserve soil moisture, insulate them to keep soil temperatures from fluctuating, prevent weed seed from germinating by blocking them from light, and—for organic mulches such as straw, compost, or wood chips—will lightly fertilize your plants as they decompose. Because it provides benefits beyond its neat and aesthetic appeal, you should always consider mulching around your vegetables. A layer of mulch, 1–2 in. (25–50 mm) thick, usually is adequate for young vegetable plants. Keep the mulch away from the plant stems, however, as it can trap moisture that encourages fungal diseases or hide rasping insects that may eat your young plants.

Keep new seedlings evenly moist until their roots have become established. If humidity is low, occasionally mist their foliage to keep it well hydrated. Apply foliar fertilizer—water-soluble nutrients absorbed by the leaves and stems of the plant—to give new transplants a boost. A feeding mixed at half the strength advised on the package directions and applied every other watering for the first 3 weeks will ensure that your plants get a strong, vigorous start. Apply water to them beneath their foliage thereafter.

EARLY-SEASON FROST PROTECTION

Freezing temperatures damage plant tissue by rupturing cell walls as sharp-edged ice crystals grow within them. Frost-burned plants may recover if their damaged foliage is pruned away and they receive tender care, but it's best to cover your seedlings to prevent frost damage.

Cover individual plants with a cloche—a bell-shaped glass cover—or with disposable hot caps made of stiff waxed paper. For large areas, breathable, lightweight, transparent fabric sheets known as floating row covers can be draped directly on the plants or supported over them on a system of wooden stakes or lathe.

For midsized beds, use arched plastic-film row covers made like tiny greenhouses, stretch clear landscape fabric over ribs of PVC pipe, or keep frost off your young seedlings with sheet acrylic plastic set on block supports.

(Top) Hot caps made of waxed paper can give temporary frost protection to plants. Bury their flanged edges in the soil or fasten them in place with stakes.

(Above) Applying a layer of straw mulch, 3–4 in. (75–100 mm) thick, will help insulate the soil during chilly nights, holding in the heat trapped by the hot cap.

(Right) Apply foliar fertilizer that is absorbed directly by the foliage immediately after planting nursery starts and transplants. Combine with a surfactant to help retain moisture and prevent wilting.

ROW COVERS AND MULCHING

Using Row Covers

1 After the bed is seeded, install the preformed row cover sections over the furrow, setting its anchors deep into the soil.

A row cover is used to insulate and protect tender young seedlings from frost and cold rains, while mulch cloth—also known as weed-barrier fabric—helps warm the soil and blocks light to prevent seed germination. Apply each to your young vegetables, following these simple steps:

2 For early-season plantings, install end sections made of row cover material to create a mini green-house for your plants.

3 The seed will sprout and grow beneath the transparent row cover. When the temperatures warm, remove the end sections.

Planting with Mulch Cloth

1 After leveling and raking the soil, lay porous mulch cloth, overlapping seams at least 8 in. (20 cm) and pinning it to the ground with U-shaped metal stakes.

2 At each planting location, make X-shaped cuts with a sharp knife. Each should be slightly larger than the transplants' rootballs.

3 Peel back the flaps and plant through the mulch cloth, into the soil beneath. Close the flaps to tightly surround the plant.

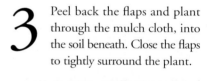

STAKING AND SUPPORTING

In the last chapter, you were shown how to install frames, stakes, wood supports, and trellises before planting most of your heavy vegetables [see Supporting Plants, pg. 32]. Supports also can be added to your garden after your seedlings emerge or when you transplant them to their final spots in your beds, using stakes and string that they can climb.

Besides efficiently using vertical space to grow more vegetables in a given area, supports hold vines above the moisture in the soil or mulch beneath them, keeping burrowing and crawling insects at bay, along with any fungal disease spores. Vigorous branching plants such as gourds, pumpkin, and squash may require both training to the supports and some careful pruning to limit the number of branches they are allowed to bear. While the amount of fruit produced by your plants will be reduced by this pruning, the size of each of them will be larger and your yield per plant will be nearly identical by weight as compared to plants that are grown in the usual fashion.

Some vining vegetable plants naturally have tendrils or so-called holdfasts to support their stem's weight. Others need your assistance to help them cling to their supports, provided by stretchy plastic plant tape, string, or plastic-coated wire ties. Remember to carefully wind the vines and stalks around the supports as they grow, binding their fleshy vines loosely to stakes or trellises while allowing them some flexibility of movement and preventing the ties from girdling them as they grow. Your attention might be required several times each week to perform this task while your young vines are growing rapidly.

Heavy fruit from plants grown on vertical supports usually will develop thick, strong stems to support themselves. You should aid unusually heavy fruit such as pumpkin or winter squash by wrapping it loosely in stretch nylon net and tying the net to the supports. Visitors to your garden will be amazed to see large gourds, melons, pumpkins, and squash dangling in midair from your supporting frames and trellises.

(Right) Vegetables with heavy fruit such as gourds, melons, pumpkins, and squash benefit from growing up through and sprawling over a pyramid support of stout timber.

(Below) Bind vines to stakes and trellises as their stems grow. Leave the ties loose to avoid girdling.

(Bottom) Dangling, heavy fruit occasionally needs an assist. Drape nylon netting loosely around the fruit, then tie it securely to its support frame.

INSTALLING TOMATO CAGES

Tomatoes are heavy, sprawling plants that perform best when supported. For large plantings, use string trellises [see Installing String Trellises, pg. 33]. For individual plants in small-space gardens, welded-wire tomato cages are best. Choose a stout cage that is at least 4 ft. (1.2 m) tall, measured from the bottom ring. Gather your cage, wooden support stakes at least 3 ft. (90 cm) long, a mallet, pliers, and wire ties, then follow these simple steps:

1 Center the cage on the young tomato plant. Carefully push the cage's wire prongs down into the soil until its bottom ring is about 4 in. (10 cm) above the soil.

2 Drive 3 stakes alongside the wire cage and parallel with the uprights, using a mallet or hammer. A mature tomato plant can stand 6 ft. (1.8 m) or taller, requiring extra support.

3 Use the pliers and wire ties to attach the cage firmly to the stakes, which will give the cage added support and prevent it from tipping as the tomato sets fruit and it matures.

4 As the tomato plant grows, train vines that extend from the cage back into its center, tying them or pruning excess growth if necessary.

Good garden care means quality when it's time to harvest. Learn the best ways to cultivate, fertilize, and water, as well as other methods used for garden care

Caring for Vegetables

The most common elements of caring for your vegetable garden include the regular acts of irrigating, cultivating, fertilizing, directing growth by pinching and pruning, and inspecting and controlling pests and diseases that sometimes can infest or infect your plants. As compared to planning, preparing, and planting, these tasks take little effort and time. You'll likely find them the most enjoyable part of vegetable gardening other than harvesting your bounty of fresh greens and fruit when they ripen.

Nature sometimes gives us water to grow our vegetables through precipitation. More often, however, you'll need to augment rain with irrigation by hand, hose, or automatic system. In this chapter, you'll learn the amount of water to apply, how frequently to irrigate, and how to gauge when your plants need more or less. The correct way to water also will be demonstrated, with different methods to use for each type of vegetable, depending on its growth habit.

Next, you'll see how to keep weeds from growing in your garden, blocking them from competing with your vegetable plants for nutrients and sunlight. You'll cultivate to uproot their seedlings and loosen the soil as you work in air and deeply mix nutrients around your vegetables' roots.

Feeding your vegetables is another care task that should be repeated at regular intervals throughout the growing season. You'll learn the differences between types of fertilizer and how to consult package labels, which give useful information about which fertilizer to use. There's more than nutrients, too. You'll find which trace minerals and micronutrients are needed for vegetables, as well as learn about helpful organic mixtures such as kelp extract that boast growth enzymes that will give your plants vigor.

Finally, you'll learn to inspect your garden to note your plants' health and overall development. You'll discover when and how to thin, pinch, or prune, and when to allow plants room to grow. If you notice a pest or a disease, you'll find information on how to identify and control both in the pages that follow. Because you plan to eat your produce, the emphasis will be on environmentally sound and sustainable control methods with little impact to you, your family, your pets, or the environment as a whole.

The fruits of vegetables such as eggplant should be thinned to one to two per branch, or three to four total per plant. Reducing the number of fruit helps each eggplant grow larger and mature more quickly than if it has to compete with many others for the nutrients provided by the plant's roots.

WATERING

Key to the irrigation of vegetable plants is a regular and sufficient application of water followed by a length of time to allow the water to be absorbed into the soil. Either too much or insufficient water can cause vegetables to fail.

Water applied too quickly will saturate the soil and cause either puddles or fast runoff, eroding the soil and exposing plant roots. Because they need air as well as water around their roots, plants left too long in saturated soil are subject to suffocation, root damage, and fungal infection. Always apply water at a rate that allows it to be absorbed, and wait to apply more whenever puddling or runoff occurs. A good goal is to fully saturate the top 4–6 in. (10–15 cm) of soil with water at each watering. For most garden soils, this means applying the equivalent of about 1 in. (25 mm) of water across the soil surface, and watering every 3–4 days.

(Right) Whether your plants are in a container or in the garden, it's always best to water them at their base and to avoid wetting foliage. Apply water slowly at the rate it is absorbed, avoiding runoff or erosion.

(Below) Keeping track of rain water that nature supplies will help you know when to irrigate your garden. Most vegetables need the equivalent of 1–2 in. (25–50 mm) of water applied per week.

Watering lightly and too frequently causes plants to become shallow-rooted and subject to drought. When the root zone is dry, the plants grow hair roots near the surface to gather moisture. It's easy to check for shallow watering. If you find that the soil remains dry 3–4 in. (10–15 cm) beneath the surface after watering, you should slow the rate of application and lengthen the time of irrigation until all of the soil is saturated.

Allow the soil surface to dry between waterings. This usually takes 2–4 days, though it may take longer if it rains. The soil at the root zone, a depth of 8–16 in. (20–40 cm), should be evenly moist yet should maintain good texture and hold sufficient air.

Soils that are loose and sandy drain too quickly. You should balance this tendency by watering more frequently and amending your soil with compost before you plant [see Amending Soil, pg. 24].

Use one of the watering methods demonstrated to ensure your plants will receive adequate and regular moisture during the growing season [see Watering Techniques, opposite pg.].

(Right) Drip irrigation can be used for vegetable plantings. Emitters that drip water at the base of plants are the most popular, but small spray heads also can be used, as seen here.

WATERING TECHNIQUES

Several methods are used to water vegetables, depending on the nature of the plants and the methods you prefer. They include soaker hose irrigation, drip irrigation, overhead misting, trench irrigation, and moat irrigation. Each option is described below, and tips are given for its use:

Soaker Hose Irrigation

A Avoid runoff, conserve water, and limit weed growth by delivering water directly to the plants with a soaker hose. It's always best to keep the hose from touching plants.

Drip Irrigation

B Automate watering, conserve water, and limit weed growth with drip irrigation delivered directly to each plant. Lay supply hose from a timer-controlled valve to each plant, choose the emitter type—drip, spray, or bubbler—and match its flow rate to the needs of your vegetable plants.

Trench Irrigation

C Apply water by filling a trench alongside your row vegetables and allow it to penetrate deeply into the root zone before watering again to promote strong, drought-tolerant plants.

Overhead Misting

D Best used with cool-season vegetables. Apply early in the day, setting a hose-end nozzle to a fine mist and slowly saturating the soil. The plants will dry thoroughly before temperatures drop in the evening.

Moat Irrigation

E Used with hill crops, a moat surrounds each plant and delivers a subsurface cone of water to each plant's roots. As with trenches, allow the water to penetrate deeply, and water only when the soil surface completely dries.

CULTIVATING AND WEED PREVENTION

Proper soil preparation, mulching, and point-irrigation using drip systems or soaker hoses will do much to control weeds in your vegetable garden. Still, it is beneficial to cultivate your soil regularly during the season. Cultivating—working the surface layer of soil with a cultivating tool, hoe, or rake—prevents a hard crust from forming on the topsoil that otherwise would cause precipitation or irrigation water to run off before it penetrated the soil. Working the soil also breaks up clods and allows air to penetrate down to the root zone, and it helps carry to the roots some nutrients such as phosphorus and potassium that tend to bind to minerals in the soil.

An important side benefit of cultivating is the uprooting of young weed plants before they can become established. All garden soil contains some weed seed. When you turn the soil to prepare it for planting, you also bring this seed to the surface, where it germinates in the ideal moisture and light conditions of your vegetable garden. Once established, weeds are deep-rooted and challenging to eradicate. It's best to uproot them by cultivating while they are young or pull the sprouts as they appear. Always avoid allowing weeds growing near your vegetable garden to go to seed, as their offspring can be troublesome in the following season.

Remember when cultivating that the intent is to work the top 4 in. (10 cm) of soil, avoiding deeper soil penetration that can harm your vegetable plants' roots. Also keep your tool 3–4 in. (75–100 mm) away from their stems.

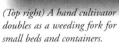

(Top right) A hand cultivator doubles as a weeding fork for small beds and containers.

(Top, above) Pulling weeds by hand requires time, effort, and care. To be effective, pull the weeds before they reach mature size and begin to produce seed, and always pull or dig out all of their roots.

(Above) Most garden weeds can be composted because the heat of the compost pile kills any seed they may contain. Burn or destroy all pest-infested and disease-infected foliage.

(Right) Use a cultivating tool to uproot weeds and break the crust on compacted garden soil, working away from the stem of the plant to prevent damage to roots. The cultivator shown combines both a hoe and tine.

CULTIVATING A GARDEN

Cultivating is an essential part of garden care that benefits plantings by loosening soil, controlling competitive weeds, aiding water penetration, and improving overall appearance. For small areas, use a hand fork or tined tool; in larger areas, use a hoe, cultivator, or specialty fork. Limit cultivating to the top 2–4 in. (50–100 mm) of soil, avoiding deeper penetration that could harm plant roots. Gather your tools, then follow these easy steps:

Cultivating Containers, Beds, and Hills

A Carefully loosen compacted soil in containers with a hand fork, turning the soil to a depth of 2–4 in. (50–100 mm) and removing any weeds that have sprouted.

B In raised beds, work carefully alongside your vegetable plants using a small, sharp-pointed cultivating tool. Work the soil around each plant to at least 2–4 in. (50–100 mm) deep.

C For plants grown in hills or mounds, turn the soil in the moat and its surrounding levy, then rebuild the mound and moat, adjusting their width as the plants grow.

Cultivating in the Garden

1 Unearth 4–6 in. (10–15 cm) of soil near the plants, removing weeds, rocks, and debris. Avoid disturbing plant roots. Break up clods. Incorporate compost or other amendements.

2 Work the soil more deeply about 1 ft. (30 cm) out from the plants. Bring buried soil, 10–12 in. (25–30 cm) deep, to the surface.

3 Work backwards down the row and around any hill plantings. Avoid walking on and compacting finished areas.

FERTILIZING

Nutrients that vegetable plants need to grow, mature, and set and ripen fruit are naturally present in most undisturbed soils and those prepared for planting [see Site and Soil, pg. 22]. Because nitrate salts and some of the micronutrients and trace elements are water-soluble and other nutrients are used by the plants as they grow, soil that once was adequate can become exhausted in short order. This especially is true for soils used to grow plants in containers.

The best way to provide nutrients for your plants is by thoroughly preparing your soil prior to planting [see Incorporating Fertilizers and Amendments, pg. 25]. During the season, use organic mulches such as salt hay, compost, or straw, which decompose slowly and release their nutrients into the soil, to replace most of the nutrients needed by your plants, especially as you work them in while cultivating your garden. If necessary, when you water add additional nutrients and trace elements by fertilizing with an organic liquid fertilizer such as fish emulsion or a tea made by soaking manure in water. Using this approach will provide low levels of the nutrients that your vegetables need and will still avoid any hazard of burning them by applying too much nitrogen fertilizer.

Solid organic fertilizers are another option when vegetable plants show signs of nutrient deficiency, which include yellowing or purpling of foliage, stunted growth, lack of vigor, or susceptibility to pests or diseases. Choose well-rotted or composted manures, bloodmeal, or manure-fortified composts of decomposed plant matter. Avoid bonemeal made from ground, sterilized bones of cows, pigs, and other slaughtered animals because they may harbor infectious proteins called "prions" that could cause neural disease if inhaled or ingested. It is believed that prions are the cause of so-called mad cow disease, or *spongiform encephalitis,* and also could be a hazard to humans.

Most organic fertilizers are balanced with roughly equal amounts of the three nutrients—nitrogen (N), phosphorus (P), and potassium (K)—plus many micronutrients and trace minerals. Exceptions include mineral phosphate, guano, and raw manure, all of which have abundant nitrogen and cause rapid growth at the expense of flowers and fruit. It's always best to use balanced, slow-release, low-concentration fertilizers for vegetables.

Organic compost that you make yourself using clippings, foliage, and other organic matter is ideal for use when you fertilize or mulch vegetables. Such compost contains both nutrients and living organic matter that improve soils. Build a compost bin or obtain one from your garden center or hardware retailer. Turn the compost every few weeks to speed decomposition.

SYNTHETIC & LIQUID FERTILIZERS

It is true that plants use both organic, natural fertilizers and those that are synthesized from petroleum by-products and other chemicals in similar ways. Synthetic fertilizers can be mixed to include specific amounts of nutrients, but they seldom contain the full range of nutrients, micronutrients, trace elements, and living soil organisms found in their natural fertilizer equivalents.

When you add the environmental impact of using non-renewable resources and the energy consumed during manufacture, the benefit of choosing organic and natural fertilizer options is clear. For your vegetable garden, select fertilizers that will feed your plants and soils, and which will make your produce most nutritious while leaving the least footprint on the earth. In many areas, agricultural runoff into groundwater, streams, and lakes is a serious concern. Choose those gardening practices that are wholesome for you and for everyone and everything around you.

An exception may be made for foliar fertilizers, which are water-soluble, dry, synthetic mixtures that, when sprayed on the foliage and stems of plants, are absorbed directly and used for photosynthesis. They are an essential aid when plants fall ill, roots become diseased, or plants struggle to become established. Because their nutrients are absorbed directly by the green parts of the plant and avoid the roots, they sometimes will help a plant survive a challenging time. Otherwise, use natural, organic fertilizers in your garden.

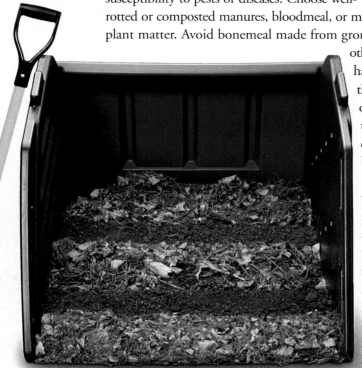

APPLYING ORGANIC FERTILIZERS

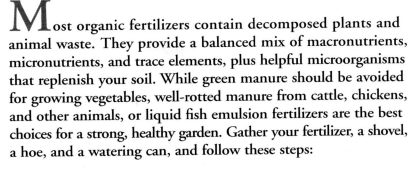

M ost organic fertilizers contain decomposed plants and animal waste. They provide a balanced mix of macronutrients, micronutrients, and trace elements, plus helpful microorganisms that replenish your soil. While green manure should be avoided for growing vegetables, well-rotted manure from cattle, chickens, and other animals, or liquid fish emulsion fertilizers are the best choices for a strong, healthy garden. Gather your fertilizer, a shovel, a hoe, and a watering can, and follow these steps:

Applying Organic Fertilizer

1 Cultivate around your plants before you fertilize to remove all competing weeds and loosen the soil.

2 Apply a layer of fertilizer, ½–1 in. (12–25 mm) deep, leaving the soil around the plant stems bare in a circle, 4–6 in. (10–15 cm) wide.

3 Thoroughly mix the fertilizer into the soil, using a hoe to cultivate and incorporate it at least 3–4 in. (75–100 mm) into the top of the bed.

4 After you apply fertilizer to your vegetable plants, always irrigate them thoroughly. The water will carry the fertilizer into the soil and dilute it.

Applying Liquid Organic Fertilizer

1 Dilute the concentrated liquid according to the package label directions, stirring thoroughly to mix the fertilizer and water.

2 Apply water mixed with diluted fertilizer to the soil around each plant, avoiding wetting the plant's foliage.

3 Irrigate after each application to dilute the fertilizer and carry it into the soil.

CONTROLLING GROWTH

Most plants grow to predetermined shapes depending on their habit, which may be low and prostrate, mounding, branching, or tall and upright. Genetically controlled, these forms may be influenced by the conditions that plants experience during growth such as prevailing wind and by events, including breakage, insect infestation, or browsing by rabbits or deer. You may direct your vegetable plants' growth by taking advantage of their reaction to pinching, pruning, or cutting and alter the size and quantity of the fruit that they produce. Besides these goals, you also may wish to keep a plant's size to suit a certain area of your garden or train it to grow vertically up a trellis, stake, or other support.

Active growth normally takes place at the buds found at the ends of branches and vines or on top of tall, upright plants. Chemical messengers within the plant signal that this bud, the so-called dominant bud, is the place where growth should be sustained. Intermediate buds, which occur all along the branch or stem, remain dormant as long as this dominant bud is actively growing, a process called "apical dominance." If the terminal bud is damaged or removed, the bud nearest the end of the stem will become dominant and start to actively grow.

Remember that your vegetable plants are very adaptable. As the quantity of fruit they bear is reduced, they compensate by making each fruit larger. When they grow excess foliage, they compensate by reducing the number of flowers and fruit that they set. You can increase the yield from your plants by pinching off flowers and removing some leaves. Each of the remaining blossoms that set fruit will be larger than they would be had the competing flowers and foliage remained on the plant. On vining plants such as cucumber and squash, entire branching stems can be removed, leaving a single runner to train vertically on a trellis. By so doing, you will reduce the plant's footprint from more than 20 sq. ft. (1.9 m²) to as little as 1 sq. ft. (929 cm²). Combining pruning and vertical supports allows you to plant more densely and reap larger harvests.

To avoid open wounds which invite disease organisms, use sharp, clean shears, washing them between pruning cuts in a solution of one part isopropyl alcohol mixed with nine parts water. Bypass pruners—shears with blades that slide past each other rather than stopping on an anvil—are best because they cut cleanly and avoid crushing stems. For new buds, pinch tender stems between your thumb and fingernail; use a pruning knife to cut tough and woody vines.

Many branching plants such as this tomato can require frequent pinching and pruning of shoots to train their growth up a trellis. Remember to always leave some shoots bearing buds and flowers.

LODGING AND BLANCHING

Lodging and blanching are two unusual techniques used with some vegetables. Root vegetables such as garlic, onion, and shallots are lodged by bending or tying their foliage to limit its growth and prevent the plants from forming seed heads, forcing the plant's energy to grow larger bulbs underground. Vegetables that are more appealing when white such as asparagus, Belgian endive (chicory), and cauliflower, are blanched by wrapping them with black paper, placing them into bags, or tying their leaves up over their stems and flower heads to keep light from reaching their chlorophyll.

When lodging, use care to avoid breaking off the stem, yet bend it sharply to crease the veins inside and limit sap flowing from the roots to the foliage. Tie the foliage to keep it bent, or tie the foliage in an overhand knot to hold its place.

Begin blanching as soon as heads—in asparagus, shoots—appear. It is important to block all light, so bury the wrapping deeply in the soil surrounding the plant. Belgian endive usually is transplanted indoors to a container set in a dark place.

PINCHING AND PRUNING

Controlling the growth of your vegetables enhances both the size and quality of the fruit they produce and improves their appearance. There are two primary methods, pinching and pruning. Pinching is used frequently as plants grow to remove growth buds, flowers, or immature fruit; pruning is a corrective action necessary to remove entire branches or prevent spread of the plant outside its growing area. Choose your option, gather the tools shown, and follow these steps:

Pinching to Increase Yield

1 Redirect your plant's energy by regularly pinching some foliage growth buds between your fingernail and thumb. This will cause the latent buds on the stem to grow, creating a denser, fuller plant.

2 For fruit-bearing vegetables, pinch off a third to one-half of the flowers as they appear. The remaining fruit will be larger and will mature more quickly.

3 After fruit has set, pinch away any that crowds, is deformed or diseased, or which receives limited light and air circulation. Pinch away all foliage in contact with or surrounding the fruit.

Pruning to Redirect Growth

1 For plants with excess foliage and little fruit, use sharp bypass pruners to remove any branches that cross the centerline of the plant, opening it to light and air circulation.

2 For plants that have become leggy, cut growing stems back to the first or second branch to promote dense, compact growth and flower production.

3 For plants with infection or infestation, prune away the affected foliage and discard or burn it. Sterilize your pruning shears between each cut by dipping them in isopropyl alcohol.

VEGETABLE GARDEN PESTS

The most serious care concerns for a vegetable garden usually occur as a result of insect or animal pests eating, damaging, or trampling fruit or foliage. Fortunately, over 90 percent of the insects you may see on vegetable plants are either harmless or beneficial—predators that attack harmful insects, other bugs, or their eggs. In a similar fashion, the number of animal pests are few, and most can be excluded from the garden by erecting fences, caging your vegetables, or otherwise blocking them from damage.

Most insect pests attack plants using one of four strategies: chewing, sucking, scoring or rasping, and boring. Most insects that harm plants are large and easily seen; only a few are microscopic. Nearly all have some natural enemies. Because of these traits and characteristics, controlling insect pests usually is easily accomplished by following a series of progressive steps [see Integrated Pest Management, pg. 68].

Mammals—especially those of large size such as deer, opossum, rabbit, and raccoon—are capable of inflicting serious damage on your garden and its plants. They are attracted to tender young vegetables and can strip plants bare or browse them to the ground in a single evening. Rodents will eat berries, corn, and many types of fruit, while gophers dine on succulent roots and moles uproot plants as they seek burrowing insects to eat.

Of other animal pests, birds are especially fond of tender shoots and ripening berries, while mollusks such as slugs and snails will devour and score sufficient foliage to denude plants to their branches.

Two approaches generally are successful for animal pests: exclusion and trapping. Fences are best for larger animals. For deer, either a single fence 8 ft. (2.4 m) or more tall or two perimeter fences, 6 ft. (1.8 m) tall and set 3 ft. (90 cm) apart, is effective. A few large deer may be able to hurdle a single tall fence, but all become uncertain when faced with two shorter fences and a long horizontal distance. For smaller mammals, individual fencing of beds may be sufficient [see Fences and Animal Pests, pg. 30].

In gardens prone to burrowing animals, set wire cages below your plantings and bury perimeter fences at least 18 in. (45 cm) deep in the soil, or try trapping. A variety of humane and live traps is available for both burrowing and above-ground pests. You even can use traps to attract snails and slugs, using beer as the bait. Once caught in a low saucer of beer, these mollusks drown or can be collected and destroyed.

(From top) A gallery of vegetable garden pests: deer, birds, rodents, cabbageworms, tomato hornworms, and snails. While large mammals can cause massive damage in a single evening, most pests are small-scale, opportunistic feeders that you can note during your regular garden inspections.

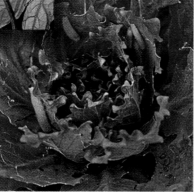

APPLYING GARDEN CHEMICALS

1 Wear protective clothing, gloves, and respirator and read completely all package label directions. Measure and mix as directed only the required quantity of the control agent, using a disposable container and utensils.

Garden chemicals—pesticides, fungicides, and herbicides, as well as some fertilizers, insecticidal soaps, and other compounds—should be applied only as a last resort after other control methods have failed, and then only in limited application directly to the infestation or infection. Choose a control that is approved for both the specific condition and the vegetable plant, read all directions and warnings, and follow them completely. On a wind-free day, gather your control, a measuring cup, implements, an applicator, rubber gloves, protective clothing, and a respirator, then follow these steps:

2 Fill the applicator with the mixed control, taking care to avoid any spillage.

3 Apply the control directly to the pest or infected foliage, wetting it. Apply the control to leaf undersides, branches, and stems that may hide pests, their eggs, and fungal spores. Avoid spraying large areas.

Warning

All garden chemicals pose personal hazard if ingested or upon contact with skin or eyes. Always wear eye protection, gloves, protective clothing, and a respirator to mix, apply, or dispose of garden chemicals.

4 Thoroughly wash the applicator when finished. Dispose of mixing utensils, any mixed and unused control agents, and any empty bottles as directed on the package.

5 Wash protective garments and gloves with soap and water, then set out to dry. Use these garments only for applying garden chemicals. Always wash your hands thoroughly with bar soap and water when you finish spraying.

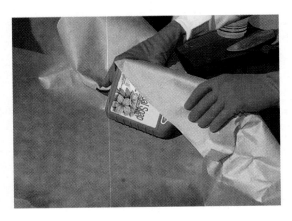

INTEGRATED PEST MANAGEMENT

Protecting the environment and working with nature to control outbreaks of pests should be a priority for every vegetable gardener seeking healthy, tasty crops. In study after study, organic growing methods reap produce and fruit equal in quality and quantity to those drawn from fields treated with pesticides. How can this be so?

The answer lies in the dynamic of insect populations. As for other animal groups, insects are divided into two large groups: the herbivores—those that eat foliage—and the carnivores, which eat other insects. For any given population of herbivores, a small number of predators exists to keep the population in balance. Pests that harm vegetable plants are drawn from the more numerous herbivore group. These plant-eating insects reproduce quickly because their ranks are easily depleted by predator insects, which reproduce more slowly.

When pesticides are applied to an insect population, most of the plant eaters and nearly all of the predatory insects are killed. Of the small number of each type that remain, the herbivores bounce back faster than the carnivorous insects, since few predators remain to stem their tide. Even more pesticide is needed to control this population boom, and the natural balance that once held the two populations in check is destroyed.

Scientists studying these outcomes have reached general concensus about the best ways to control infestations of harmful insects. The USDA now recommends following an approach called "Integrated Pest Management," or IPM, to best take advantage of the natural dynamics of insect populations. Using IPM, a small amount of residual crop damage occurs, but surprisingly little more than would be the case in fields treated with pesticides.

IPM calls for using progressive steps of control depending on the severity of the infestation. The first defense is planting vegetables that are healthy and naturally resistant to common diseases and some insects. Keep your garden healthy by employing good watering, fertilizing, and cultivating practices. Healthy plants are best able to fend off early attacks by insects until predator populations can bring them under conrol.

Separate your plantings by dividing large numbers of plants into groups for different spots in your garden. Insect pests are specific to each species, and separation limits large populations.

Inspect your garden at least weekly, looking closely for signs of insect activity. Eradicate all weeds, since native plants frequently host pests. Turn over leaves and look for chewed or rasped stems. Finding an infestation is the best way to limit its spread.

If you find pests, pick them from the plants or wash them off using a spray of clean water. Prune infested foliage and destroy it. Seek out egg cases and remove them. Most infestations can be controlled easily at this early stage.

When an infestation proves resistant to hand controls, apply minimally toxic controls such as horticultural oils, soaps, or insecticidal soaps directly to the pests, avoiding broadcast spraying. As a last resort for very stubborn infestations, apply botanical pesticides such as neem oil, rotenone, or pyrethrin according to their package directions, choosing a control that specifically names the insect and edible plants you intend to treat and observing all cautions.

(From top) Organic controls for pests include beneficial insects such as ladybird beetles, snail traps that are filled with beer, toads, and pheromone-baited, sticky white-fly traps that lure and hold insects.

PEST SYMPTOMS, CAUSES, CURES

Symptom	Cause	Remedies
Leaves curled and twisted, often with a black, sooty appearance. Deformed or stunted blooms on new growth.	Aphids. Look for soft-bodied, round, black, gray, green, or yellow insects, 1⁄16–1⁄4 inch (1.5–6 mm) long. Found on many plants. Frequently found in combination with ants.	Wash off light infestations with a strong stream of water. If ineffective, spray with superior oil. Spray with botanical neem or pyrethrin as a last resort.
Green parts of leaves are chewed, removed, or left in place stripped to veins. Later, leaves are dry and skeletonized.	Beetles, including Colorado potato beetles, Japanese beetles, and beetle larvae. Hard-shelled beetles are most active in the heat of the day.	Hand pick beetles after shaking plant in early morning while they are inactive. Apply milky spore *(Bacillus popilliae)* for Japanese beetle grubs, *Bacillus thuringiensis* (BT) for Colorado potato beetles. Spray with neem or pyrethrin as a last resort.
Seedlings cut off at ground level.	Cutworms. Look for smooth, gray brown, worm-like moth larvae under plant debris or just below soil surface.	Install cardboard collars (e.g., toilet-paper rolls) around plant stems, and sink 2 in. (50 mm) into the soil.
Foliage is eaten and stems are scored or eaten. Black or brown droppings, 1⁄20 in. (1.2 mm) wide are left on foliage. Moths and butterflies are seen resting on plants.	Various larvae and caterpillars, white cabbage moth, tomato hornworm, wormlike larvae, and loopers. Look at undersides of leaves and along stems for pests during midday.	Hand pick caterpillars from center leaves of plant. Release parasitic wasps and flies. Spray with *Bacillus thuringiensis* (BT). Apply horticultural oil in summer.
White trails on or within leaves; papery yellow or brown blotches on foliage.	Leaf miners. Look for small, pale larvae and 1⁄6-in. (4.2-mm) tiny, green or black, flying insects active during the day.	Hand pick larvae. Remove infested leaves. Release lady beetles. Spray foliage with neem oil extract solution as a last resort.
Stunted, discolored, spotted plants with deformed roots, sometimes bearing swollen galls; loss of vigor.	Nematodes, microscopic wormlike creatures that live in soil and feed on plant roots.	Release beneficial nematodes. Remove and destroy affected plants. Replant with unrelated species. Solarize bed for 3–4 weeks prior to planting by covering soil with clear plastic and allowing sunlight to raise soil temperature to 140°F (60°C).
Leaves with brown or black spots. Roots and shoots may be deformed.	Plant bugs. Look for greenish yellow or tan insects 1⁄4 in. (6 mm) long.	Hand pick. Spray with insecticidal soap. If infestation is severe, spray affected areas with pyrethrin or rotenone as a last resort.
Brown-, silver-, or white-speckled leaves; may be gummy or deformed. Blooms are deformed and fail to open.	Thrips. Shake foliage and blossoms over white paper and look for moving, winged specks. Thrive in hot, dry conditions.	Release lady beetles. Remove and destroy infested foliage. Wash foliage with water; spray pests with insecticidal soap.
Yellow leaves and stunted, sticky plants. When foliage is shaken, a cloud of white insects may fly up.	Whiteflies. Shake foliage and look for 1⁄20-in. (1.2-mm) mothlike, flying insects. Inspect leaf undersides for scalelike, gray or yellow eggs.	Catch with sticky traps. Spray with soap solution. Spray infested foliage with insecticidal soap. Spray foliage with horticultural oil or neem oil extract solution. Spray with pyrethrin as a last resort.
Ripe and half-ripened fruit and berries bear numerous cuts and holes. Partially eaten produce covers the ground, accompanied by bird droppings.	Birds. Look for songbirds, crows, and other fruit-eating species that forage on or near the ground.	Mount silver-foil streamers over vegetables. Cover beds with floating row covers as fruit and berries begin to ripen. Hang and move frequently owl and hawk silhouette decoys.
Uprooted plants; foliage eaten to ground level; bulbs and roots eaten, leaving dying stalks and leaves.	Deer and rodents. Look for hoof and paw prints, burrows, mounds, tunnels.	Plant resistant plants. Install fence barriers or cages when planting, including beneath-soil barriers. Trap and remove rodents. Avoid bonemeal, fish emulsion use.
Chewed leaves and blossoms; silvery mucus trails.	Slugs and snails. After dark, look for shelled and unshelled mollusks on foliage or soil.	Remove leaf litter, which is used as a hiding place. Hand pick after dark; use copper foil barriers around beds or containers; dust with diatomaceous earth; use beer-filled traps; use non-toxic baits containing iron phosphate; use bait gel.

DISEASES AFFECTING VEGETABLES

The most common diseases to infect vegetable plants are either viral or fungal in nature. A few bacterial infections also occur but seldom are seen in vegetables. Depending on the specific disease and infected plants, treatments and care may vary.

Treating established viral infections usually is beyond the capabilities of even professional horticulturists. The most prevalent viral diseases—although each susceptible vegetable usually has readily available resistant varieties for planting—include cabbage yellows and tobacco mosaic. Yellows infects, weakens, and can kill broccoli, brussels sprouts, cabbage, cauliflower, and kale, while mosaic generally stunts and kills tomatoes and its relatives. Your best bet for thwarting viral diseases is to choose plants resistant to the most common viral strains found in your region and vary your plantings each year.

(From top) Common plant diseases that might infect your vegetables include the gray stipple of powdery mildew and brown, withered stem seed in damping off—both caused by fungal spores and suitable for treatment—and mosaic virus, an incurable disease.

Gardeners who use tobacco products should be aware that tobacco mosaic virus inadvertently may be spread to susceptible garden vegetable plants by contact with cigarettes, cigars, or chewing tobacco. Always wash your hands thoroughly after smoking when handling tomato plants, or wear rubber gloves while touching, pruning, or harvesting.

If your vegetables should contract a viral disease, it is important to prevent the infection's spread. Uproot and burn—or otherwise dispose of plant matter outside of the garden—all infected plants once you recognize the disease condition. Do not compost diseased foliage, and avoid planting the related species in beds that experienced infection during prior seasons.

By contrast, even established fungal and bacterial infections are treatable, and in many cases resistant-plant varieties are available. The most common infections of vegetable plants are cucumber anthracnose, powdery mildew, scab, fusarium wilt, and verticillium wilt. Each has distinctive characteristics that will help you recognize the condition and can be treated using organic approaches [see Disease Symptoms, Causes, Cures, next pg.].

Another condition caused by fungal disease that you may encounter early in spring is damping-off. Actually, several different fungi can infect newly sprouted starchy seeds planted in moist, cool soil, all causing similar results. The stem of the seedling develops a telltale brown score at the soil line, then rots completely through. Avoid damping off by planting large-seeded species when the soil temperature has reached at least 60°F (16°C).

Most fungal diseases can be prevented by proper spacing, ample air circulation, and good watering practices. All fungal diseases stem from spores found naturally in the soil or carried by the wind. To germinate, the spores must find a dark, moist environment with plant tissue for food. Keeping foliage dry is of the essence for fungal-disease prevention. Always water your vegetables at the soil line and avoid splashing or spraying their foliage unless you irrigate early in the morning of a warm, dry day when the sun and wind quickly will dry your plants' leaves. Using these care techniques will prevent both downy and powdery mildew.

You can reduce further the hazard of communicable plant diseases from your garden by avoiding large, single-species plantings and promptly removing all fallen, decayed leaves and plant matter from around your vegetables. By inspecting your plants frequently and taking these simple precautions, your garden will be a healthy place filled with thriving vegetation filled with fruit and leafy greens.

DISEASE SYMPTOMS, CAUSES, CURES

Symptom	Cause	Remedies
Black, tan, or red spots on leaves; leaves yellow and drop. Black cankers on stems, with a general wilt of branch tips.	Anthracnose, a fungal disease that occurs in late spring and summer, typically after humid conditions.	Remove infected leaves and branch tips. Collect and destroy infected fallen leaves. Thin excessive growth to promote air circulation. Spray with bordeaux mixture, a copper sulfate and lime–based fungicide.
Leaves are mottled with black spots, eventually yellow and die. Powdery black or brown dusting on foliage and blossoms; leaves may drop.	Black spot and leaf spot, fungal diseases, found on many plants. Spreads by spores blown onto moist plant leaves. Common in shady, crowded plantings.	Space plantings to allow good air circulation. Remove shading foliage. Apply water at base of plant. Strip and destroy infected leaves. Spray with bordeaux mixture, a copper sulfate and lime–based fungicide.
Flowers wilt and foliage tips curl, yellow, and die. Oozing cankers form at base of shoots with main stem. Affected foliage may have a strong odor.	Blight and scab, several bacterial diseases caused when soil containing bacteria is splashed onto cut and bruised foliage or is carried to flowers by pollinating insects.	Remove and dispose of affected plants. Apply water at base of remaining plants. Install floating row covers and pollinate by hand. Rotate plantings annually to new beds. Spray with bordeaux mixture, a copper sulfate and lime–based fungicide.
Flowers and foliage collapse under heavy fuzz of brown or gray fungal spores.	Botrytis rot, also known as gray mold.	Remove affected blossoms, foliage, or entire plant; space plants for more air circulation; reduce nitrogen fertilizer.
Gray scabs form on the blossom ends of maturing tomatoes and peppers.	Blossom-end rot, a developmental and cultural disorder rather than bacterial or fungal infection caused by stress and mineral deficiency.	Strip affected fruit from plants. Fertilize with 5–10–10 formula and mulch soil surface with organic compost. Water deeply and regularly. Shade affected plants from hot midday sun.
Brown stains and softened tissue near base of stem or crown of plant; leaves may yellow or drop.	Crown or stem rot. Look for decaying stems. Usually associated with keeping soil overly moist.	Rarely curable; remove infected foliage, dipping pruning shears in isopropyl alcohol solution between cuts. Reduce watering. Repot to soil-free, well-drained mix. Root cuttings of healthy growth.
Gray, cottony masses shroud brown-spotted, dying foliage. Stems are discolored.	Downy mildew, a fungal disease common in cool, moist conditions.	Space plantings to allow good air circulation. Remove shading foliage. Apply water at base of plant. Strip and destroy infected leaves. Rotate plantings annually to new beds.
Flowers wilt and foliage tips curl, yellow, and die. Gray, powdery spores and fibers sometimes are seen on leaf undersides.	Fusarium wilt, a fungal disease common in cool, moist conditions caused by spores in soil entering plants through roots. Most prevalent in plants experiencing stress, mineral deficiency.	Space plantings to allow good air circulation. Remove shading foliage. Strip and destroy infected leaves. Fertilize with 0–5–10 formula and mulch soil surface with organic compost. Apply water at base of plant. Rotate plantings annually to new beds.
Streaked and mottled foliage, deformed blooms; stunting; loss of vigor.	Mosaic virus, an incurable plant disease.	Remove and destroy affected plants. Promptly control aphid, spider mite, thrips infestations, which can spread viral infection. Plant resistant cultivars.
Leaves have white to grayish, powdery patches, as though they have been dusted with flour.	Powdery mildew, a fungal disease prevalent when days are hot and nights are cool, with high humidity. Mostly attacks new leaves.	Thin branches to improve air circulation. Spray with a 0.5% solution of baking soda (sodium bicarbonate): 1 tsp. (5 ml) baking soda per quart [1 l] of water. Rotate plantings annually to new beds.
Foliage is marked with pale spots above, brown, red, round spots on their undersides; leaves may brown and drop.	Rust, a fungal disease, common on corn. Wipe affected foliage on white cloth, which stains orange, pink.	Plant resistant cultivars. Fertilize with nitrogen monthly until symptoms subside. Rotate plantings annually to new beds.
Plants lose vigor and wilt in hot weather. Leaves drop. Plants die.	Verticillium wilt, a fungal disease caused by spores in soil entering plants through roots.	Plant resistant cultivars. Remove and destroy affected plants. Rotate plantings annually to new beds.

Harvesting and Preserving

Picking produce at its peak of flavor is a treat reserved for those who grow their own vegetables. By comparison to market vegetables, those grown in your garden can be allowed to ripen naturally, fill with sweetness, and develop tender flesh and rich, succulent flavor. While most times your goal will be to consume your garden's fruit immediately after picking, sometimes you will be blessed with an overabundance of vegetables that will warrant freezing, preserving or canning them for later use.

Whether you pick your vegetables to eat raw in salads or as crudités, to cook them as accompaniments to a main course, or for preserving, recognizing the right time to harvest will give you a big payback in terms of taste. Each vegetable has its own telltale signs of ripeness, which you should learn to recognize.

Some vegetables reach a pinnacle of ripeness and a peak of flavor all at once, just as the plant matures; these include eggplant, melon, and squash. Other vegetables offer many opportunities throughout the season for gathering and tasting: amaranth, all of the leaf lettuces, sorrel, and spinach. Then there are root crops such as beets, carrots, and turnips, which can be stored right in the garden even after they mature, under a protective covering of mulch. You can dig them as you need them over a period of months.

To help you prepare for the coming and continuous bounty your vegetable garden will offer, take a few moments to review each plant's maturity and harvest information [see Encyclopedia of Vegetables, pg. 79]. In it, you'll find convenient estimates of the maturity dates for most garden vegetables, recommendations for their ideal means of short- and long-term storage, as well as methods and techniques for preserving them.

In the pages that follow, you'll find a brief survey of when vegetables should be harvested to achieve peak taste, how fresh produce should be picked, prepared, and stored, and an overview of options for preserving vegetables. Because freezing has become a popular storage method that gives good results in terms of texture and flavor, you'll also find step-by-step directions showing how to blanch and freeze vegetables.

Beauty to behold matched by uncommon fresh taste are the payoffs you will receive from your garden throughout the season.

HARVESTING VEGETABLES

Recognizing the peak of ripeness is a skill honed over time. Still, there are some tips for getting off to a good start. Here are some suggestions for recognizing ripeness and assuring good texture and flavor:

Leafy green vegetables such as bok choy, cabbage, endive, horseradish greens, lettuce, mustard greens, sorrel, spinach, and Swiss chard are at their tender best when the plants are young. Thinning not only provides delicately flavored early salad ingredients, it alleviates overcrowding and competition for nutrients and water. Use the outside leaves, allowing the central growth bud to form new leaves until it begins to bolt, or form a seed head. Water the evening before harvest.

Root vegetables such as carrot, parsnip, radish, rutabaga, and turnip are good candidates for long-season picking. When young, their flavor is mild and their texture is tender. By maturity, they develop the rich flavors and sturdy flesh desired for stews and soups. Mulch over the ripe root crops when the first frosts start, and you'll be able to have fresh vegetables until the hard freezes begin.

(Right) Pumpkins should be cut from the vine when their stalks dry and turn brown, then left in the field in the sun for a week to develop a tough rind, a process called curing.

(Below) Pick cane berries such as blackberry, blueberry, currant, and raspberry every day during their season. Frequent harvesting causes them to form new buds.

(Bottom) Cut artichokes from their stalks when they reach desired size, then chill them in ice water. They taste best when they are steamed immediately after harvest.

Vine vegetables such as beans, cucumber, gourds, peas, pumpkin, and squash should be picked when they reach full size and color, or when legume pods first fill with plump peas and beans. You can hand pick small fruit and pods, but use a sharp pair of bypass pruning shears to cut the sturdy stems of larger fruit. An exception should be made for berry vines, which require daily picking as their fruit achieves full color.

Tomatoes come in two varieties, determinate and indeterminate. Cultivars grown commercially and those used for cooking or paste usually are determinate—all their fruit forms and ripens at once—while home and heritage cultivars set a stream of new tomatoes until the vine is killed by frost. In either case, pick tomatoes when their flesh is fully colored and their skin becomes tender; test it with your thumbnail to see if it will mark slightly with light pressure, a sure sign of ripeness.

Stalk and bush vegetables such as broccoli, brussels sprouts, cauliflower, corn, eggplants, and peppers will reach ripeness in successive groups. Carefully peel back the husk of the fullest ear of corn 1–2 in. (25–50 mm) after its silk turns brown. If kernels near the tip are swelling, the corn is at its peak flavor. Pick it, submerging it immediately in ice water, and cook it right away; each hour after harvest some of its sugar turns to woody-tasting starch. Cole vegetables such as broccoli, brussels sprouts, and cauliflower should be picked just as their flowers begins to swell but before they open. Pick eggplants and peppers using the same coloration and skin-bruising tests as you would for tomatoes.

Aromatic bulb vegetables such as garlic, onion, and shallot will begin to send up pompon-shaped flower heads when they near maturity. Forestall this tendency by lodging their stems [see Lodging and Blanching, pg. 64]. This technique ensures that the remaining growth will take place in the swelling bulb. When the foliage begins to yellow, it's time to pull your bulb vegetables and put them in a warm, sheltered, airy spot to cure and dry.

HARVEST TECHNIQUES

Each vegetable has a preferred method of harvesting. Some must be cut, others picked, still others dug. For best flavor and nutrition, use or preserve vegetables soon after harvesting by one of the following options:

Leafy Green Vegetables

A For leafy vegetables, use a sharp knife to cut them at their base. Immerse them immediately in cold water.

Root Vegetables

B Use a garden fork to carefully unearth tubers or roots. Pull carrots and beets. Set them on a tarp in a protected, shady spot to dry, then brush soil from them and store them in a dark, dry spot.

Vine Vegetables

C Use sharp bypass pruners or lopping shears to cut ripe fruit from the vine. Refrigerate or set them on a tarp in a shady, protected location to cure for 1–2 days, then store them in a dark, dry spot.

Continuous Harvest Vegetables

D Pick beans and peas every few days as they mature to encourage new flowers and fruit to form. Immerse them immediately in cold water.

Stalk and Bush Vegetables

E Break or cut corn, eggplants, peppers, and tomatoes from their stalks as they mature. Immerse them immediately in ice water for best flavor.

Onion and Garlic

F Lodge the stalks when they begin to form seed, then wait 2–3 weeks for the bulbs to form underground. Pull as needed. Set them on a tarp in a protected, shady spot to cure, then hang them in a dark, dry spot.

STORAGE, PRESERVING, AND DRYING

While the primary purpose of growing vegetables is to eat them picked fresh from the garden, many of us like to extend their flavors throughout the year by storing and preserving any excess that remains.

Some garden vegetables such as berries, corn, English peas, and radishes begin losing taste and texture from the moment that they are picked. There's no substitute for eating them fresh. Many others, including root and tuber vegetables, winter squash, pumpkin, and sweet potato, can be stored successfully to extend fresh taste into autumn and winter. Still others such as cabbage or cucumber can be preserved in brine or pickled. Other popular means of storing and preserving vegetables are dehydration and drying. Finally, you can pressure-can some produce in glass jars; make jellies, jams, and chutneys; or, with some preparation, blanch, pack, and freeze it [see Preparing Vegetables for Freezing, opposite pg.].

Storing fresh vegetables requires sorting them into groups depending on the conditions they need. Choose a dark, warm, dry spot for gourds, winter melons, potatoes, pumpkins, and squash—about 55–65°F (13–18°C) is right. Cool and dry is the best choice for sun-dried vegetables, including beans, peas, peppers, and tomatoes, and for dried and dehydrated chives, garlic, leeks, onion, and shallots. For them, the temperature should be 40–50°F (4–10°C). A household refrigerator's vegetable keeper is the best spot for produce that needs cool and moist storage, including green beans, cucumbers, eggplants, melons, okra, peppers, and summer squash. Finally, store asparagus, beets, broccoli, cabbage, celery, leafy greens, leeks, lettuce, green onions, fresh peas, radishes, and rhubarb in moist conditions, at temperatures from 34–38°F (1–3°C), as in a porous paper bag placed in the lower areas of a home refrigerator.

Experts agree that deep-freezing at very low temperatures is the best way to store fresh vegetables for periods as long as 6 months. Gone are the efforts associated with hot brines and syrups, pressure cookers, and the extensive effort needed for home canning. Any firm-fleshed vegetable that can be cut into small pieces, mashed, or pureed is suitable for freezing. Blanching—a prefreezing immersion in boiling water for 1–2 minutes—helps retain optimum flavor and texture. After draining, pack and quick-freeze them to 0°F (−18°C).

(Above) Tomatoes that have been dried in a vegetable dehydrator have the same sweet, rich flavor as their traditional, sun-dried counterparts.

(Below) Home-canned preserves must be processed in a pressure cooker for sufficient time to kill any bacteria they contain. Highly acidic preserves such as pickled asparagus, beans, and cucumbers can be processed in boiling water if they contain sufficient salt and vinegar, or they can be refrigerated after boiling until they cure. Most vegetable gardeners use freezing to preserve their vegetables.

CANNING AND PICKLING

Home canning using mason jars with one-time-use lids and tight metal rings has faded from popularity. Unlike pickling, which relies on salt brine to preserve vegetables, or sweet condiment processes that produce jams and jellies and sterilize naturally because of their high sugar content, canning relies solely on high-heat processing and careful attention to prevent bacterial growth and health hazard.

To be successful, canning jars and their contents all must be presterilized by boiling, packed using clean tools while still hot, carefully sealed, and placed into a pressure cooker for treatment at temperatures of as much as 230°F (110°C) for times that vary by the vegetable and the pressure cooker model used. Vegetables that are canned incorrectly may bear a hazard for causing botulism due to the tasteless, odorless, fatal, botulin toxin, as well as other spoilage diseases that can cause jars to burst.

By contrast, pickled cucumbers and sauerkraut need simple packing in a boiling brine made of salt and vinegar. They are sealed and boiled for 15–20 minutes in an open saucepan on a stove before cooling and storage. Fresh pickles and sauerkraut may be made by brining washed, raw cucumbers and shredded cabbage in a loosely covered crock stored in a cool, dark spot at 35-45°F (2–7°C) for 4–6 weeks, then packing them loosely into jars and setting them in a household refrigerator for use in 2–4 weeks.

Always follow a recipe to can or pickle—they often are included in boxes of canning jars.

PREPARING VEGETABLES FOR FREEZING

Freezing has become the most popular preserving technique to use for most vegetables. It retains the most nutrients and holds garden-fresh flavor for up to 6 months of storage. The secret to freezing is twofold: blanching and quick-freezing. For best results, follow these simple steps:

1 Chill fleshy vegetables after harvest to avoid having their sugars turn to starch.

2 Shuck legumes and prepare other vegetables for blanching by peeling and cutting. Cutting them into pieces helps them freeze quickly.

3 For processed vegetables, cook, mash or puree, then cool and strain, and package for freezing.

5 Pack vegetables tightly in containers or in resealable or special vacuum bags. Remove all excess moisture and air, then seal or use a vacuum sealer to exhaust all air and seal.

4 For vegetables frozen whole or in slices, blanch them in boiling water for 1–2 minutes, then immerse them immediately in an ice-water bath to stop the cooking process. When they are cold, drain and pack for freezing.

6 Quick-freeze in a deep freezer set to its lowest temperature, allowing air to circulate between the vegetable packages. Quick-freezing avoids formation of ice crystals that rupture plant cell walls and affect texture.

T he needs of vegetable gardeners for information differ from those of flower and landscape gardeners. While a few vegetables are bulbs, biennials, or perennials, most are annuals that begin their growth from seed, mature, and form the fruit or leafy greens we treasure in the course of a single gardening season. Each plant has traits that affect the degree of success it will have for filling its life mission, and you will want to note each vegetable's specific needs.

The 68 vegetables and more than 35 herbs showcased in this chapter are accompanied by detailed descriptions to help you plan, plant, grow, harvest, and preserve or store them. It has been organized conveniently in a uniform format under topic headings to help you quickly locate the information and find detailed answers to your questions.

Keep in mind that many new cultivars are introduced each season for the popular species of vegetable plants, along with many hundreds of favorite cultivars that have weathered the test of time. Most of the new cultivars were chosen by growers because of qualities that make them superior to others of their kind, including resistance to common diseases or pests, special colors or flavors, quality or size of fruit, and many other characteristics. It's fun to experiment by planting new options even as you enjoy growing vegetables that have been successful for you in the past.

Among the useful information you will find for each plant are estimates of how many should be planted to yield sufficient produce for your family, detailed requirements for planting seed and seedlings, notes on which vegetables should be planted in successions or rotated around the garden from year to year, ideal planting and growing temperatures, and soil and moisture needs. There also are suggestions for watering, fertilizing, cultivating, mulching, and pruning, along with notes about resistance or susceptibility to pests and diseases, companion plants, time to maturity, when to harvest, and how to store or preserve your produce. Everything you need to know about the most popular vegetables can be found in these pages.

> A gallery of the most popular and widely planted vegetables, with all the facts you will need to grow them successfully in your garden.

Encyclopedia of Vegetable Plants

(From top) Hot peppers, artichoke, sweet peppers, cucumbers, radishes, carrots, cauliflower, and summer squash—just a few of the favorites found in home vegetable gardens.

Amaranth:: Warm season. Leafy green vegetable similar in both taste and appearance to spinach, amaranth is grown primarily in the tropics where it is successful in regions where spinach is subject to early bolting. It is seldom cultivated in the continental United States or Canada.

Yield: Allow 4–6 plants per household member.

Planting: Sow seed in full sun in spring for summer harvest when soil warms to 60–80°F (16–27°C). Sow seed ¼ in. (6 mm) deep, 8–12 in. (20–30 cm) apart, thinning to 4–6 in. (10–15 cm) apart, in rows 8–12 in. (20–30 cm) apart. Plant seedlings when 3–3½ in. (75–90 mm) tall, spaced 4–6 in. (10–15 cm) apart, in rows 8–12 in. (20–30 cm) apart.

Growing Temperature: 72–86°F (22–30°C). Best in warm climates with high humidity, a greenhouse, or other protected site. Protect plants from temperatures below 60°F (16°C).

Soil: Moist, well-drained soil. Fertility: Rich. 5.5–7.0 pH. Prepare soil at least 2 ft. (60 cm) deep.

Care: Challenging. Keep evenly moist; avoid wetting foliage. Fertilize semi-weekly with 10–10–10 formula or organic liquid fertilizer. Mulch. Cultivate. Pinch plants back when 7–8 in. (18–20 cm) tall for greater production.

Companion Plants: Compact, leafy green vegetables, radishes, and strawberries.

Maturity/Harvest: 42–70 days. Thin outer leaves when plant is 6–8 in. (15–20 cm) tall, then pick greens again when 4–5 new leaves emerge for continuous harvest of tender, edible leaves.

Storage/Tips: Fresh in vegetable keeper of refrigerator for 1–2 weeks. Leaves are primarily used raw in salads or steamed for use as a cooked vegetable similar to spinach.

Artichoke: Cool-season perennial. An edible thistlelike relative of cardoon, artichokes are tasty and prolific, and they require abundant space—mature plants are 6 ft. (1.8 m) wide and 3–4 ft. (90–120 cm) high—so consider garden placement with eventual size in mind.

Yield: Allow 1 plant per 1–2 household members. For preserving, allow 2–4 plants, yielding 4 qts. (3.8 l) of artichoke hearts.

Planting: Sow seed indoors in late winter–early spring 2 weeks before last expected frost. Set out seedlings and root divisions in full sun when soil warms to 50–85°F (10–29°C). Sow seed ½ in. (12 mm) deep and 6 in. (15 cm) apart, thinning to 6–8 ft. (1.8–2.4 m) apart, in rows 6–8 ft. (1.8–2.4 m) apart.

Growing Temperature: 40–75°F (4–24°C). Zones 8–10; grow as annual, zones 4–7. Shade plants in full sunlight at temperatures over 95°F (35°C). Prefers mild winters and cool summers with constant temperatures and frequent precipitation. Layered with heavy mulch, they sometimes survive temperatures to 0°F (–18°C). In short-season, cold-winter climates, plant artichoke in large, movable containers for relocation indoors before first frost.

Soil: Damp, well-drained, sandy soil. Fertility: Rich. 6.0–6.8 pH. Prepare soil at least 3 ft. (90 cm) deep.

Care: Moderate. Keep evenly damp; allow soil surface to dry between waterings. Water deeply. Fertilize in spring and autumn with 5–10–10 formula. Mulch. Cut stalks and leaves to the soil after harvest, forcing new growth. Replace plants every 3–4 years. Aphid, earwig and powdery mildew susceptible.

Companion Plants: Asparagus, rhubarb.

Maturity/Harvest: Cut immature buds when 3–4 in. (75–100 mm) wide before scales loosen or flowers form, in spring of second season and annually thereafter for steaming; to 3 in. (75 mm) wide for preserved hearts. Fan scales and clean thoroughly under abundant running water, clipping off thorns and outer leaves with scissors.

Storage/Tips: Fresh in vegetable keeper of refrigerator for 5–7 days; cooked and frozen, 2–3 months; pickled or canned, 1–2 years. Steam or boil until tender (about 20 minutes). Serve hot or cold, with butter or salad dressing; the soft part of the outer leaves, entire heart, and stem are edible. Buds allowed to go to seed produce attractive purple thistlelike flowers for cutting or drying.

Asparagus: Cool-season perennial. This member of the lily family is a prized, early-spring delicacy. Plants grown from seed require 3 years to become established and produce spears but yield ample harvests annually for 20 or more years. The edible green female spears are capped with a bud-forming top; allowed to go to seed, the buds will sprout feathery, fernlike foliage.

Yield: Allow 10–15 plants per household member.

Planting: Sow seed indoors in flats 12–14 weeks before last expected frost and harden seedlings 7–10 days before transplanting. Set out seedlings when soil warms to 50–85°F (10–29°C). Sow seed 1½ in. (38 mm) deep, 2 in. (50 mm) apart, thinning to 6 in. (15 cm) apart, in rows 2 ft. (60 cm) apart. Alternatively, plant root crowns in late winter or early spring for harvest during the second season, 18 in. (45 cm) apart, in trenches 1 ft. (30 cm) deep, backfilled with organic compost until 8 in. (20 cm) deep. Bury crowns with a layer of soil 2 in. (50 mm) deep, adding more soil over the plants in spring as their spears emerge, gradually filling the trench.

Growing Temperature: 60–85°F (16–29°C). Zones 3–10. Shade plants in full sunlight at temperatures over 95°F (35°C) to prevent bolting.

Soil: Moist, well-drained soil. Fertility: Rich. 6.0–6.8 pH. Prepare soil at least 1 ft. (30 cm) deep.

Care: Challenging. Keep evenly moist. Fertilize in early spring and after harvest with 10–5–5 formula supplemented with garden lime. Mulch. Cultivate. Cut back feathery foliage to 1 in. (25 mm) above soil when it turns brown. Mulch heavily in cold-winter climates to protect root crowns from freezing and frost heaving. To grow white spears, blanch asparagus by covering the bed with black plastic supported on stakes before spears emerge. Rodent susceptible. Insect pest and disease resistant.

Companion Plants: Artichokes, basil, parsley, and tomatoes.

Maturity/Harvest: Spring of third season, then annually. Cut spears when ¼–½ in. (6–12 mm) in diameter and 10 in. (25 cm) tall. Avoid cutting any spears from earlier-season growth.

Storage/Tips: Fresh in vegetable keeper of refrigerator for 2–3 weeks; blanched and frozen, 4–6 months; pickled or canned, 1–2 years. Steam until tender. Avoid using metal utensils that discolors asparagus.

Beans, Broad; Fava; Horse; or Windsor: Cool season. Member of the vetch family that produces large pods on a plant to 4½ ft. (1.4 m) tall, bearing somewhat flat, oval-shaped beans in a variety of colors, including green, pinkish red, white, and yellow. They may be harvested green for immediate use or for canning, or dried for storage.

Yield: Allow 4–8 plants per household member.

Planting: In short-season climates, sow seed indoors 3–4 weeks before last frost and harden seedlings 7 days before transplanting. In average climates, sow seed in early spring through midseason, depending on cultivar, when soil warms to 50–85°F (10–29°C); in mild-winter climates, in autumn for late winter or early-spring harvest. Sow seed 1 in. (25 mm) deep, 4–5 in. (10–13 cm) apart, thinning to 6 in. (15 cm) apart, in rows 3 ft. (90 cm) apart. Plant successions.

Growing Temperature: 60–65°F (16–18°C). If sustained temperatures exceed 100°F (38°C) and are accompanied by low humidity, plants may fail; avoid planting in direct sunlight or sites with excessive heat.

Soil: Moist, well-drained, sandy soil. Fertility: Rich. 6.0–6.8 pH. Prepare soil at least 1 ft. (30 cm) deep. Rotate plantings with leafy green and cole-family vegetables to avoid nitrogen depletion.

Care: Moderate. Keep evenly moist until flowers form pods; water regularly thereafter. Fertilize monthly with 5–10–10 formula. Mulch. Cultivate. Pest and disease resistant.

Companion Plants: Cucumbers, potatoes, and summer savory.

Maturity/Harvest: 80–100 days. Pick pods when 2–3 in. (50–75 mm) long for use fresh; after mature and pods have dried on the vine, as for dried beans.

Storage/Tips: Fresh in vegetable keeper of refrigerator for 5–7 days; dried in porous, fabric bags stored in a cool, dry location, 1 year. Best eaten fresh, steamed and dressed with olive oil or butter, then garnished with chopped fresh tomato.

Beans, Dried: Warm season. Dried beans are an excellent source of protein in a convenient, storable form easily used for cooking. Broad, kidney, lima, navy, pinto, and white beans are the most commonly dried legumes.

Yield: Allow 4–8 plants per household member, yielding 2–3 lbs. (0.9–1.4 kg).

Planting: Sow seed in full sun in spring when soil warms to 60–85°F (16–29°C). Sow seed 1½–2 in. (38–50 mm) deep, 1 in. (25 mm) apart, thinning to 4 in. (10 cm) apart, in rows 18–30 in. (45–75 cm) apart or in a circle planted around a pole.

Growing Temperature: 60–85°F (16–29°C). Best in mild-summer climates. Prepare soil 12–16 in. (30–40 cm) deep.

Soil: Moist, well-drained, sandy soil. Fertility: Rich. 6.0–6.8 pH. Prepare soil at least 1 ft. (30 cm) deep. Rotate legume crops throughout the garden to naturally boost soil nitrogen levels.

Care: Easy. Keep evenly moist until flowers form pods; damp thereafter. Fertilize monthly with 5–10–10 formula or well-rotted manure. Avoid deep cultivation that could cut through the shallow, widespread roots. Powdery mildew susceptible.

Companion Plants: Carrots, cauliflower, cucumbers, potatoes, and summer savory.

Maturity/Harvest: 65–70 days. Pick pods when mature and beginning to wither, spread them on a flat surface in a warm, protected spot, and dry thoroughly; in arid climates, allow pods to dry on vines. Fully dry pods will split open naturally to reveal the dried beans; mature pods also can be dried in a vegetable dehydrator.

Storage/Tips: Dried in porous, fabric bags stored in a cool, dry location, to 1 year; sealed in plastic bags and frozen, to 2 years. Some dried-bean cultivars picked at the green, shelling stage known as "shuckies"—especially French flageolet, French horticultural, and great northern white beans—also may be eaten steamed with butter or cooked in soups and casseroles as you would snap beans and peas.

Beans, Garbanzo or Gram; Chickpeas: Warm season. Fernlike bush 2–2½ ft. (60–75 cm) tall, related to true beans and peas, with bulging green pods containing 1–2 tan-colored, pealike seeds. Although edible when green, garbanzos most often are dried for later use. Their unique flavor and texture make them popular for use whole in salads; combined with grains and baked, they make a nutritious, protein-rich, cholesterol-free meat substitute.

Yield: Allow 4–8 plants per household member for eating fresh; for drying, allow 10–15 plants, yielding 2 lbs. (0.9 kg).

Planting: In average climates, sow seed in partial shade in spring, when soil warms to 65–80°F (18–27°C); in mild-winter climates, in late autumn. Sow seed 1½–2 in. (38–50 mm) deep, 3–6 in. (75–150 mm) apart, thinning to 8–12 in. (20–30 cm) apart, in rows 2 ft. (60 cm) apart.

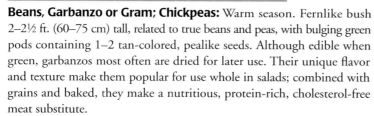

Growing Temperature: 60–70°F (16–21°C). Flowers may fail to set fruit at temperatures above 90°F (32°C).

Soil: Moist, well-drained loam. Fertility: Rich. 6.0–6.8 pH. Prepare soil at least 18 in. (45 cm) deep. Rotate legume crops throughout the garden to naturally boost soil nitrogen levels.

Care: Easy. Keep evenly moist during flowering and pod formation; allow soil surface to dry between waterings thereafter. Fertilize semi-monthly with 5–10–10 formula. Avoid deep cultivation that could cut through the shallow, widespread roots. Pest and disease resistant.

Companion Plants: Celery, corn, cucumbers, potatoes, strawberries, and summer savory.

Maturity/Harvest: 100 days. Pick pods when 1 in. (25 mm) long for use fresh; picked after pods have dried on the vine or when mature pods have withered, spread on a flat surface in a warm, protected spot, as for dried beans.

Storage/Tips: Fresh in the vegetable keeper of a refrigerator for 5–7 days; dried in porous, fabric bags stored in a cool, dry location, to 1 year; blanched, sealed in plastic bags, and frozen, to 6 months; canned using a pressure cooker, 3 years. Fresh, boiled garbanzo beans, mashed to a paste with tahini spices, lemon juice, garlic, and olive oil, provide a tasty Middle-Eastern dip known as hummus for crudités, crackers, chips, and crisps.

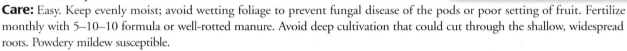

Beans, Lima or Butter: Warm season. Both bush and pole varieties bear clusters of pods containing 3–4 large, flat, oval beans, taking longer to mature than other beans. Shell and steam fresh beans, or dry them for storage and later use in cooking. Miniature or baby lima cultivars mature quickly but yield smaller beans.

Yield: Allow 4–8 plants per household member.

Planting: In average climates, sow seed in spring when soil warms to 65–85°F (18–29°C); in mild-winter climates, in autumn and late winter. *Bush:* Sow seed 1½–2 in. (38–50 mm) deep, 3–6 in. (75–150 mm) apart, thinning to 3 in. (75 mm) apart, in rows 2–3 ft. (60–90 cm) apart. *Pole:* Sow seed 1½–2 in. (38–50 mm) deep, 6–10 in. (15–25 cm) apart, thinning to 6 in. (15 cm) apart, in rows 30–36 in. (75–90 cm) apart, installing stakes at time of planting. Plant successions.

Growing Temperature: 60–70°F (16–21°C). Flowers may fail to set fruit at temperatures over 80°F (27°C); cold, wet conditions cause flowers to drop.

Soil: Moist, well-drained, sandy soil. Fertility: Rich. 6.0–6.8 pH. Prepare soil 12–16 in. (30–40 cm) deep.

Care: Easy. Keep evenly moist; avoid wetting foliage to prevent fungal disease of the pods or poor setting of fruit. Fertilize monthly with 5–10–10 formula or well-rotted manure. Avoid deep cultivation that could cut through the shallow, widespread roots. Powdery mildew susceptible.

Companion Plants: *Bush:* celery, corn, cucumbers, potatoes, strawberries, and summer savory. *Pole:* scarlet runner beans, corn, summer savory, and sunflowers. Succession planting sequence includes spinach, early radish, lima bean, then beets or potatoes.

Maturity/Harvest: *Bush:* 65–80 days. *Pole:* 80–95 days. Pick pods when first plump for green, shelled beans; when pods are full and begin to wither for drying. Regular picking encourages production of new flowers and a sustained harvest.

Storage/Tips: Fresh in vegetable keeper of refrigerator for 1–2 weeks; blanched and frozen, 3–4 months; pickled or canned in a pressure cooker, 2–3 years; dried in porous, fabric bags stored in a cool, dry location, 1 year. Rehydrate dried lima beans by soaking them in hot water at least 4 hours prior to use; beans added directly to soups and stews will remain tough.

Beans, Snap; Pinto; Romano; or Wax: Warm season. Both bush and pole varieties bear many flat or round pods containing 6–8 kidney-shaped beans in green, purple, yellow, and speckled colors. Many new cultivars are offered each season along with old favorites. Bush beans mature more quickly than pole varieties but yield fewer pods. Steam fresh beans, or dry them for storage and later use in cooking.

Yield: Allow 4–8 plants per household member.

Planting: In average climates, sow seed in spring when soil warms to 60–85°F (16–29°C); in mild-winter climates, in autumn–late winter. *Bush:* Sow seed 1½–2 in. (38–50 mm) deep, 2 in. (50 mm) apart, thinning to 3 in. (75 mm) apart, in rows 18 in. (45 cm) apart. *Pole:* Sow seed 1½–2 in. (38–50 mm) deep, 4–6 in. (10–15 cm) apart, thinning to 6 in. (15 cm) apart, in rows 3 ft. (90 cm) apart, installing stakes at time of planting. Plant successions 3–4 weeks apart.

Growing Temperature: 60–70°F (16–21°C). Best in mild climates.

Soil: Moist, well-drained, sandy soil. Fertility: Rich. 6.0–6.8 pH. Prepare soil at least 1 ft. (30 cm) deep.

Care: Easy. Keep evenly moist. Fertilize monthly with 5–10–10 formula or well-rotted manure. Avoid deep cultivation that could cut through the shallow, widespread roots. Choose disease-resistant cultivars.

Companion Plants: *Bush:* celery, corn, cucumbers, potatoes, rosemary, strawberries, and summer savory. *Pole:* scarlet runner beans, corn, rosemary, summer savory, and sunflowers. Rotate plantings annually with cole-family vegetables.

Maturity/Harvest: *Bush:* 45–60 days. *Pole:* 60–85 days. Pick when 3 in. (75 mm) long as they first begin to bulge for snap beans; when pods are full and begin to wither for drying. Regular picking encourages production of new flowers and a sustained harvest.

Storage/Tips: Fresh in vegetable keeper of refrigerator for 7–10 days; blanched and frozen, 3 months; pickled or canned in a pressure cooker, 2–3 years; dried in porous, fabric bags stored in a cool, dry location, 1 year. Fresh-pack blanched snap beans into sterile jars and cover with boiling, seasoned brine, then refrigerate for 2–3 weeks before use.

Beets: Cool season. Grown primarily for their bulb-shaped roots in gold, white, yellow, and concentric- or candy cane–striped colors, beets also produce tasty greens. Beets are popular as a hot side dish, used as a fresh-cooked salad vegetable when chilled and sliced, and sometimes are pickled and canned.

Yield: Allow 5–10 plants per household member.

Planting: In average climates, sow seed in early spring when soil warms to 50–80°F (10–27°C), plant new successions every 3 weeks until temperatures reach 80°F (27°C), then resume planting 6–8 weeks before the first frost for autumn harvest; in mild-winter climates, plant successions every 3 weeks thoughout the year while temperatures remain below 80°F (27°C). Sow seed ½ in. (12 mm) deep, 1 in. (25 mm) apart, thinning when 3 in. (75 mm) tall to 4 in. (10 cm) apart, in rows 18–24 in. (45–60 cm) apart. Sift fine sand or compost to cover seed with a layer ¼ in. (6 mm) deep.

Growing Temperature: 45–75°F (7–24°C). Tolerate varied temperatures.

Soil: Moist, well-drained, sandy soil. Fertility: Rich. 6.0–6.8 pH. Prepare soil at least 1 ft. (30 cm) deep.

Care: Easy. Keep evenly moist; beets tend to become woody if waterings are irregular. Fertilize semi-monthly with 10–10–10 formula. Cultivate. Inspect frequently for root damage by boring pests.

Companion Plants: Carrots, garlic, kohlrabi, onions, and radishes.

Maturity/Harvest: 45–65 days. Pull roots when 2–3 in. (50–75 mm) wide, carefully uprooting, rinsing to remove soil, then allowing them to dry. Cut outer leaves while young and tender, leaving the central growth bud to resprout.

Storage/Tips: *Roots:* fresh in vegetable keeper of refrigerator for 1–2 months; fresh in damp sawdust in a dark, cool spot, 3–4 months; sliced, steamed and canned or pickled, 1 year. *Greens:* fresh in vegeable keeper of refrigerator for 5–7 days; steamed and frozen, 3 months.

Berries, Blackberry: Cool-season perennial. Trailing, canelike vines to 8 ft. (2.4 m), with invasive root runners, bear cup-shaped berries in shades of red and black. Wild and domesticated cultivars have been hybridized, including boysenberry, loganberry, marionberry, and ollalieberry, in thornless and thorn-bearing varieties; thornless varieties tend to yield fewer berries. Choose cultivars known to be successful in your region.

Yield: Allow 4–6 plants per household member. For jams or jellies, allow 12–16 plants, yielding 4–5 qts. (4.4–5.5 l).

Planting: In cold-winter climates, set out bare-root divisions in partial shade in early spring when soil warms to 35–55°F (2–13°C); in mild-winter climates, in early spring or autumn. *Erect:* Set out bare-root divisions in a trench 6 in. (15 cm) deep, 30 in. (75 cm) apart, in rows 10 ft. (3 m) apart. *Trailing:* Set out bare-root divisions 1 ft. (30 cm) deep, 5–8 ft. (1.5–2.4 m) apart, in rows 10 ft. (3 m) apart. Install root-guard barriers, at least 18 in. (45 cm) deep, to prevent roots from spreading beyond the bed, as well as trellises or support wires, 6–8 ft. (1.8–2.4 m) tall. Cover roots with 1 in. (25 mm) of soil until they sprout, then gradually backfill until the trench is filled.

Growing Temperature: 55–80°F (13–27°C). Zones vary by variety (*erect:* zones 3–9; *trailing:* 4–10). Best in mild climates with maximum of 5 hours of direct sun daily.

Soil: Moist, well-drained soil. Fertility: Rich. 5.5–6.8 pH. Prepare soil at least 2 ft. (60 cm) deep.

Care: Moderate. Keep evenly moist until fruit matures; reduce watering thereafter to limit cane growth. Fertilize quarterly with acidic 10–10–10 formula supplemented with garden sulfur. Mulch. Cultivate. Tie trailing varieties onto wire supports. Prune away old canes after fruiting ends, leaving new canes to produce fruit the following season.

Companion Plants: Other berry, cane, and vine plants.

Maturity/Harvest: Late spring and summer of second season, then annually. Pick berries when full colored, sweet, plump, and easily pulled from canes; avoid washing. Regular picking encourages production of new flowers and a sustained harvest.

Storage/Tips: Fresh in vegetable keeper of refrigerator for 1–2 weeks; frozen whole or as pie fillings, 1 year; preserved as jams or jellies, 3 years.

Berries, Blueberry: Cool-season perennial. Highbush, rabbit-eye, and lowbush cultivars, 3–6 ft. (90–180 cm) tall, bear round, smooth-skinned, blue berries on new branches in early summer. In autumn, their foliage turns colorful copper, orange, and red. Highbush cultivars are best for cool, cold-winter climates, while rabbit-eye blueberries grow best in warm and arid or humid climates with mild winters, and lowbush types perform best in cool, coastal and cold-winter areas.

Yield: Allow 3–5 plants per household member. For jams or jellies, allow 10–12 plants, yielding 4 qts. (4.4 l).

Planting: Set out highbush cultivars in partial shade in early spring when soil warms to 35–55°F (2–13°C); rabbit-eye and lowbush cultivars, in late autumn or winter. Set out seedlings 12–18 in. (30–45 cm) deep, 5 ft. (1.5 m) apart, in rows 5 ft. (1.5 m) apart.

Growing Temperature: *Highbush:* 55–80°F (13–27°C). Zones 4–8. *Rabbit-eye:* 60–90° (16–32°C). Zones 8–11. *Lowbush:* 45–80°F (7–27°C). Zones 2–8.

Soil: Moist, well-drained soil. Fertility: Rich–average. 4.0–5.5 pH. Prepare soil at least 2 ft. (60 cm) deep.

Care: Moderate. Keep evenly moist. Fertilize annually in spring with acidic 5–10–10 formula supplemented with garden sulfur or evergreen-needle compost. Mulch. Avoid cultivating; blueberries have shallow surface roots. Protect ripening berries from birds with netting. In spring, trim tops lightly to limit spreading; in autumn, prune fruiting branches; in winter, prune lowest, overlapping, or weak branches.

Companion Plants: Acidic soil–tolerant ornamental and vegetable species.

Maturity/Harvest: 60–80 days after first bloom, annually thereafter. Pick berries when full colored, sweet, plump, and easily pulled from the cluster; avoid washing. Yields abundant fruit for several weeks.

Storage/Tips: Fresh in vegetable keeper of refrigerator for 2–3 weeks; frozen whole or as pie fillings, 6 months; preserved in jams or jellies, 3 years. Bush blueberries make excellent garden borders.

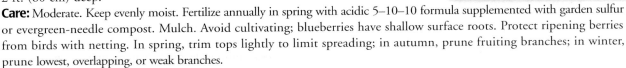

Berries, Currant or Gooseberry: Cool-season perennial. Closely related, currants and gooseberries are cold-tolerant, compact shrubs, 4–5 ft. (1.2–1.5 m) tall, bearing edible berries. Currants are black, red, or white, smooth skinned, sweet flavored, and a good source of vitamin C. Gooseberries are green and red, bristly skinned, strongly fragrant, and larger. Both are grown as decorative plantings as well as for their fruits.

Yield: Allow 1–2 plants per household member. For jams or jellies, allow 4 plants, yielding 3–4 qts. (3.3–4.4 l).

Planting: In cold-winter climates, set out bare-root divisions in full sun to partial shade in early autumn when soil temperature drops to 45–60°F (7–16°C); in mild-winter climates, in winter. *Currants:* Plant root divisions 5–6 in. (13–15 cm) deep, 4 ft. (1.2 m) apart, in rows 10 ft. (3 m) apart. *Gooseberries:* Plant nursery starts 3–4 in. (75–100 mm) deep, 5 ft. (1.5 m) apart, in rows 12 ft. (3.7 m) apart. For both berry types, install trellises or support wires at least 6 ft. (1.8 m) tall at time of planting.

Growing Temperature: 60–85°F (16–29°C). Zones 4–10.

Soil: Moist, well-drained loam. Fertility: Rich. 5.5–6.8 pH. Prepare soil at least 3 ft. (90 cm) deep.

Care: Moderate. Keep evenly moist until berries form and begin to ripen; reduce watering thereafter. Avoid wetting foliage. Fertilize semi-annually in spring and autumn with acidic 5–10–10 formula. In alkaline soils, apply chelated iron quarterly. Mulch. Prune annually after fruiting is completed to maintain open form with good air circulation, and remove basal suckers. Currant worm and white pine blister rust susceptible; cultivation prohibited in some jurisdictions.

Companion Plants: Acidic soil–tolerant ornamental and vegetable species.

Maturity/Harvest: Late spring–early summer of second season, then annually. Pick berries when full colored, plump, and easily pulled from the cluster.

Storage/Tips: Fresh in vegetable keeper of refrigerator for 2–3 weeks; frozen whole or as pie fillings, 6 months; preserved in jams or jellies, 3 years. Tart-flavored currants and gooseberries are natural companions for sweet fruits such as strawberries.

Berries, Raspberry: Cool-season perennial. Trailing canes to 8 ft. (2.4 m), with invasive root runners, bear black, red, and yellow, cup-shaped berries. Both foliage and clustered fruit grow on canes, which bear fruit in their second and subsequent seasons. Summer-bearing raspberries are red, while autumn-bearing cultivars are black; each type requires specific pruning care.
Yield: Allow 3–5 plants per household member. For jams or jellies, allow 12–16 plants, yielding 4–5 qts. (4.4–5.5 l).
Planting: In cold-winter climates, set out bare-root divisions in partial shade in early spring when soil warms to 35–55°F (2–13°C); in mild climates, in early spring or late autumn. Plant root divisions 3 in. (75 mm) deep, 2 ft. (60 cm) apart, in rows 4–6 ft. (1.2–1.8 m) apart, installing edge boards or root-guard barriers, at least 18 in. (45 cm) deep, to prevent roots from spreading beyond the bed, as well as trellises or support wires, 6–8 ft. (1.8–2.4 m) tall.
Growing Temperature: 55–80°F (13–27°C). Zones 3–10; best in cool-summer areas of zones 5–8. Best with maximum of 6 hours of direct sun daily.
Soil: Moist, well-drained, sandy soil. Fertility: Rich. 6.0–6.8 pH. Prepare soil at least 2 ft. (60 cm) deep.
Care: Moderate. Keep evenly moist until berries form and begin to ripen; reduce watering thereafter. Fertilize quarterly with acidic 10–10–10 formula supplemented with garden sulfur. Mulch. Cultivate. Tie onto wire supports. Protect ripening berries from birds with netting. *Red summer bearing:* Prune away old canes after fruiting ends, leaving new canes to produce fruit the following season. *Black autumn bearing:* Head new canes in spring to force branching; new berries will form on branches in summer. Prune after fruiting ends. *Everbearing:* Produce berries on top of cane in autumn; remove top after fruiting ends. Berries will develop in summer of following season on lower stem; remove spent canes after summer fruiting ends.
Companion Plants: Other berry, cane, and vine plants.
Maturity/Harvest: Summer or autumn of second season; depending on cultivar, annually or semi-annually thereafter. Pick berries when full colored, sweet, plump, and easily pulled from cane; avoid washing.
Storage/Tips: Fresh in vegetable keeper of refrigerator for 2–3 weeks; frozen whole or as pie fillings, 6 months; preserved as jams or jellies, 3 years. Raspberries and strawberries complement each other, making superb pies.

Berries, Strawberry: Cool-season perennial. Low-growing plants, to 8 in. (20 cm) tall, bear red, heart-shaped, berrylike fruit unique for having their seeds on their fruits' exterior skins. They are divided into spring-bearing and everbearing cultivars. Strawberries reproduce by extending foliage runners that start new plants, by root division, and by seed.
Yield: Allow 20 plants per household member. For jams or jellies, allow 40 plants, yielding 4–5 qts. (4.4–5.5 l).
Planting: In cold-winter climates, set out root divisions in full sun in early spring when soil warms to 45–60°F (7–16°C); in mild-winter climates, in late autumn or early spring. Plant root divisions 12–14 in. (30–36 cm) apart, in mounds 6 in. (15 cm) high and wide, 2 ft. (60 cm) apart. In containers, plant root divisions 12–14 in. (30–36 cm) apart.
Growing Temperature: 70–90°F (21–32°C). Zones 3–11. Best with at least 6 hours of direct sun, in mild-summer climates.
Soil: Moist, well-drained, sandy soil. Fertility: Rich. 5.8–6.5 pH. Prepare soil at least 1 ft. (30 cm) deep.
Care: Easy. Keep evenly moist; avoid wetting foliage. Fertilize monthly with 5–10–10 formula supplemented with potassium sulfate. Mulch as fruit spurs develop to lift berries above soil, preventing contact. Remove mulch when fruiting ends, and cut plants back to the soil. In cold-winter climates in autumn, transplant to flats filled with moist sawdust and store in a cool, dark place until spring. Replace parent plants every 3 years, retaining runner starts. Slug, snail and downy and powdery mildew susceptible.
Companion Plants: Beets, carrots, and radishes.
Maturity/Harvest: 90–120 days. Pick fruit when full colored, sweet, plump, and full flavored; avoid washing.
Storage/Tips: Fresh in vegetable keeper of refrigerator for 7–10 days; frozen whole or as pie fillings, 6 months; preserved as jams or jellies, 3 years. Good for small-space, container gardens.

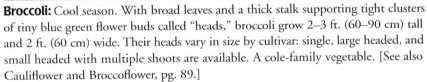

Bok or Pak Choy; Celery Mustard: Cool season. Swiss-chardlike bok choy is an Asian green, 12–20 in. (30–50 cm) tall, with broad, shiny, white-veined leaves and cream or red, fleshy stems, prized for cooking in stir-fried dishes. A cole-family vegetable.
Yield: Allow 12–15 plants per household member.
Planting: In average climates, sow seed outdoors in full sun in spring when soil warms to 45°F (7°C) and in autumn after heat has broken and 2 months of warm weather remains; in mild-winter climates, in autumn when soil temperature drops to 65°F (18°C). Sow seed ¼–½ in. (6–12 mm) deep, 4 in. (10 cm) apart, thinning to 12–16 in. (30–40 cm) apart, in rows 24 in. (60 cm) apart. Plant successions every 2 weeks.
Growing Temperature: 45–75°F (7–24°C). Zones 3–10. Best in mild climates. Avoid planting in areas with more than 6 hours of daily sunlight. Bolts in temperatures over 80°F (27°C) and when daylight hours lengthen in summer.
Soil: Damp, well-drained, sandy soil. Fertility: Rich. 6.5–7.5 pH. Prepare soil at least 18 in. (45 cm) deep. Rotate plantings with legumes to avoid nitrogen depletion.
Care: Easy. Keep damp; allow soil surface to dry between waterings. Fertilize monthly with 10–3–3 formula supplemented with garden lime. Mulch. Cultivate. Aphid, cabbage looper, cabbageworm, cutworm, root maggot and powdery mildew susceptible.
Companion Plants: Brussels sprouts, cabbage, and cauliflower.
Maturity/Harvest: 45–80 days. Thin outer leaves by cutting at base when 5 in. (13 cm) long; harvest by cutting at soil line when plants reach 1 ft. (30 cm) tall. Young leaves have delicate texture and sweet taste; allow plants to mature for best flavor.
Storage/Tips: Fresh in vegetable keeper of refrigerator for 3–4 weeks; steamed and frozen, 3–4 months; sliced, steamed, and frozen as filling for Asian dishes, soups, and stews, 4–6 weeks. Good as a steamed vegetable to accompany meat dishes or as a subtitute for Swiss chard or spinach in filled pasta dishes; raw leaves can be eaten with other leafy greens as a salad vegetable; entire plant can be stir-fried with other vegetables and meat for use in Asian dishes.

Broccoli: Cool season. With broad leaves and a thick stalk supporting tight clusters of tiny blue green flower buds called "heads," broccoli grow 2–3 ft. (60–90 cm) tall and 2 ft. (60 cm) wide. Their heads vary in size by cultivar: single, large headed, and small headed with multiple shoots are available. A cole-family vegetable. [See also Cauliflower and Broccoflower, pg. 89.]
Yield: Allow 2–3 plants per household member.
Planting Time: In average climates, sow seed indoors 5–6 weeks before last expected frost and harden seedlings 4–5 days before transplanting; in mild-winter climates, in autumn. Set out seedlings in open shade when soil warms to 50–85°F (10–29°C). Sow seed ¼–½ in. (6–12 mm) deep, 2 in. (50 mm) apart, thinning when 6 in. (15 cm) tall to 14–18 in. (36–45 cm) apart, in rows 24–30 in. (60–75 cm) apart.
Growing Temperature: 45–75°F (7–24°C). Bolts in temperatures over 85°F (29°C) and when daylight hours lengthen in summer.
Soil: Moist, well-drained soil. Fertility: Rich–average. 6.0–6.8 pH. Prepare soil at least 18 in. (45 cm) deep. Rotate plantings with legumes to avoid nitrogen depletion.
Care: Easy. Keep evenly moist; avoid wetting foliage. Fertilize monthly with 10–10–10 formula. Mulch. Cultivate. Aphid, cabbage looper, cabbageworm, cutworm, root maggot and powdery mildew susceptible.
Companion Plants: Beets, celery, herbs, onions, and potatoes.
Maturity/Harvest: 70–100 days. Pick heads when buds are still tight and green, cutting the main stem below the head and leaving secondary shoots to develop new, slightly smaller heads. After harvesting, soak heads for 3–5 minutes in 1 qt. (1.1 l) lukewarm water mixed with ¼ cup (60 ml) vinegar and 2 tbsp. (30 mg) salt to remove pests, then rinse and dry.
Storage/Tips: Fresh in vegetable keeper of refrigerator for 2 weeks; blanched and frozen, 3 months. Broccoli florets can be eaten raw as crudités with dip or as a salad vegetable, steamed with butter or cream sauces to accompany meat dishes, stir-fried with other vegetables and meat for use in Asian dishes, or used as a flavoring and filler for soups, stews, and casseroles. While mild temperatures continue, broccoli will continue to produce new shoots after harvesting until killed by frost.

Brussels Sprouts: Cool season. Small, cabbage-shaped sprouts, 1–2 in. (25–50 mm) wide, grow in alternating rows along an upright, thick stalk, to 3 ft. (90 cm) tall, bearing broad, toothed leaves. Sprouts mature from the bottom up; use them as they mature or pinch the stalk when 20 in. (50 cm) tall to force its sprouts to mature together. Cool temperatures enhance and sweeten the flavor of the sprouts. Fresh brussels sprouts are an excellent raw appetizer when halved and accompanied with an herb-seasoned sour cream dip. A cole-family vegetable.

Yield: Allow 1 plant per household member, yielding 50–75 sprouts.

Planting: In average climates, sow seed indoors 16–20 weeks before the last frost and harden seedlings 5–7 days before transplanting; in mild-winter climates, in autumn, after heat has broken. Set out seedlings in partial shade when soil warms to 50–85°F (10–29°C). Sow seed ¼–½ in. (6–12 mm) deep, 2 in. (50 mm) apart, thinning to 12–18 in. (30–45 cm) apart, in rows spaced 24–30 in. (60–75 cm) apart.

Growing Temperature: 45–75°F (7–24°C).

Soil: Moist, well-drained soil. Fertility: Rich. 6.5–7.5 pH. Prepare soil at least 18 in. (45 cm) deep. Rotate plantings with legumes to avoid nitrogen depletion.

Care: Moderate. Keep evenly moist; avoid wetting foliage. Fertilize monthly with 10–10–10 formula. Mulch. Cultivate. Aphid, cabbage looper, cabbageworm, cutworm, root maggot and powdery mildew susceptible.

Companion Plants: Beets, celery, herbs, onions, and potatoes.

Maturity/Harvest: 100–110 days. Pick sprouts as they ripen when 1–1½ in. (25–38 mm) wide and still tight, cutting at base of sprout stem. Water the evening before harvest for mildest flavor. Best flavor after frost. Tender young leaves growing between sprouts may be eaten raw or steamed as greens. In late autumn in cold-winter climates, cut remaining stalks and hang in a cool, dry spot.

Storage/Tips: Fresh in vegetable keeper of refrigerator for 3–4 weeks; blanched and frozen, 4 months.

Cabbage: Cool season. Available in cultivars with many different foliage colors, head shapes, sizes, and maturity ranges from as short as 7 weeks to as long as 4 months. Red and curly-leaved savoy hybrids are mildest in flavor. A cole-family vegetable. [See also Bok or Pak Choy; Celery Mustard, pg. 87].

Yield: Allow 4–8 plants per household member. For sauerkraut, allow 6 plants, yielding 10–12 qts. (9.5–11.4 l).

Planting: In average climates, sow seed indoors 4–6 weeks before last expected frost and harden seedlings 5–7 days before transplanting; in mild-winter climates, in partial shade in spring, autumn, or winter when soil is 45–90°F (7–32°C). Sow seed ½ in. (12 mm) deep and 1 in. (25 mm) apart, thinning to 24–30 in. (60–75 cm) apart, in rows 2–4 ft. (60–120 cm) apart. Plant successions 3–4 weeks apart.

Growing Temperature: 45–75°F (7–24°C). Tolerates light frosts. Bolts in temperatures over 80°F (27°C) and when daylight hours lengthen in summer; avoid planting in areas with more than 3–4 hours of daily sunlight.

Soil: Moist, well-drained soil. Fertility: Rich. 6.5–7.5 pH. Prepare soil at least 18 in. (45 cm) deep. Rotate plantings with legumes and leafy greens to avoid nitrogen depletion.

Care: Easy. Keep evenly moist; avoid wetting foliage. Fertilize monthly with 10–3–3 formula. Mulch. Cultivate. Aphid, cabbage looper, cabbageworm, cutworm, root maggot and powdery mildew susceptible.

Companion Plants: Beets, celery, herbs, onions, and potatoes.

Maturity/Harvest: 50–60 days for early cultivars; 90–120 days for late cultivars. Cut heads from basal stalk when full, firm, and 4–10 in. (10–25 cm) in diameter, discarding outer leaves.

Storage/Tips: Fresh in vegetable keeper of refrigerator for 3–4 months; cured with brine as sauerkraut and refrigerated, 5–6 months; brined and canned, 1 year. Blanched or steamed leaves, rolled tightly around an herb-seasoned filling of ground meat and rice, produce savory cabbage rolls.

Carrots: Cool season. Usually grown for their flavorful crisp orange roots, 3–10 in. (75–250 mm) long, depending on cultivar and soil texture, carrots may be conical and tapered, cylindrical, or ball shaped. Short cultivars generally are easier to grow and tend to be sweeter than the tapered varieties.

Yield: Allow 20–30 plants per household member.

Planting: In average climates, sow seed in full sun in early spring–late summer when soil warms to 40–85°F (4–29°C) and until 80 days before first frost; in mild-winter climates, in autumn–early spring. Sow seed ¼–½ in. (6–12 mm) deep, ½ in. (12 mm) apart, thinning to 1½–2 in. (38–50 mm) apart, in rows 1–2 ft. (30–60 cm) apart. Plant successions every 2–3 weeks.

Growing Temperature: 45–75°F (7–24°C). Best in mild climates.

Soil: Moist, well-drained, sandy loam. Fertility: Rich–average. 5.5–6.8 pH. Prepare soil at least 1 ft. (30 cm) deep.

Care: Easy. Keep evenly moist. Fertilize monthly with 5–10–10 formula supplemented with wood ash or garden potash to provide ample potassium; cultivate and water after fertilizing. Mulch. Pest and disease resistant.

Companion Plants: Chives, leeks, onions, peas, rosemary, and tomatoes.

Maturity/Harvest: 50–75 days; 30–40 days for thinned baby carrots. Pull roots when 3 in. (75 mm) long for tapered cultivars; ¾ in. (19 mm) wide for round cultivars.

Storage/Tips: Fresh in vegetable keeper of refrigerator for 1–2 months; sliced, blanched, and frozen, 6 months; brined and pickled, 1 year. In mild-winter climates, store mature carrots in-ground until ready for use; in cold-winter climates, dig before first frost, avoid washing, and store in damp sawdust in a dark, cool spot, 3–4 months. Carrots are an excellent source of beta-carotene, a nutrient recognized for multiple health benefits.

Cauliflower and Broccoflower: Cool season. Broad-leaved plants, 18–24 in. (45–60 cm) tall and wide, with headlike, tightly formed, curd-shaped, edible, cream, green, purple, white clusters consisting of immature flowers. A cauliflower and broccoli hybrid, broccoflower bears green, broccoli-like heads and tastes similar to cauliflower. Fast-maturing cultivars available. Cole-family vegetables [see also Broccoli, pg. 87.]

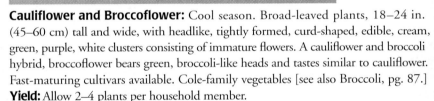

Yield: Allow 2–4 plants per household member.

Planting: In average climates, set out seedlings in indirect sun–partial shade in early spring–midsummer when soil warms to 65–85°F (18–29°C); in mild-winter climates, after heat has broken in autumn–winter. Sow seed ½ in. (12 mm) deep, 1 in. (25 mm) apart, thinning to 15–24 in. (38–60 cm) apart, in rows 2–3 ft. (60–90 cm) apart.

Growing Temperature: 60–65°F (16–18°C). Best in mild, humid climates. Bolts in temperatures over 85°F (29°C) and when daylight hours lengthen in summer; provide shade-cloth protection in hot, arid climates, or plant in autumn.

Soil: Moist, well-drained soil. Fertility: Rich. 6.0–6.8 pH. Prepare soil at least 18 in. (45 cm) deep. Rotate plantings with legumes to avoid nitrogen depletion.

Care: Moderate. Keep evenly moist; avoid wetting foliage. Fertilize monthly with 5–10–10 formula. Mulch. Cultivate. Blanch to ensure white heads by loosely tying leaves over developing heads when 2 in. (50 mm) wide, or choose self-blanching cultivars. Aphid, cabbage looper, cabbageworm, cutworm, root maggot and powdery mildew susceptible.

Companion Plants: Beets, celery, herbs, onions, and potatoes.

Maturity/Harvest: 70–120 days; 55–80 days for seedlings. Cut heads from basal stalk when firm and 4–8 in. (10–20 cm) wide. After harvesting, soak broccoflower heads for 3–5 minutes in 1 qt. (1.1 l) lukewarm water mixed with ¼ cup (60 ml) vinegar and 2 tbsp. (30 mg) salt to remove pests, then rinse and dry.

Storage/Tips: Fresh in vegetable keeper of refrigerator for 2–3 weeks; blanched and frozen, 3–4 months; brined and canned or pickled, 1 year. Cauliflower florets can be eaten raw as crudités with dip or as a salad vegetable, steamed with butter or cream sauces to accompany meat dishes, or used as a flavoring and filler for soups, stews, and casseroles.

Celery or Celeriac: Cool season. Grown for celery stalks and celeriac roots, both plants, 15–20 in. (38–50 cm) tall, descend from harsh-tasting wild marsh plants. Careful selection and hybridizing have created the familiar snack, salad, seasoning, and cooking vegetables known for their mild, distinctive flavor. Celery must be blanched during growth to protect it from sun; unblanched celery has a strong flavor and woody texture. Choose self-blanching cultivars for best results.

Yield: Allow 5 plants per household member.

Planting: In average climates, sow seed indoors 6–8 weeks before last expected frost and harden seedlings 7–10 days before transplanting; in mild-winter climates, in spring, autumn, or winter. Set out transplants when 4–6 in. (10–15 cm) tall and soil warms to 50–65°F (10–18°C). Sow seed ¼–½ in. (6–12 mm) deep, 3–5 in. (75–125 mm) apart, thinning to 6–10 in. (15–25 cm) apart, in rows 2 ft. (60 cm) apart. Install floating row covers after planting to limit access by pests.

Growing Temperature: 60–70°F (16–21°C). Best in long-season, cool, mild climates. Bolts in temperatures over 75°F (24°C) and when daylight hours lengthen in summer.

Soil: Moist, well-drained, sandy soil. Fertility: Rich. 5.8–6.8 pH. Prepare soil at least 1 ft. (30 cm) deep.

Care: Challenging. Keep evenly moist; allow soil surface to dry between waterings. Fertilize monthly with 5–10–15 formula or liquid organic fertilizer. Mulch. Cultivate. Blanch celery to ensure white stems when 1 ft. (30 cm) tall by mulching with straw or wrapping with opaque, waterproof paper, or choose self-blanching cultivars. Aphid, borer, cabbage looper, leafhopper, nematode and blight susceptible.

Companion Plants: Lettuce, English peas, and spinach.

Maturity/Harvest: 100–120 days. Cut bunch below crown when 12–18 in. (30–45 cm) tall, or cut outer stalks as needed, leaving the central growth bud to grow new stalks; celery roots may be harvested for use as for celeriac. Dig celeriac roots when 2–3 in. (50–75 mm) wide at crown. Wash both thoroughly and allow to dry. For more intense flavor, withhold water from celery plants 2 days before harvest; enhance mild flavor by watering 4–8 hours before harvest.

Storage/Tips: Fresh in vegetable keeper of refrigerator for 4–6 weeks.

Chayote; Chuchu; Christophine; or Mirliton: Warm-season perennial. A gourd family member, chayote bears insignificant flowers and green, bristly, pear-shaped, large-seeded fruit, tasting of both nuts and squash, in autumn, on vines to 50 ft. (15 m) long. Choose cultivars known to be successful in your region.

Yield: Allow 1 vine per 4 household members, yielding 100–150 or more fruit per vine; a minimum of 2 plants is required to ensure adequate cross-pollination and fruit production.

Planting: Sow seed or whole fruit in full sun in spring when soil warms to 65–85°F (18–29°C). Sow seed 6–8 in. (15–20 cm) deep, 2 ft. (60 cm) apart, thinning to 10 ft. (3 m) apart, in rows 10–12 ft. (3–3.7 m) apart, or plant seedlings 10 ft. (3 m) apart, installing sturdy trellises or wire supports, 10 ft. (3 m) tall, at time of planting.

Growing Temperature: 65–80°F (18–27°C). Zones 7–11; grow as annual, zones 4–6. Best in mild-winter, mild-summer climates.

Soil: Moist, well-drained, sandy soil. Fertility: Rich. 6.0–6.8 pH. Prepare soil at least 30 in. (75 cm) deep.

Care: Easy. Keep evenly moist. Fertilize monthly during growth with 10–10–10 formula or well-rotted manure. Mulch before first frost, zones 7–8. Avoid deep cultivation that could cut the shallow, widespread roots. Train vines onto trellises or wire supports. Aphid, vine borer, squash bug and fungal disease susceptible.

Companion Plants: Corn, peppers, pumpkin, and squash.

Maturity/Harvest: Autumn of first season, annually thereafter. Pick fruit when 4–6 in. (10–15 cm) in diameter.

Storage/Tips: Fresh in vegetable keeper of refrigerator for 4–6 weeks; steamed and canned, 1 year. All parts are edible: fruit, steamed or sautéed; soft seeds, sliced and eaten in salads or chopped and used as a nut substitute with a flavor and texture that resembles squash; tender young vine tips, eaten raw in salads or stir-fried; leaves, steamed for greens; tubers, boiled or baked.

Chicory; Belgian Endive; French Endive; or Radicchio: Cool-season perennial. Small-rooted cultivars bear greens prized for salads, while fleshy-rooted cultivars produce roots that can be dried and ground as a coffee substitute or flavoring. Radicchio is a broad-leaved cultivar of chicory with red foliage and a biting, tangy flavor. Belgian or French endive bears dense, white leaves with a crisp texture and mildly bitter taste (see Care, below).

Yield: *Chicory:* Allow 2–4 chicory plants per household member. *Belgian Endive* and *Radicchio:* Allow 8–10 plants per household member.

Planting: In average climates, sow seed in spring and early summer when soil warms to 50–85°F (10–29°C); in mild-winter climates, in autumn and winter. Sow seed ¼ in. (6 mm) deep, 1–2 in. (25–50 mm) apart, thinning to 6–12 in. (15–30 cm) apart, in rows 2–3 ft. (60–90 cm) apart.

Growing Temperature: 45–75°F (7–24°C). Zones 3–11. Bolts in temperatures over 80°F (27°C) and when daylight hours lengthen in summer. Cool weather or mild frost causes radicchio to develop distinctive purplish red foliage and become milder in taste.

Soil: Moist, well-drained, sandy soil. Fertility: Rich. 5.0–6.8 pH. Prepare soil at least 1 ft. (30 cm) deep.

Care: Moderate. Keep evenly moist. Fertilize monthly with 10–10–10 formula supplemented with garden sulfur. Mulch heavily with straw around radicchio to force head formation. Cultivate. *Belgian Endive:* Use Belgian endive 'Witloof' leaves raw in salads for first year. When frosts begin, trim remaining leaves to 1 in. (25 mm) from central growth bud, dig carefully, and transplant angled into damp sand at 45°, barely covering the tip. Place in a cool, dark location and water regularly; buds will form the distinctive tight, pale-green heads of Belgian endive.

Companion Plants: Beets, carrots, lettuce, radishes, and spinach.

Maturity/Harvest: 85–100 days. *Chicory:* When 5–6 in. (13–15 cm) in height, cut 1 in. (25 mm) above the growth bud to allow plant to resprout. *Radicchio:* When heads are red, tightly formed, and 3–5 in. (75–125 mm) wide, cut at the base of the leaves. *Belgian Endive:* When blanched heads are tightly formed and 3–5 in. (75–125 mm) wide, cut above the growth bud to allow plant to resprout.

Storage/Tips: Fresh greens in vegetable keeper of refrigerator for 1 week; fresh roots, 4–5 months.

Collards: Warm-season biennial or short-lived perennial. An open, leafy plant, 1–3 ft. (30–90 cm) tall and wide, with a stout, central stalk bearing bluish green leaves. Collards are close relatives of cabbage and cauliflower. The plants tolerate sustained heat and grow into late-autumn frosts, improving in flavor after temperatures drop. A cole-family vegetable.

Yield: Allow 2–3 plants per household member.

Planting: In average climates, sow seed indoors 4–6 weeks before last expected frost and harden seedlings 4–7 days before transplanting; in mild-winter climates, in spring, autumn, or winter. Set out seedlings in partial shade when soil warms to 50–85°F (10–29°C). Sow seed ¼ in. (6 mm) deep, 2 in. (50 mm) apart, thinning to 18–24 in. (45–60 cm) apart, in rows 3 ft. (90 cm) apart. Plant successions 2–3 weeks apart.

Growing Temperature: 45–75°F (7–24°C). Best in warm, humid climates.

Soil: Moist, well-drained soil. Fertility: Rich. 5.5–6.8 pH. Rotate plantings with legumes to avoid nitrogen depletion.

Care: Easy. Keep evenly moist. Fertilize monthly with 10–10–10 formula or well-rotted manure. Mulch. Cultivate. In cold-winter climates, in autumn trim remaining leaves from the stalks and carefully dig the roots; heel roots into moist wood chips or sand, store in a cool place, watering occasionally, then replant in spring; in mild-winter climates, leave plants in beds under mulch.

Companion Plants: Husk tomatoes, southern peas, peppers, and tomatoes.

Maturity/Harvest: 60–90 days. Cut greens sparingly from central stem beginning when plants reach 12 in. (30 cm) tall. As new leaves emerge, additional greens may be harvested.

Storage/Tips: Fresh in vegetable keeper of refrigerator for 1 week; steamed and frozen, 3–4 months. Use thinned leaves as tender, tasty greens for salads.

Corn, Sweet; Popcorn; or Ornamental Corn: Warm season. First noticed by European explorers to the Western Hemisphere and now a worldwide staple, corn forms tassels at its stalk tip and several ears midway up the stalk, which can reach 9 ft. (2.7 m) tall on many cultivars. Pollen from the flowering tassel, which is carried by the wind, pollinates sticky, silky threads on each ear of corn. Each of the threads connects to an unfertilized kernel, and the ear develops as many kernels as silks that are pollinated. Shaking the stalks while they are in tassel produces fuller ears of corn. Corn varieties include sweet corn, field corn, popcorn, and ornamental corn, in early, midseason, and late cultivars, bearing kernels of many different colors and sweetnesses.
Yield: Allow 10–15 plants per household member.
Planting: Sow seed in full sun in spring when soil warms to 50–90°F (10–32°C); sow separate beds of early and late cultivars for a sustained harvest. Avoid planting 2 cultivars nearer together than 20 ft. (6 m), or in rows perpendicular to prevailing winds, due to cross-pollination. Sow seed 1–2 in. (25–50 mm) deep, 4–6 in. (10–15 cm) apart, thinning to 12–18 in. (30–45 cm) apart, in at least 4 rows 2–3 ft. (60–90 cm) apart, forming a square or rectangle for good pollination. Plant successions 3–4 weeks apart.
Growing Temperature: 50–95°F (10–35°C). Requires at least 6 hours of sunlight daily.
Soil: Moist, well-drained soil. Fertility: Rich. 5.8–6.8 pH. Prepare soil at least 18 in. (45 cm) deep.
Care: Moderate. Keep evenly moist. Fertilize with 10–5–5 formula or well-rotted manure when stalks reach 12 in. (30 cm) tall; repeat when 30 in. (75 cm) tall. Cultivate. Corn earworm susceptible.
Companion Plants: Beans, cucumbers, peas, potatoes, pumpkins, and squash.
Maturity/Harvest: 60–100 days. Cut ears from stalk when silks turn brown and kernels yield a white milky fluid when pierced. Immerse immediately in ice water; chilling prevents sugars from turning to starches and preserves texture.
Storage/Tip: Fresh in vegetable keeper of refrigerator for 2–4 days; blanched, cut from cob, and frozen, 3–6 months. Late-season varieties have larger kernels, sweeter flavor, and more vigorous growth habits than early varieties.

Cucumbers: Warm season. Vining plants, to 5 ft. (1.5 m) long, usually with bristly, heart-shaped leaves, bear cylindrical fruit with smooth or prickly, deep green, white, or yellow skin and a greenish white, crisp, juicy interior and many soft seeds, though some cultivars are seedless. Choose disease-resistant cultivars by letter codes: anthracnose (A), leaf spot (LS), downy mildew (DM), mosaic virus (M), scab (S), and wilt (BW or FW).
Yield: Allow 4–6 plants per household member. For pickling, allow 18–20 plants of each cultivar, yielding 5 qts. (4.7 l).
Planting: Sow seed or set out seedlings in full sun in spring when soil warms to 60–90°F (16–32°C). *Mounds:* Sow 4–6 seeds, ½ in. (12 mm) deep, 4 in. (10 cm) apart, in mounds 16 in. (40 cm) wide, 10 in. (25 cm) high, and 4 ft. (1.2 m) apart, thinning to 2 seedlings per mound. *Rows:* Sow 2–3 seeds, ½ in. (12 mm) deep, 18 in. (45 cm) apart, in rows 6 ft. (1.8 m) apart, thinning to 2 seedlings per drill, 3 ft. (90 cm) apart for ground plantings, or 18 in. (45 cm) apart for plants grown on trellises or supports 3–4 ft. (90–120 cm) high.
Growing Temperature: 60–90°F (16–32°C). Prepare soil at least 18 in. (45 cm) deep.
Soil: Damp, well-drained, sandy soil. Fertility: Rich. 5.5–6.8 pH. Flowers may fail to set fruit at temperatures below 75°F (24°C).
Care: Easy. Keep evenly damp; allow soil surface to dry between waterings. Fertilize monthly with 5–10–10 formula. Vines may temporarily wilt on hot days, recovering overnight. Beetle, whitefly and slug, snail susceptible.
Companion Plants: Beans, corn, peas, pumpkins, and squash.
Maturity/Harvest: 55–65 days. Pick fruit when 6–10 in. (15–25 cm) long for slicing; 1–6 in. (25–150 mm) long for pickling (sweet or baby dills); 3–4 in. (75–100 mm) long for pickling (regular dills); 12–15 in. (30–38 cm) long for English or Armenian cultivars. Harvest frequently to extend development of new flowers and fruit.
Storage/Tips: Fresh in vegetable keeper of refrigerator for 1–2 weeks for table and pickling cultivars or 2–3 days for Armenian and English cultivars; brined and pickled, 2 years. Hot caps encourage early sprouting and flowering.

Eggplant: Warm season. Bushy plants, to 3 ft. (90 cm) tall and wide, bear large, rough, oval, lobed leaves and tubular or pear-shaped, meaty fruit, 5–12 in. (13–30 cm) long and to 2 pounds (0.95 kg) in weight, with glossy, smooth, green, purple, white, yellow, or striped skin. Popular in Mediterranean and vegetarian dishes, as a substitute for pasta, and deep-fried as an appetizer.
Yield: Allow 1–2 plants per household member.
Planting: In average climates, sow seed indoors at time of last expected frost and harden seedlings 7–10 days before transplanting; in mild-winter climates, in spring. Set out seedlings 3–4 in. (75–100 mm) tall in full sun when soil warms to 65–70°F (18–21°C); hasten warming by covering beds with black plastic. Sow seed ¼–½ in. (6–12 mm) deep, 6 in. (15 cm) apart, thinning to 2 ft. (60 cm) apart, in rows 3 ft. (90 cm) apart.
Growing Temperature: 65–90°F (18–32°C). Protect plants from temperatures below 50°F (10°C); flowers will drop at low temperatures. Shade plants at temperatures over 100°F (38°C).
Soil: Moist, well-drained, sandy soil. Fertility: Rich. 5.5–6.8 pH. Prepare soil at least 2 ft. (60 cm) deep. Amend soil prior to planting with calcium-rich ground oyster shells. Rotate plantings to prevent accumulation of disease organisms in soil; avoid sites where peppers, potatoes, tomatoes previously were grown.
Care: Moderate. Keep evenly moist; allow soil surface to dry between waterings. Fertilize monthly with 10–10–10 formula, liquid organic fertilizer, or well-rotted manure. Mulch. Cultivate. Pinch large-fruited cultivars to one fruit per main branch or a total of 4–6 per plant. Support fruit if necessary to maintain above the soil surface. Aphid, flea beetle, whitefly and verticillium wilt susceptible.
Companion Plants: Bush beans and southern peas.
Maturity/Harvest: 100–140 days. Pick fruit when firm, glossy, full color, and desired size. Chill after harvesting. Harvest promptly before seeds color; leaving fruit on plant causes mushy texture.
Storage/Tip: Fresh in vegetable keeper of refrigerator for 1 week.

Endive, Curly or Escarole: Cool-season biennial. Endive is a loose-headed, curly-fringed, lettucelike green, to 8 in. (20 cm) tall, with a strong flavor; escarole is generally similar but bears smooth leaves. Endive is related to sunflower; Belgian endive is an unrelated plant [see Chicory; Belgian Endive; French Endive; or Radicchio, pg. 91].
Yield: Allow 2–3 plants per household member.
Planting: In average climates, sow seed in full sun in early spring when soil warms to 50–85°F (10–29°C); in mild-winter climates, in autumn. Sow seed ¼ in. (6 mm) deep, 1–2 in. (25–50 mm) apart, thinning to 8–12 in. (20–30 cm) apart, in rows 18–24 in. (45–60 cm) apart. Plant successions.
Growing Temperature: 50–80°F (10–27°C). Cool temperatures produce highly prized, bitter-tasting greens; provide shade to plants in full sunlight at temperatures over 85°F (29°C).
Soil: Moist, well-drained, sandy soil. Fertility: Rich. 5.0–6.8 pH. Prepare soil at least 1 ft. (30 cm) deep.
Care: Easy. Keep evenly moist; avoid wetting foliage. Fertilize monthly with 5–5–5 formula. Cultivate. Blanch to ensure white foliage by loosely tying outer leaves over developing head when 4–5 in. (10–13 cm) tall; avoid blanching when foliage is wet, and loosen ties following rain to allow foliage to dry. Aphid, armyworm, flea beetle, leafhopper, slug, snail and mildew susceptible.
Companion Plants: Beets, parsnips, radishes, and turnip.
Maturity/Harvest: 85–100 days. Cut outer leaves from stem beginning when 5–6 in. (13–15 cm) long; early-harvest greens are tender and mild flavored. Continue harvesting throughout season, cutting all remaining leaves when stalks begin to form seed heads. Wash throughly and allow to dry before chilling.
Storage/Tips: Fresh in vegetable keeper of refrigerator for 2 weeks. Endive leaves can be eaten raw as flavorful, somewhat bitter salad greens.

Garlic: Cool-season bulb. Garlic is a flat-leaved plant bearing bulbous heads consisting of many tear-shaped cloves wrapped in a papery tunicate sheath. Used raw, garlic is intensely flavored; roasted or baked garlic is mild flavored and popular for appetizers. Long believed by herbalists to possess preservative and curative powers, garlic's beneficial effects on the immune system, efficacy in reducing cholesterol levels, and aid in lowering blood pressure are now medically documented. An onion-family vegetable.

Yield: Allow 12–16 plants per household member.

Planting: In average climates, plant outer cloves in full sun in early spring and again in early autumn; in mild-winter climates, in spring, autumn, and winter, while soil temperatures remain 35–90°F (2–32°C). Set cloves 1 in. (25 mm) deep, 4–8 in. (10–20 cm) apart, in rows 15 in. (38 cm) apart; reserve small central cloves for cooking. Use seed stock; grocery garlic often is treated to prevent sprouting.

Growing Temperature: 45–85°F (7–29°C). Zones 3–11. Garlic tolerates varied growing conditions; once stalks develop, they require 2 months at 32–50°F (0–10°C) for bulbs to fully develop.

Soil: Moist, well-drained soil. Fertility: Rich. 5.5–6.8 pH. Prepare soil at least 1 ft. (30 cm) deep.

Care: Moderate. Keep evenly damp during active growth; allow soil surface to dry between waterings. Fertilize monthly with 0–10–10 formula. Mulch. Cultivate. Pinch off all seed heads when they form, then lodge plants by gently doubling over stems and tying them. Lodging hastens the drying of plant tops, redirects nutrients to the root, and increases head size. After 1 month, withhold water. Garlic is susceptible to soil-borne root maggots; rotate plantings every year.

Companion Plants: Beets, lettuce, strawberries, summer savory, and tomatoes.

Maturity/Harvest: 90–100 days. Pull heads when fully formed 2–3 weeks after lodging, brushing away any clinging soil and allowing heads to cure for 3–4 weeks in a warm, shady space protected from rain until their outer skins turn papery.

Storage/Tips: Fresh and dried, in a nylon net bag in a dark, dry, cool place, for 4–6 months; peeled and frozen, 6–8 months; blanched and canned, 1 year. Braid cured garlic heads and stalks into decorative strands for short-term storage.

Gourds: Warm season. Closely related to squash, gourds are vining plants, 10–15 ft. (3–4.5 m) long, with pumpkinlike leaves and bearing tough-skinned, seedy fruit used mostly for decoration, rustic utensils, and even for birdhouses and musical instruments. Exfoliating sponges used for cosmetic cleansing are the dried pithy cores of loofah gourds.

Yield: Allow 1–2 plants of each cultivar, yielding 10–15 gourds.

Planting: In average climates, sow seed indoors at time of last expected frost and harden seedlings 5–7 days before transplanting; in mild-winter climates, in late winter. Set out seedlings in full sun in spring when soil warms to 68–86°F (20–30°C). Sow 2–3 seeds, 2 in. (50 mm) deep, 1 ft. (30 cm) apart, thinning to 2–4 ft. (60–120 cm) apart, in rows or hills 4 ft. (1.2 m) apart, installing trellises or support wires 3–5 ft. (90–150 cm) tall at time of planting. Separate plantings 50–75 ft. (15–23 m) to prevent cross-hybridization between cultivars.

Growing Temperature: 50–90°F (10–32°C). Flowers may drop or fail to set fruit at temperatures below 50°F (10°C).

Soil: Moist, well-drained, sandy soil. Fertility: Rich. 5.5–6.8 pH. Prepare soil at least 2 ft. (60 cm) deep.

Care: Easy. Keep evenly moist; avoid wetting foliage. Withhold water when flowers appear. Fertilize only at time of planting with 5–10–10 formula. Mulch. Cultivate. Avoid direct contact of gourds with soil. Cucumber beetle and fungal disease susceptible.

Companion Plants: Beans, corn, and peas.

Maturity/Harvest: 85–100 days. Cut fruit when vines have dried and stems turn tan, before frost. Cure for 3–4 weeks in a shady, warm dry spot until seed rattles inside when gourds are shaken.

Storage/Tips: Dried, gourds store indefinitely; enhance their beauty by painting with shellac or other clear sealing finish. For loofah sponges, cook mature fruit in barely boiling water for 4–5 hours; when sodden and pliable, cool. Remove skin and flesh from the gourds' tough, fibrous cores, then bleach, rinse thoroughly, trim, and dry in a warm, sunny spot protected from rain.

HERBS

While the horticultural definition of herbs includes many plants reputed to have beneficial use in cooking or medicine, most common to vegetable gardeners are the culinary herbs:

Angelica *(Angelica archangelica).* Zones 3–10. Hardy biennial herb, to 6 ft. (1.8 m) tall, with oval, pointed, divided leaves on stout, hollow stalks and green flowers in branching clusters, forming many seed. Mild, sweet-flavored stalks and sharply sweet seed; use stalks for candied preserves, leaves as flavoring for deserts, roots for soups and stews.

Anise *(Pimpinella anisum).* Annual herb, to 2 ft. (60 cm) tall, with simple basal leaves, feathery upper leaves, and tiny white flowers in branching clusters on tall stalks in late summer, forming many tiny seed. Mild to strong licorice fragrance; use leaves for salad greens, seed for toppings on bread, confections, and desserts.

Basil *(Ocimum basilicum).* Annual herb, to 30 in. (75 cm) tall, with oval, pointed leaves and small, white flowers in spiking clusters in summer. Strong, sweet fragrance; use as flavoring for oil, vinegar and in pesto sauce for pasta.

Bay Laurel *(Laurus nobilis).* Zones 8–11. Broad-leaved evergreen tree, to 40 ft. (12 m) tall, with leathery, oval, pointed leaves and inconspicuous white flowers in spring; ideal for container plantings and topiary. Strongly aromatic; use for flavoring stock, sauces, poultry, meat, and fish dishes.

Bee Balm *(Monarda didyma).* Zones 2–10. Very hardy perennial herb, to 4 ft. (1.2 m) tall, with oval, pointed leaves and red, scythe-shaped flowers in round-headed spiking clusters in summer. Mint-basil fragrance; use leaves for cold and hot herbal tea, flavoring and garnish for salads, light meat and poultry dishes.

Borage *(Borago officinalis).* Hardy annual herb, to 3 ft. (90 cm) tall, with broadly oval, veined leaves and bright blue flowers in clusters on long stalks in summer. Mild cucumber-like flavor; use leaves and flowers as flavoring for teas, garnish, and greens for salads.

Caraway *(Carum carvi).* Hardy biennial herb, to 2 ft. (60 cm) tall, with feathery leaves and tiny pinkish white flowers in flat-headed clusters in spring, forming many seed. Unique flavor. Use seed for flavoring casseroles, soups, and stews or as topping on baked breads and confections; use leaves as salad greens.

Chamomile *(Chamaemelum nobile).* Zones 3–10. Hardy, low, perennial herb, to 1 ft. (30 cm) tall, with feathery light green leaves and daisylike, rayed flowers in early summer. Strong apple or pear fragrance; use for herbal tea. False chamomile, *Matricaria recutita,* is a similar plant more frequently grown for dried flowers, which are also used for herbal tea.

Chervil *(Anthriscus cerefolium).* Annual herb, to 2 ft. (60 cm) tall, with parsleylike, divided leaves with tiny white flowers in branching clusters in late spring, forming many seed. Mild parsley and anise flavor; use leaves before flowers form for flavoring salads, sauces, soups, and egg dishes.

Chives *(Allium schoenoprasum).* Zones 3–10. Hardy, bunching, rhizomatous perennial bulb with round, hollow, grasslike leaves, to 2 ft. (60 cm) tall, bearing pink, ball-shaped flowers in late spring. Mild onion flavor; use as a garnish and flavoring for dips, soups, and salads.

Coriander or **Cilantro** *(Coriandrum sativum).* Annual herb, to 3 ft. (90 cm) tall, with finely divided upper and broadly lobed lower leaves, and tiny pink, purple, or rose flowers in summer. Sharply flavored leaves, sweetly fragrant seed; use leaves as flavoring for Asian, Mediterranean, and Mexican dishes, seed for flavoring casseroles, curries, and ground meat, or for stewed dishes.

Cumin *(Cuminum cyminum).* Annual herb, to 6 in. (15 cm) tall, with threadlike leaves and small pink, white flowers surrounded by bracts in summer, forming many seed. Strongly fragrant seed; use crushed seed as flavoring for Asian, Mexican dishes.

Dill *(Anethum graveolens).* Annual herb, to 4 ft. (1.2 m) tall, with feathery leaves, bearing tiny yellow flowers in flat-headed clusters in summer, forming many seed. Strong dill flavor; use leaves as garnish and flavoring for dips and salads, seed for pickling, sauces, fish dishes.

Fennel *(Foeniculum vulgare).* Zones 4–11. Hardy perennial herb, to 5 ft. (1.5 m) tall, with lacy, dill-like leaves and tiny yellow flowers in flat-headed clusters in summer. Mild anise flavor; use tender young leaves for garnish and salad greens, milder seeds for herbal tea and baked fish and poultry dishes. Florence fennel, *F. var. azoricum,* is a closely related plant grown for its swollen root, eaten cooked or raw.

Ginger *(Zingiber officinale).* Zones 9–10. Tender rhizomatous perennial bulb, to 2 ft. (60 cm) tall, with narrow, spear-shaped leaves, canelike stems, and multicolored flowers of green, pink, white, and yellow in summer. Very fragrant root; use in Asian and savory dishes, confections, sauces.

Horseradish *(Armoracia rusticana).* Zones 5–10. Hardy, deep-rooted, perennial rhizomatous herb, to 18 in. (45 cm) tall, with large, coarse, paddlelike leaves on long stalks, bearing tiny white flowers in late spring. Intense, pungent-flavored roots, milder leaves; use roots grated as flavoring for dips and sauces, leaves in salad greens.

Hyssop *(Hyssopus officinalis).* Hardy, semi-evergreen, shrubby herb, to 2 ft. (60 cm) tall, with oval, pointed leaves and blue, purple, red, white flowers in late summer. Strong mintlike fragrance; use as flavoring for game, pâté, soups, stews.

Lavender *(Lavandula angustifolia).* Zones 6–11. Hardy perennial herb, to 3 ft. (90 cm) tall, with narrow, gray, textured leaves and blue, lavender, purple flowers in spiking clusters on tall, reedy stalks. Pleasantly aromatic; use flowers to flavor oil, vinegar.

Lemon Balm *(Melissa officinalis).* Zones 3–10. Hardy perennial herb, to 2 ft. (60 cm) tall, with light green, oval, toothed leaves and tiny white flowers in whorled clusters in spring. Lemony fragrance; use leaves for herbal tea and as flavoring for confections, desserts.

Lemon Verbena *(Aloysia triphylla).* Zones 8–11. Tender perennial shrub, 6–8 ft. (1.8–2.4 m) tall, with bladelike, pointed leaves, bearing white flower spikes in late summer. Strong lemon scent; use for herbal tea and as a flavoring in desserts.

Lovage *(Levisticum officinale).* Zones 4–10. Hardy perennial herb, to 6 ft. (1.8 m) tall, with oval, deeply cut leaves and greenish yellow flowers in flat-headed clusters in summer, forming many seed. Yeasty celery-like fragrance; use leaves as flavoring for soups, sauces, and casseroles, tender young leaves as salad greens, and seed as flavoring for baked and vegetarian dishes.

Marjoram *(Origanum majorana).* Zones 8–11. Tender branching perennial herb, to 2 ft. (60 cm) tall, with oval, gray green leaves and tiny white flowers surrounded by flowerlike bracts in spiking clusters in summer. Intensely fragrant; use leaves for Italian pasta, pizza, sauces.

Mint *(Mentha* sp.). Zones 3–10. Many species of hardy perennial herbs, 2–3 ft. (60–90 cm) tall, with oval, textured, finely toothed leaves and tiny pink or purple flowers in whorled, spiking clusters in summer. Intense to mild minty fragrance, depending on species; use leaves as flavoring for drinks and herbal tea, as a salad green, or for seasoning vegetarian casseroles and vegetable dishes.

Oregano *(Origanum vulgare).* Zones 3–9. Hardy perennial herb, to 30 in. (75 cm) tall, with broadly oval leaves and pink flowers in whorled spiking clusters in summer. Strongly fragrant; use as flavoring for Italian dishes, sauces, pizza.

Parsley *(Petroselinum crispum).* Hardy biennial herb, to 3 ft. (90 cm) tall, with curly or flat, divided leaves and tiny, yellow green flowers in flat clusters in summer. Strongly fragrant; use leaves as garnish and flavoring for sauces, egg, fish, poultry dishes and as an ingredient for bouquet garni.

Pot Marigold *(Calendula officinalis).* Annual herb, to 2 ft. (60 cm) tall, with narrow, rounded leaves and gold, orange, yellow, double-daisylike flowers in spring to summer. Mildly bitter flavor; use leaves for salad greens, flower petals as coloring, garnish, and flavoring for dips, rice dishes, soups.

Rosemary *(Rosmarinus officinalis).* Zones 7–11. Tender evergreen perennial shrub, 2–4 ft. (60–120 cm) tall, with needle-shaped, flat leaves and tiny, bright blue flowers in whorled clusters in spring. Intensely fragrant, somewhat reminiscent of resin; use leaves as flavoring for meat dishes, omelets, stuffings, and casseroles, flowers for garnish in salads.

Rue *(Ruta graveolens).* Zones 8–11. Tender perennial shrub, to 3 ft. (90 cm) tall, with narrow, gray green, textured leaves and purple or yellow flowers in summer. Intensely fragrant; use as flavoring in dips, salads, sauces, condiments.

Sage *(Salvia officinalis).* Zones 5–11. Hardy erect perennial herb, to 2 ft. (60 cm) tall, with blade-shaped, textured leaves and purple, red, or white flowers in whorled spiking clusters in early summer. Mildly to intensely fragrant; use as flavoring for meat, poultry, soups, stews, and stuffings.

Sorrel *(Rumex acetosa).* Zones 3–9. Hardy perennial herb, to 3 ft. (90 cm) tall, with broadly oval, light green leaves and insignificant greenish flowers. Sour to bitter flavor; use for salad greens and as flavoring for sauces, soups.

Summer Savory *(Satureja hortensis).* Annual herb, to 18 in. (45 cm) tall, with very narrow leaves and light pink, white flowers in whorled spiking clusters in summer. Mildly fragrant; use leaves for flavoring cheese, egg, light meat, poultry, and vegetarian dishes, sauces, soups, and stocks.

Sweet Cicely *(Myrrhis odorata).* Zones 5–10. Hardy perennial herb, to 3 ft. (90 cm) tall, with fernlike leaves and tiny white flowers in dill-like clusters in summer, forming many large seed. Mild licorice fragrance; use leaves as salad greens, seed for flavoring fruit dishes.

Tarragon *(Artemisia dracunculus).* Zones 4–9. Hardy upright rhizomatous perennial, to 5 ft. (1.5 m) tall, with narrow, needlelike leaves, bearing greenish white flowers in early summer. Strong licorice fragrance; use for flavoring vinegar, sauces, fish, poultry dishes, and as ingredient in fines herbes.

Thyme *(Thymus vulgaris).* Zones 3–11. Very hardy, shrubby perennial herb, to 1 ft. (30 cm) tall, with tiny oval leaves and inconspicuous pink flowers in early summer. Strongly fragrant; use leaves as flavoring in meat dishes, sauces, and soups, and as an ingredient in bouquet garni.

Winter Savory *(Satureja montana).* Zones 5–9. Hardy, shrubby, evergreen perennial herb, to 1 ft. (30 cm) tall, with very narrow leaves and tiny pink, white flowers in summer. Strongly fragrant; use leaves as flavoring for bean, game, meat dishes and casseroles.

Woodruff *(Galium odoratum).* Zones 3–11. Hardy, low, perennial herb, to 1 ft. (30 cm) tall, with oval, pointed leaves and white flowers in branching clusters in summer. Grassy fragrance; use as flavoring for herbal teas, May wine.

Husk Tomatoes; Ground Cherries; or Tomatillos: Warm-season annual or perennial. Shrublike bushy plants, to 2–4 ft. (60–120 cm) tall, with toothed, oval leaves and bearing fruit superficially similar to green or yellow cherry tomatoes encased in a green or tan papery husk. Peeling back the husk will reveal a green, yellow, or purple, seedy, solid fruit with flavors either sweet or tangy, depending on species, used for making jams, pies, or salsas. Similar in cultivation to tomatoes, but tolerates inconsistent temperatures. A relative of ornamental Chinese lantern plant.

Yield: Allow 1–2 plants per household member.

Planting: In average climates, sow seed indoors at time of last expected frost and harden seedlings 5–7 days before transplanting; in mild-winter climates, in full sun in spring when soil warms to 65–85°F (18–29°C). Sow seed ⅛ in. (3 mm) deep, 2 in. (50 mm) apart, thinning to 10 in. (25 cm) apart, in rows 2 ft. (60 cm) apart.

Growing Temperature: 50–85°F (10–29°C). Best in mild climates with hot days.

Soil: Moist–damp, well-drained soil. Fertility: Rich. 6.0–6.8 pH. Prepare soil at least 30 in. (75 cm) deep.

Care: Moderate. Keep damp; allow soil surface to dry between waterings. Cultivate. Protect from frost; extend harvest in autumn by covering plants with clear plastic supported on stakes above foliage when nighttime temperatures fall below 50°F (10°C).

Companion Plants: Beans, corn, and tomatoes.

Maturity/Harvest: 120 days. For tangy salsas, pick fruit when green and firm; for sweet preserves, harvest when ripening husks turn tan, split open, and fruit separates easily from the plant. Leave fruit in husk until ready for use. Fruit sweetens after light frosts.

Storage/Tips: Fresh in husks in vegetable keeper of refrigerator for 2–3 weeks; chopped and frozen, 6 months; preserved by canning as jam, preserves, or salsa, 1 year.

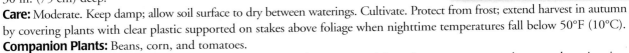

Jerusalem Artichokes or Sunchokes: Warm-season perennial. Close relative of sunflower, a bushy, spreading plant, 6–10 ft. (1.8–3 m) tall, topped with yellow-rayed flowers with golden centers, bearing a tuber similar in appearance to a potato but flavored like water chestnut. The name Jerusalem artichoke likely derives from English corruption of the French name for sunflower, *girasol.*

Yield: Allow 2–3 plants per household member.

Planting: In average climates, plant tubers in full sun in spring when soil warms to 50–85°F (10–29°C); in mild-winter climates, in late winter. Set tubers 4–6 in. (10–15 cm) deep, 2 ft. (60 cm) apart, in rows 36–40 in. (90–102 cm) apart, installing edge boards or root-guard barriers, at least 2 ft. (60 cm) deep, to prevent roots from spreading beyond the bed.

Growing Temperature: 65–90°F (18–32°C). Zones 4–11. Tolerates hard freezes when protected under a thick layer of mulch.

Soil: Moist, well-drained, sandy loam. Fertility: Rich. 5.8–6.2 pH. Prepare soil at least 2 ft. (60 cm) deep.

Care: Easy. Keep evenly moist. Fertilize annually in spring with 5–10–10 formula or well-rotted manure. Mulch in winter, zones 4–7. Avoid deep cultivation that could cut the shallow, widespread tubers, 8–16 in. (20–40 cm) from the stalk, beneath the outer edge of the foliage. When leaves turn yellow in autumn, lodge or cut stalks to 3 in. (75 mm) above soil, or lift several tubers as seed stalk, and store them over winter packed in loose, damp sawdust, placed in a cool, dry location. Carefully remove all tubers from soil to prevent volunteer shoots from sprouting. Pest and disease resistant.

Companion Plants: Corn, peanuts, and rhubarb.

Maturity/Harvest: 110–150 days. Lift tubers with a garden fork when flowers fade and they are 3–4 in. (75–100 mm) wide. Best flavor when harvested after light frost.

Storage/Tips: Fresh in vegetable keeper of refrigerator for 2–3 weeks; in damp sawdust in a dark, cool location, 6 months; in ground, throughout winter. Lacking starches that turn to sugar during digestion, they are an excellent alternative to rice and potatoes for diabetics. As ornamental plantings, they also provide effective and attractive windbreaks.

Kale: Cool season. Either curly edged or smooth, to 2 ft. (60 cm) tall, with blue, gray, green, white, yellow, or red-veined leaves, kale has a distinctive, sweet, cabbagelike taste which improves after early frosts. Use kale in Asian stir-fried dishes, serve it steamed or lightly sautéed in butter, or chop it as a flavorful addition to braised meats, soups, and stews. A cole-family vegetable.

Yield: Allow 4–5 plants per household member.

Planting: Sow seed or set out seedlings in full–partial sun in spring or autumn, when soil warms to 55–75°F (13–24°C). Sow seed ¼ in. (6 mm) deep, 1 in. (25 mm) apart, thinning to 1 ft. (30 cm) apart, in rows 2 ft. (60 cm) apart. Set out seedlings 12–16 in. (30–40 cm) apart, in rows 2 ft. (60 cm) apart. Plant successions every 3–4 weeks.

Growing Temperature: 45–75°F (7–24°C). Best in mild-summer climates. Protect plants from heat, sun at temperatures above 80°F (27°C); from freezing at temperatures below 10°F (–12°C). Kale is generally tolerant of even hard frosts.

Soil: Moist, well-drained, sandy loam. Fertility: Average. 5.5–6.8 pH. Prepare soil at least 18 in. (45 cm) deep. Rotate plantings with legumes to avoid nitrogen depletion.

Care: Easy. Keep evenly moist. Fertilize only when signs of deficiency occur. Mulch every 2 months with organic compost; when plants are 6 in. (15 cm) tall, apply loose straw around stems. Cultivate. Inspect frequently for foliage damage or egg clusters on underleaves due to larvae of white cabbage butterfly; wash infested plants with dilute soap solution to remove and kill the eggs. Aphid, cabbage looper, cabbageworm, cutworm, root maggot and powdery mildew susceptible.

Companion Plants: Beets, celery, herbs, onions, and potatoes.

Maturity/Harvest: 55–75 days. Begin harvesting when plants reach 8–10 in. (20–25 cm) tall, thinning outer leaves, leaving the central growth bud to resprout. Cut stalks 2 in. (50 mm) above the soil when plants mature, before bolting, leaving their roots; in mild climates, the roots will sprout in 1–2 weeks, growing a new plant.

Storage/Tips: Fresh in vegetable keeper of refrigerator for 1–2 weeks; blanched and frozen, 6 months. Remove the leaves' middle ribs before eating, reserving them for dicing into soups, stews.

Kohlrabi: Cool season. The swollen stem of kohlrabi resembles an above-ground turnip; long-stemmed green or purple leaves sprout in a fan from a globelike central stem, 2–3 in. (50–75 mm) wide. A cole-family vegetable.

Yield: Allow 4–5 plants per household member.

Planting In average climates, in full sun–partial shade in spring for early summer harvest or late summer for autumn harvest when soil temperature is 50–85°F (10–29°C); in mild-winter climates, in autumn for early winter harvest or in late winter for early spring harvest. Sow seed ¼–½ in. (6–12 mm) deep, 1 in. (25 mm) apart, thinning to 5–8 in. (13–20 cm) apart, in rows 30 in. (75 cm) apart. Plant successions 3–4 weeks apart.

Growing Temperature: 40–75°F (4–24°C). Best in mild-summer climates. Protect plants from heat, sun at temperatures above 80°F (27°C). Kohlrabi is generally tolerant of even hard frosts.

Soil: Moist, well-drained, sandy soil. Fertility: Rich. 5.5–6.8 pH. Prepare soil at least 18 in. (45 cm) deep. Rotate plantings with legumes to avoid nitrogen depletion.

Care: Easy. Keep evenly moist. Fertilize semi-monthly with acidic 5–10–10 formula. Mulch; when plants are 4–5 in. (10–13 cm) tall, apply organic compost to soil around stems. Cultivate. Inspect frequently for foliage damage or egg clusters on underleaves due to larvae of white cabbage butterfly; wash infested plants with dilute soap solution to remove and kill the eggs. Aphid, cabbage looper, cabbageworm, cutworm, root maggot and powdery mildew susceptible.

Companion Plants: Beets, celery, herbs, onions, and potatoes.

Maturity/Harvest: 45–60 days. Cut bulbs and leaves when stems reach 2–3 in. (50–75 mm) wide. Overmature kohlrabi bulbs are woody and have less flavor than those with tender, young stems.

Storage/Tips: Fresh in vegetable keeper of refrigerator for 1–2 weeks. Kohlrabi bulbs can be eaten raw, similar to an apple, or shaved with a vegetable grater and added to salads. Use the tangy, cabbage-flavored leaves as salad greens or for steaming.

Leeks: Cool season. With stems of white becoming green, 24–30 in. (60–75 cm) tall, and topped with deep green fanlike foliage, leeks mature slowly and are prized for their mild yet zesty flavor. With potato, chicken broth, and cream, a principal ingredient of vichyssoise, a cold soup. An onion-family vegetable.

Yield: Allow 12–15 plants per household member.

Planting: In average climates, sow seed indoors in flats at least 3 in. (75 mm) deep, filled with loose potting soil, 8–10 weeks before last expected frost, and harden seedlings 6–9 days before transplanting; in mild-winter climates, in full sun–partial shade in early autumn or late winter. Sow seed in trenches 4–6 in. (10–15 cm) deep, ⅛ in. (3 mm) deep, 1 in. (25 mm) apart, thinning to 4–6 in. (10–15 cm) apart, in rows 18 in. (45 cm) apart. Set out seedlings in trenches 4–6 in. (10–15 cm) deep, 4–6 in. (10–15 cm) apart. Plant successions every 2–3 weeks.

Growing Temperature: 45–85°F (7–29°C). Shade plants at temperatures over 90°F (32°C).

Soil: Damp, well-drained, sandy loam. Fertility: Rich. 6.0–6.8 pH. Prepare soil at least 1 ft. (30 cm) deep.

Care: Easy. Keep evenly damp; water when soil surface dries. Fertilize monthly with 5–10–10 formula; cultivate and water after fertilizing. Mulch. Blanch to ensure white root heads by gradually filling planting trench with sand as plants grow, mounding to base of first leaf junction. Pest and disease resistant.

Companion Plants: Carrots, celery, garlic, and onions.

Maturity/Harvest: 120–170 days. Best harvested as needed. Pull when stems are 1–2 in. (25–50 mm) wide and stalks are 16–24 in. (40–60 cm) tall. In cold-winter climates, in autumn pull roots and heel into moist wood chips.

Storage/Tips: Fresh, heeled in wood chips and placed in a dark, cool, moist spot, for 2 months [see Maturity/Harvest, above]. Good accompaniment to roasted potatoes, yams, and other mild-flavored tubers.

Lettuce, Butterhead or Bibb: Cool season. Leafy green plants, to 1 ft. (30 cm) tall, bear loose heads of wavy-fringed, light green leaves with cream yellow centers. Crisp textured and delicate in flavor, cultivars include those with heads to 7 in. (18 cm) wide and miniatures only 4 in. (10 cm) wide.

Yield: Allow 6–10 heads per household member. A square bed, 16 sq. ft. (1.5 m²) in area, yields enough salad greens for a family of 3 for 4–6 weeks.

Planting: In average climates, sow seed indoors 4–6 weeks before last expected frost or, after frost hazard has passed, in spring–early autumn; in mild-winter climates, in full sun–partial shade in spring–early winter. Harden seedlings 5–7 days before transplanting when soil warms to 40–75°F (4–24°C). Sow seed ¼ in. (6 mm) deep, 1–2 in. (25–50 mm) apart, thinning to 6–8 in. (15–20 cm) apart, in rows 16–24 in. (40–60 cm) apart, or broadcast over an area and thin to 1 ft. (30 cm) apart. Avoid overcrowding. Plant successions every 3–4 weeks. Install floating row covers after planting to limit access by pests.

Growing Temperature: 45–75°F (7–24°C). Bolts in temperatures over 85°F (29°C) and when daylight hours lengthen in summer. Protect plants from temperatures below 35°F (2°C).

Soil: Moist, well-drained, sandy loam. Fertility: Average. 6.0–6.8 pH. Prepare soil at least 1 ft. (30 cm) deep.

Care: Easy. Keep evenly moist; avoid wetting foliage. Fertilize only at planting with 0–5–5 formula. Mulch. Cultivate. As plants mature, avoid overhead watering in direct sun to prevent leaf blemish. Chewing insect and slug, snail susceptible.

Companion Plants: Carrots, cucumbers, radishes, and strawberries.

Maturity/Harvest: 65–80 days. Best harvested as needed. Begin harvesting when plants reach 10 in. (25 cm) tall, 5–6 weeks from sowing, thinning outer leaves, leaving the central growth bud to resprout. Cut heads 2 in. (50 mm) above the soil when plants mature, before bolting. Pull roots and reseed bed; roots left in the soil will resprout with coarser, less flavorful foliage.

Storage/Tips: Fresh in vegetable keeper of refrigerator for 2–3 weeks. Good eaten raw as leafy green in salads; steamed as wrap over ground-meat fillings as for cabbage rolls.

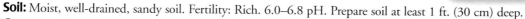

Lettuce, Celtuce; or Asparagus Lettuce: With foliage similar in appearance and taste to romaine, upon reaching maturity celtuce forms stout central stalks, to 18 in. (45 cm) tall, which may be substituted for asparagus or celery in raw salads, served as crudités, or used in Asian stir-fried dishes. Romaine is a closely related species [see also Lettuce, Romaine; or Cos, opposite pg.].

Yield: Allow 4–6 heads per household member.

Planting: In average climates, sow seed in full sun–partial shade in late summer to early autumn; in mild-winter climates, in autumn–winter, when soil temperature drops to 40–75°F (4–24°C). Sow seed ¼ in. (6 mm) deep, 2 in. (50 mm) apart, thinning to 1 ft. (30 cm) apart, in rows 18 in. (45 cm) apart, or broadcast over an area and thin to 1 ft. (30 cm) apart. Install floating row covers after planting to limit access by pests.

Growing Temperature: 45–75°F (7–24°C). Protect plants from temperatures below 40°F (4°C). Bolts in temperatures over 85°F (29°C) and when daylight hours lengthen in summer.

Soil: Moist, well-drained, sandy soil. Fertility: Rich. 6.0–6.8 pH. Prepare soil at least 1 ft. (30 cm) deep.

Care: Easy. Keep evenly moist; avoid wetting foliage. Fertilize only at planting with 5–10–10 formula. Mulch. Cultivate. Blanch celtuce to ensure white stems when 1 ft. (30 cm) tall by mulching with straw or wrapping with opaque, waterproof paper, or choose self-blanching cultivars. Chewing insect and slug, snail susceptible.

Companion Plants: Carrots, cucumbers, radishes, and strawberries.

Maturity/Harvest: 65–90 days. Begin harvesting when 5–8 in. (13–20 cm) tall, removing alternate outer leaves, leaving the central growth bud to sprout additional leaves; avoid excessive stripping of leaves. Cut stem 2 in. (50 mm) above the soil when 4–6 in. (10–15 cm) tall but before it bolts to produce flower buds.

Storage/Tips: Fresh in vegetable keeper of refrigerator for 2 weeks. Leaves are good eaten raw as leafy green in salads; use sliced stalks for flavoring in sauces, soups, and stews as for celery.

Lettuce, Crisphead or Iceberg: Cool season. With a firm, compact head of pale green, crisp leaves on a basal rosette of open leaves, the tight, perfect spheres of crisphead are both the most often grown and the most challenging lettuce. Fortunately, the flavor and texture of open-leaved crispheads are every bit as tasy as their idealized sisters.

Yield: Allow 6–10 heads per household member.

Planting: In average climates, sow seed in full–partial sun in early spring when soil warms to 40–75°F (4–24°C), or in late summer; in mild-winter climates, in autumn. Sow seed ¼ in. (6 mm) deep, 1–2 in. (25–50 mm) apart, thinning to 1 ft. (30 cm) apart, in rows 16–24 in. (40–60 cm) apart, or broadcast over an area and thin to 1 ft. (30 cm) apart. Install floating row covers after planting to limit access by pests.

Growing Temperature: 45–75°F (7–24°C). Protect plants from temperatures below 40°F (4°C). Shade plants in full sunlight at temperatures above 85°F (29°C). Best in mild-summer climates.

Soil: Moist, well-drained, sandy soil. Fertility: Rich. 6.0–6.8 pH. Prepare soil at least 1 ft. (30 cm) deep.

Care: Moderate. Keep evenly moist; avoid wetting foliage. Fertilize only at planting with 5–10–10 formula. Mulch. Cultivate. Chewing insect, slug, snail and downy mildew susceptible.

Companion Plants: Carrots, cucumbers, radishes, and strawberries.

Maturity/Harvest: 80–90 days. Cut when heads are tight and turn yellowish green. Cut heads from the stem 1 in. (25 mm) above the soil, removing any loose outer leaves, leaving the central growth bud to sprout additional leaves.

Storage/Tips: Fresh in vegetable keeper of refrigerator for 2–3 weeks; discard the outer leaves, then rinse and dry to prevent premature spoilage of the head. Good eaten raw as leafy green in salads; steamed as wrap over ground-meat fillings as for cabbage rolls.

Lettuce, Leaf or Looseleaf: Cool season. Loose, open, green, purple, red, and yellow leaves with curly fringes form mounding plants, to 14 in. (36 cm) tall. Mild flavored, they are ideal for salads

Yield: Allow 6–10 plants per household member.

Planting: In average climates, sow seed in full sun–partial shade in early spring or late summer when soil warms to 40–75°F (4–24°C); in mild-winter climates, in autumn. Sow seed ¼ in. (6 mm) deep, 1–2 in. (25–50 mm) apart, thinning to 4–8 in. (10–20 cm) apart, in rows 1–2 ft. (30–60 cm) apart, or broadcast over an area and thin to 10 in. (25 cm) apart. Plant successions every 3–4 weeks.

Growing Temperature: 45–75°F (7–24°C). Shade plants at temperatures above 85°F (29°C). Bolts in temperatures over 80°F (27°C) and when daylight hours lengthen in summer.

Soil: Moist, well-drained, sandy soil. Fertility: Rich. 6.0–6.8 pH. Prepare soil at least 1 ft. (30 cm) deep.

Care: Easy. Keep evenly moist; avoid wetting foliage. Fertilize only at planting with 5–10–10 formula. Mulch. Cultivate. Chewing insect and slug, snail susceptible.

Companion Plants: Carrots, cucumbers, radishes, and strawberries.

Maturity/Harvest: 40–50 days. Begin harvesting when 4–6 in. (10–15 cm) tall, thinning outer leaves, leaving the central growth bud to resprout. Cut stem 2 in. (50 mm) above the soil when 10–12 in. (25–30 cm) tall but before it bolts to produce flower buds.

Storage/Tips: Fresh in vegetable keeper of refrigerator for 2–3 weeks. Good eaten raw as leafy green in salads.

Lettuce, Romaine; or Cos: Cool season. Oval, light green leaves with prominent ribs and veins form upright plants, 8–9 in. (20–23 cm) tall, with open, cylindrical or oval heads. Green yellow central leaves are tender, crisp, and sweeter than both the outer leaves and other cultivars. The lettuce of choice for Caesar salads. Choose dwarf cultivars for planting in containers, small-space gardens. Celtuce is a closely related species [see also Lettuce, Celtuce; or Asparagus Lettuce, opposite pg.].

Yield: Allow 6–10 plants per household member.

Planting: In average climates, sow seed indoors 4–6 weeks before last expected frost and harden seedlings 4–5 days before transplanting, or in late summer or early autumn; in mild-winter climates, in full sun in winter. Set out seedlings 3–4 in. (75–100 mm) tall when soil warms to 40–75°F (4–24°C). Sow seed ¼–½ in. (6–12 mm) deep, 1–2 in. (25–50 mm) apart, thinning to 6–8 in. (15–20 cm) apart, in rows 16–24 in. (40–60 cm) apart, or broadcast over an area and thin to 10 in. (25 cm) apart. Avoid overcrowding; best in small, separated plantings. Plant successions every 3–5 weeks.

Growing Temperature: 45–75°F (7–24°C). Shade plants at temperatures above 85°F (29°C). Bolts in temperatures over 80°F (27°C) and when daylight hours lengthen in summer. Most heat-tolerant lettuce species.

Soil: Moist, well-drained, sandy soil. Fertility: Rich. 6.0–6.8 pH. Prepare soil at least 1 ft. (30 cm) deep.

Care: Easy. Keep evenly moist; avoid wetting foliage. Fertilize only at planting with 5–10–10 formula. Mulch. Cultivate. Blanch romain to ensure white lower leaves when 6 in. (15 cm) tall by wrapping with opaque, waterproof paper. Chewing insect and slug, snail susceptible.

Companion Plants: Carrots, corn, cucumbers, radishes, and strawberries.

Maturity/Harvest: 80–85 days. Cut stem 1 in. (25 mm) above the soil when 8 in. (20 cm) tall, leaving the central growth bud to resprout. Immerse cut romaine in ice water immediately after cutting.

Storage/Tips: Fresh in vegetable keeper of refrigerator for 2–3 weeks. Good eaten raw as leafy green in salads. Dry leaves thoroughly after rinsing and tear romaine into bite-sized pieces; water dilutes the flavors of both the lettuce and most salad dressings. Can be steamed as wrap over ground-meat fillings as for cabbage rolls.

Melons, Summer: Warm season. Summer melons—early-ripening musk-melons (termed erroneously "cantaloupe") and watermelons—are vining plants, to 20 ft. (6 m) long, bearing round or oval fruit with firm rinds surrounding light green, orange, red, or yellow, succulent flesh and seeds. Muskmelons have thin, textured skins and generally are small; watermelons are thick skinned, solid green or striped, seedless or seed bearing, to 30 lbs. (11 kg) or more. Choose disease-resistant cultivars by letter codes: fusarium wilt (F) and powdery mildew (PM). True cantaloupes are a related species grown mostly in Europe and seldom seen in North American gardens.

Yield: Allow 2–3 plants per household member, pinching back flowers to permit only 4 fruits to form per vine.

Planting: In all climates, sow seed in full sun when soil warms to 60–90°F (16–32°C). Sow 4–6 seeds, 1 in. (25 mm) deep, 1 ft. (30 cm) apart, thinning to 2 plants per drill, in rows 6–8 ft. (1.8–2.4 m) apart, or in mounds 2–3 ft. (60–90 cm) tall, 2 ft. (60 cm) wide, spaced 6–8 ft. (1.8–2.4 m) apart, installing sturdy tripod supports at time of planting.

Growing Temperature: 70–90°F (21–32°C). Requires sustained temperatures over 80°F (27°C) to set flowers and develop fruit; flowers may drop if temperatures during bloom exceed 90°F (32°C).

Soil: Moist, well-drained soil. Fertility: Rich. 6.0–6.8 pH. Prepare soil at least 2 ft. (60 cm) deep.

Care: Challenging. Keep evenly moist; avoid wetting foliage. Fertilize at planting with 5–10–10 formula, monthly thereafter with 10–10–10 formula. Cultivate. Keep heavy fruits from direct soil contact with supports, or place melons on boards. Powdery mildew, fusarium wilt susceptible.

Companion Plants: Corn, nasturtium, and radish.

Maturity/Harvest: 70–100 days. Pick melons when stems have turned brown, fruits are easily detached from vine, and stem holds emit a strong, sweet aroma. Limit water for 5–7 days before harvest to concentrate sugars.

Storage/Tips: Fresh in refrigerator for 1 week; preserved as canned chutneys and sweet rind pickles, 1 year; processed and frozen as sorbet, 2 months.

Melons, Winter: Warm season. Winter melons—late-ripening casabas, charentals, crenshaws, honeydews, and Persians—are vining plants, to 25 ft. (7.5 m) long, bearing a variety of melon sizes, shapes, flavors, and colors in late autumn or early winter.

Yield: Allow 2–3 plants per household member, pinching back flowers to permit only 4 fruits to form per vine.

Planting: In average climates, sow seed when soil warms to 50°F (10°C); in subtropical climates, in winter for early summer harvest. Sow 4–6 seeds, 1 in. (25 mm) deep, 1 ft. (30 cm) apart, thinning to 2 plants per drill, in mounds 2–3 ft. (60–90 cm) tall, 2 ft. (60 cm) wide, and 4–6 ft. (1.2–1.8 m) apart, installing sturdy tripod supports at time of planting.

Growing Temperature: 45–95°F (7–35°C). Requires sustained temperatures over 80°F (27°C) to set flowers and develop fruit; flowers may drop if temperatures during bloom exceed 90°F (32°C). Place fruit on aluminum reflectors in cool climates.

Soil: Moist, well-drained soil. Fertility: Rich. 6.0–6.8 pH. Prepare soil at least 2 ft. (60 cm) deep.

Care: Challenging. Keep evenly moist; avoid wetting foliage. Fertilize at planting with 5–10–10 formula, monthly thereafter with 10–10–10 formula. Cultivate. Keep heavy fruits from direct soil contact with supports, or place melons on boards. Powdery mildew, fusarium wilt susceptible.

Companion Plants: Beans, corn, nasturtium, and radish.

Maturity/Harvest: 110 days. Pick melons when stems have turned brown, fruits are easily detached from vine, and stem holds emit a strong, sweet aroma. Harvest promptly; leaving melons on vine after maturity causes mushy, seedy texture.

Storage/Tips: Fresh in refrigerator for 1 week; processed and frozen as sorbet, 2 months. Cut cubes, freeze layered flat in sealed plastic bags, mix with berries or other fruit, add sugar to taste, blend, and strain to make low-calorie fruit smoothies.

Okra: Warm season. Bushy plants, 4–7 ft. (1.2–2.2 m) tall, with narrow, toothed, textured leaves, bear deep green, red, juicy seedpods on upright stalks growing from leaf nodes. Common cultivars usually have sharp spines, though some hybrid okra are spineless; wear gloves when caring for plants.

Yield: Allow 6 plants per household member.

Planting: In average climates, sow seed in full sun in spring when soil warms to 65–95°F (18–35°C), repeating in summer; in short-season climates, sow seed indoors 4–6 weeks before soil warms and harden seedlings 5–8 days before transplanting. Sow seed ½ in. (12 mm) deep, 6 in. (15 cm) apart, thinning to 12–20 in. (30–50 cm) apart, in rows 30–48 in. (75–120 cm) apart.

Growing Temperature: 65–95°F (18–35°C). Requires sustained temperatures over 85°F (29°C) to flower and set fruit; plant northern cultivars in cooler climates.

Soil: Moist, well-drained soil. Fertility: Rich. 6.0–6.8 pH. Prepare soil at least 2 ft. (60 cm) deep.

Care: Moderate. Keep evenly moist. Fertilize monthly with 5–10–10 formula. Cultivate. Pest and disease resistant.

Companion Plants: Melons, southern peas, and peppers.

Maturity/Harvest: 55–65 days. Cut pods at stem when 3–5 in. (75–125 mm) long; harvest on alternating days to extend development of new flowers and seedpods. Wear gloves when harvesting to prevent potential skin irritation; sap permanently stains clothing and utensils.

Storage/Tips: Use immediately; avoid storage. Okra is a principal ingredient of gumbo; use it as well to thicken and give body to soups and stews, bread and deep fry it, or stir-fry with other vegetables in Asian dishes.

Onion: Cool-season bulb. The sturdy green foliage and swollen roots of onions, with papery tunicates covering their many concentric layers of crisp, juicy, distinctively pungent flesh, make onion and its close relatives—chives, garlic, leeks, and shallots—popular garden vegetables to sow from seed, set out as seedlings, or plant as sets—immature bulbs available in spring. Onions are harvested and eaten both when young and green as scallions and at maturity as easily stored brown, red, or white bulbs. An onion-family vegetable.

Yield: Allow 20–30 plants per household member.

Planting: In cold-winter climates, sow seed indoors 4–6 weeks before soil warms to 35–90°F (2–32°C) and harden seedlings 5–7 days before transplanting; in mild-winter climates, set out seedlings or sets in full sun in late autumn. Sow seed ½ in. (12 mm) deep, ½ in. (12 mm) apart, thinning to 4 in. (10 cm) apart, in rows 18–25 in. (45–63 cm) apart, or broadcast over an area and thin to 4 in. (10 cm) apart.

Growing Temperature: 45–85°F (7–29°C).

Soil: Moist, well-drained sandy soil. Fertility: Rich. 6–6.8 pH. Prepare soil at least 1 ft. (30 cm) deep. Rotate plantings with other vegetables to prevent accumulation of pest and disease organisms in soil.

Care: Easy. Keep evenly moist. Fertilize monthly during active growth with 5–10–10 formula. Mulch deeply to protect from frost. Cultivate. Lodge foliage when seed heads form and flowers open; for bunching cultivars, trim off flowers and withered stalks. Borer, thrip and nematode susceptible.

Companion Plants: Beets, lettuce, summer savory, strawberries, and tomatoes.

Maturity/Harvest: 80–150 days. Pull green onion bulbs while less than ½ in. (12 mm) wide; harvest bunching cultivars when bulbs are 1–2 in. (25–50 mm) wide, thinning from the outside of the bunch; pull drying onion bulbs when 3–5 in. (75–125 mm) wide and tops wither. Harvest promptly; leaving onions in ground causes mushy texture, bulb division.

Storage/Tips: *Green and Bunching:* Fresh in vegetable keeper of refrigerator for 2–3 weeks; chopped and frozen, 6–8 months. *Drying:* Cut 1½ in. (38 mm) above the bulb or braided into strands, cured 10–20 days in a shady, warm, dry spot, and stored in a porous fabric bag in a cool, dry place, 4–6 months; chopped, dried in a vegetable dehydrator, and sealed in airtight plastic containers, 1 year; chopped and frozen, 6–8 months.

Parsnip: Cool-season biennial. Grown for their cream to rusty tan, carrot-shaped roots, 4–9 in. (10–23 cm) long and 2 in. (50 mm) wide, parsnips are the hardiest of root crops; they can be left in the ground all winter if mulched. Cool weather prior to harvest concentrates their sugars.
Yield: Allow 10 plants per household member.
Planting: In average climates, sow seed in full sun in late spring when soil warms to 40–75°F (4–24°C); in mild-winter climates, in early summer–late autumn. Sow seed ½ in. (12 mm) deep, 1 in. (25 mm) apart, thinning to 3–4 in. (75–100 mm) apart, in rows 2 ft. (60 cm) apart, or broadcast over an area and thin to 4 in. (10 cm) apart.
Growing Temperature: 45–75°F (7–24°C). Tolerates hard freezes when protected under a thick layer of mulch.
Soil: Moist, well-drained, sandy soil. Fertility: Rich. 6.0–6.8 pH. Prepare soil at least 18 in. (45 cm) deep.
Care: Easy. Keep evenly moist. Fertilize monthly with 10–10–10 formula. In cold-winter climates before the first hard freeze, mulch with 6–10 in. (15–25 cm) of straw covered with 4–6 in. (10–15 cm) of soil; in mild climates, apply mulch when temperatures exceed 80°F (27°C). Cultivate. Pest and disease resistant.
Companion Plants: Beets, carrots, rutabagas, and other root vegetables.
Maturity/Harvest: 100–130 days. Harvest roots when desired size, digging carefully with a garden fork; best after frost. Mulch heavily for in-ground storage in winter; in mild-winter climates, complete harvest before temperatures warm in spring. Leaving parsnips in ground when weather warms causes woody, fibrous texture.
Storage/Tips: Fresh in vegetable keeper of refrigerator for 2–4 months. In all climates, store parsnips in ground throughout winter until ready for use. Roots can be steamed, mashed, or grilled as one would carrots as a side dish; diced and chopped for stews and soups.

Peanuts: Warm season. Bunching or spreading tropical legumes, to 20 in. (50 cm) tall, with potato-like, alternating leaves but related to peas, bear yellow, pealike flowers followed by a stalklike peg that grows downward into the soil, forming 2–6 seeded pods, 1–2 in. (25–50 mm) beneath the soil. Spanish peanuts bear 2 nuts per pod; Virginia cultivars, 2–6 nuts.
Yield: Allow 10–12 plants per household member, yielding 2–3 lbs. (0.75–1.1 kg) of nuts.
Planting: In average climates, sow nuts indoors at time of last expected frost and harden seedlings 7–10 days before transplanting; in mild-winter climates, in full sun in spring when soil warms to 65–85°F (18–29°C). Sow shelled nuts 1½ in. (38 mm) deep, 6–8 in. (15–20 cm) apart, in rows 3 ft. (90 cm) apart. Plant successions every 3 weeks.
Growing Temperature: 65–90°F (18–32°C). Requires sustained temperatures over 85°F (29°C) to set flowers, develop, and ripen peanuts.
Soil: Moist, well-drained, sandy loam. Fertility: Rich. 5.8–6.2 pH. Prepare soil at least 2 ft. (60 cm) deep. Rotate plantings with cole-family vegetables in alternating years.
Care: Challenging. Keep evenly moist; allow soil surface to dry between waterings and avoid wetting foliage. Withhold water when plants flower. Cultivate when plants flower, working sand mixed with gypsum into the soil surface at least 8 in. (20 cm) deep.
Companion Plants: Beets, bush peas, and potatoes.
Maturity/Harvest: 110–150 days. Harvest when leaves yellow and wither, loosening soil with a garden fork and gently pulling entire plants. Shake off clinging soil, hang plants to cure in a protected, dry, warm spot for 2–3 weeks, then remove the nuts.
Storage/Tips: Raw in shells, in porous fabric bags stored in a dry, dark spot, for up to 3 months; roasted, in an airtight container or frozen, 1 year. Make peanut butter by blending whole nuts in a household blender or food processor. Children love the unusual growing habits of peanuts.

Peas, Garden; English; or Snap: Cool season. Vining and bush-forming plants, 2–6 ft. (60–180 cm) tall, bear canoe-shaped green pods, to 5 in. (13 cm) long, with 4–10 succulent green peas. Cultivars include super-sweet and traditional English pea.

Yield: Allow 30 plants per household member.

Planting: In average climates, in full sun in early spring–midsummer when soil warms to 40–70°F (4–21°C); in mild-winter climates, in autumn, after heat has broken and 3–4 months of warm weater remains. *Bush:* Sow 2 seeds, 2 in. (50 mm) deep, 2–3 in. (50–75 mm) apart, in an alterating diagonal pattern, thinning to 4 in. (10 cm) apart, in rows 3–4 ft. (90–120 cm) apart, installing support stakes and strings 2 ft. (60 cm) tall, 1 ft. (30 cm) apart, at time of planting. *Pole:* Sow 1 seed, 2 in. (50 mm) deep, 2 in. (50 mm) apart, in a circle 16–20 in. (40–50 cm) in diameter planted around a pole, thinning to 8 plants. Plant successions every 2–3 weeks.

Growing Temperature: 50–75°F (10–24°C). Best in spring before soil warms to 80°F (27°C) and in autumn. Shade plants at temperatures over 80°F (27°C).

Soil: Moist, well-drained soil. Fertility: Rich. 5.5–6.8 pH. Prepare soil at least 18 in. (45 cm) deep. Rotate plantings with cole-family vegetables in alternating years.

Care: Easy. Keep evenly moist; avoid wetting foliage and withhold water when flowers appear. Fertilize only at planting with 5–10–10 formula. Mulch. Cultivate. Aphid and powdery mildew susceptible.

Companion Plants: Beans, carrots, corn, cucumbers, radishes, and turnips.

Maturity/Harvest: 55–70 days. Pick when pods bulge and before they develop a waxlike coating; reserve any withered or yellowed pods for drying or use as seed stock; for pods used in stir-fried dishes or raw in salads, select stringless cultivars and pick when 1–2 in. (25–50 mm) long, or plant super-sweet cultivars [see Peas, Sugar or Snow, pg. 106]. Harvest frequently to extend development of new flowers and pods. Chill in ice water and shell soon after harvest for sweetest texture and flavor.

Storage/Tips: Fresh in pod in vegetable keeper of refrigerator for 1–3 weeks; shelled, 1 week; blanched, chilled, and frozen, 4–6 months; dried and stored in porous fabric bags, 1 year. Dry shelled peas on waterproof cloth in a warm, protected spot.

Peas, Southern; Cowpeas; Crowder; or Black-Eyed Peas: Warm season. Several beanlike, vining or bushy legumes, with vinelike stems to 12 ft. (3.7 m) long, bearing cream, green, or pink seedpods resembling snap beans, with 8–20 usually beige, pealike seeds, each marked with a black notch. Substitute green southern peas for snap beans.

Yield: Allow 30 plants per household member.

Planting: In average climates, sow seed indoors at time of last expected frost and harden seedlings 7–10 days before transplanting; in mild-winter climates, in full sun in spring when soil warms to 60–70°F (16–21°C). Sow seed 1 in. (25 mm) deep, 2 in. (50 mm) apart, thinning to 4 in. (10 cm) apart, in rows 6–8 in. (15–20 cm) tall and wide, 3 ft. (90 cm) apart, installing stakes and string or wire supports at time of planting. Plant successions every 4 weeks.

Growing Temperature: 70–95°F (21–35°C). Requires sustained temperatures over 85°F (29°C) to set flowers and develop pods. Protect plants from temperatures below 40°F (4°C).

Soil: Moist, well-drained, sandy soil. Fertility: Rich. 6.0–6.5 pH. Prepare soil at least 18 in. (45 cm) deep.

Care: Easy. Keep evenly moist; avoid wetting foliage. Fertilize at planting and when flowers appear with 5–10–10 formula. Cultivate. Aphid and powdery mildew susceptible.

Companion Plants: Beans, carrots, corn, cucumbers, radishes, and turnips.

Maturity/Harvest: 60–70 days. Pick pods when 4–5 in. (10–13 cm) long and beginning to swell for use fresh as shucked peas or as for snap beans. Harvest when pods on the vine have dried completely but still remain closed. Dry shelled peas on a waterproof cloth in a sunny, warm, protected spot.

Storage/Tips: Fresh in vegetable keeper of refrigerator for 1–3 weeks; blanched, chilled, and frozen, 6 months; dried and stored in porous fabric bags, 1 year.

Peas, Sugar or Snow: Cool season. Vining and bushy plants, 2–6 ft. (60–180 cm) tall, bear flat green pods, to 3 in. (75 mm) long, with 4–10 tiny, immature, green peas. Cultivars of garden peas genetically selected for tender sweetness and eaten whole before seed begin to swell in their pods. A principal ingredient in many Asian stir-fried dishes and popular salad vegetable.

Yield: Allow 30 plants per household member.

Planting: In average climates, in full sun in early spring–summer when soil warms to 40–70°F (4–21°C); in mild-winter climates, in autumn, after heat has broken and 3–4 months of warm weater remains. Sow 2 seeds, 2 in. (50 mm) deep, 2–3 in. (50–75 mm) apart, in an alternating diagonal pattern, thinning to 4 in. (10 cm) apart, in rows 3–4 ft. (90–120 cm) apart, installing support stakes and strings 2 ft. (60 cm) tall, 1 ft. (30 cm) apart, at time of planting. Plant successions every 2–3 weeks.

Growing Temperature: 50–75°F (10–24°C). Best in spring before soil warms to 80°F (27°C) and in autumn. Shade plants at temperatures over 80°F (27°C).

Soil: Moist, well-drained soil. Fertility: Rich. 5.5–6.8 pH. Prepare soil at least 18 in. (45 cm) deep. Rotate plantings with cole-family vegetables in alternating years.

Care: Easy. Keep evenly moist; avoid wetting foliage and withhold water when flowers appear. Fertilize only at planting with 5–10–10 formula. Mulch. Cultivate. Aphid and powdery mildew susceptible.

Companion Plants: Beans, carrots, corn, cucumbers, radishes, and turnips.

Maturity/Harvest: 55–70 days. Pick pods when 1½–2½ in. (38–63 mm) long and peas are visible within the pods. Harvest frequently to extend development of new flowers and pods.

Storage/Tips: Fresh in vegetable keeper of refrigerator for 1–2 weeks; blanched, chilled, and frozen, 3 months.

Peppers, Hot or Chili: Warm season. Bushy, upright plants, to 3 ft. (90 cm) tall, bearing oval leaves and gold, green, red, yellow peppers, 1–7 in. (25–178 mm) long, ranging from mild to fiery hot depending on their capsaicin content. Hot peppers vary depending on their care, even those from the same plant and from hour to hour.

Yield: Plants per household member depend on cultivar. Read care tag or seed package data carefully when estimating yield.

Planting: In average climates, sow seed indoors, 5–8 in. (13–20 cm) apart in a planting tray 4–6 in. (10–15 cm) deep filled with loose potting soil, 6–8 weeks before soil is expected to warm to 65–90°F (18–32°C) and harden seedlings 5–7 days before transplanting; in mild-winter climates, in full sun in spring. Sow 2 seeds, ½ in. (12 mm) deep, 18–24 in. (45–60 cm) apart, thinning to 1 plant per drill, in rows 28–36 in. (70–90 cm) apart. Plant successions every 3–4 weeks.

Growing Temperature: 70–95°F (21–35°C). Flowers may fail to set fruit at temperatures over 105°F (41°C); shade plants in full sunlight.

Soil: Moist, well-drained, sandy loam. Fertility: Rich. 5.5–6.8 pH. Prepare soil at least 30 in. (75 cm) deep. Avoid planting in sites previously used to grow eggplants, peppers, or tomatoes to prevent accumulation of disease organisms in soil.

Warning

Pods and seed of hot peppers contain a powerful eye and skin irritant. Always wear gloves when caring for or harvesting peppers.

Care: Moderate. Keep evenly moist; allow soil surface to dry between waterings. Fertilize monthly with 5–10–10 formula. Mulch. Cultivate. Aphid, cutworm, pepper weevil, and whitefly susceptible.

Companion Plants: Beets, garlic, onions, and parsnips.

Maturity/Harvest: 60–95 days. Pick when full colored and desired size; chill after harvesting. Harvest frequently to extend development of new flowers and fruit. Water deeply 4–8 hours before harvest for mildest peppers; withhold watering 1–2 days to enhance piquant flavor.

Storage/Tips: Fresh in vegetable keeper of refrigerator for 1 week; roasted, peeled, and frozen, 6 months; dried, 1 year; processed as pickled peppers and canned, 2 years. Dry peppers by laying them out loosely in flats in the sun, using a vegetable dehydrator, or weaving and hanging as decorative strands. Peppers can be ground into powder in a food mill for use as seasoning.

Peppers, Sweet: Warm season. Bushy, compact plants, 18–24 in. (45–60 cm) tall, bearing oval leaves and gold, green, orange, purple, red, yellow peppers of many forms: banana, bell, oval, round, and tear shaped. Some sweet pepper cultivars are nearly as spicy as their near relatives, the hot peppers.

Yield: Allow 2–3 plants of each type per household member.

Planting: In average climates, sow seed indoors 6–8 weeks before soil is expected to warm to 65°F (18°C) and harden seedlings 5–7 days before transplanting; in mild-winter climates, in full sun in late spring when soil warms to 65–90°F (18–32°C). Sow 3 seeds ¼–½ in. (6–12 mm) deep, 18–24 in. (45–60 cm) apart, thinning to 1 plant per drill, in rows 30–36 in. (75–90 cm) apart. Plant successions every 3 weeks.

Growing Temperature: 65–80°F (18–27°C). Flowers may drop at temperatures over 105°F (41°C); shade plants in full sunlight.

Soil: Moist, well-drained, sandy loam. Fertility: Rich. 5.5–6.8 pH. Prepare soil at least 30 in. (75 cm) deep. Avoid planting in sites previously used to grow eggplants, peppers, or tomatoes to prevent accumulation of disease organisms in soil.

Care: Moderate. Keep evenly moist; allow soil surface to dry between waterings. Fertilize monthly with 5–10–10 formula. Mulch. Cultivate soil 8–12 in. (20–30 cm) from the plants to avoid cutting shallow, widespread roots. Aphid, cutworm, pepper weevil, and whitefly susceptible.

Companion Plants: Beets, garlic, onions, parsnips, radishes.

Maturity/Harvest: 60–95 days. Pick when full colored and desired size; chill after harvesting. Best for pickling if harvested before seed matures. Water 4–8 hours before harvest for mildest peppers; withhold watering 1–2 days to enhance piquant flavor.

Storage/Tips: Fresh in vegetable keeper of refrigerator for 2–3 weeks; blanched and frozen, 4–6 months; dried, 1 year; processed as pickled peppers and canned, 2 years. Dry peppers by laying them out in loose flats in the sun, using a vegetable dehydrator, or weaving and hanging as decorative strands. Sweet peppers can be eaten raw, roasted, sautéed, or chopped for cooking in stir-fried dishes and casseroles; or pickled whole or in relishes. Sweet peppers are a principal ingredient of Mexican *chile rellenos*—roasted, peeled and seeded, stuffed with cheese, dipped into beaten egg whites and fried.

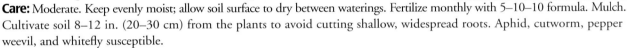

Potatoes: Cool-season perennial tuber. A close relative of tomatoes and peanuts with bushy, somewhat vining plants, to 2 ft. (60 cm) tall, bearing purple, white flowers and many oval, round, finger-shaped, or clustered, brown, purple, red, tan, or yellow tubers at their roots. Flavor and texture vary by cultivar, which is classified as early, midseason, or late season based on the length of time required for maturity. Choose disease-free or resistant cultivars known to be successful in your region.

Yield: Allow 4–5 plants per household member, yielding 20–50 potatoes.

Planting: *Early:* In average climates, sow in full sun in spring 4–6 weeks before last expected frost; in mild-summer climates, in late spring. *Midseason:* In spring when soil warms to 50–85°F (10–29°C). *Late:* In late spring. Cut seed potatoes into segments with at least 2 eyes, dust cut surfaces with garden lime, and plant 2–3 in. (50–75 mm) deep, 10–14 in. (25–35 cm) apart, in rows 30–36 in. (75–90 cm) apart. When sprouts emerge, add 2 in. (5 cm) of soil over the planting to prevent tubers from greening.

Growing Temperature: 45–80°F (7–27°C); needs vary by cultivar. Zones 2–10.

Soil: Damp, well-drained, sandy soil. Fertility: Rich. 4.8–5.4 pH. Prepare soil at least 2 ft. (60 cm) deep.

Care: Easy. Keep evenly damp; allow soil to dry between waterings. Withhold water 2 weeks before harvest. Fertilize only at planting with 5–10–10 formula. Mulch. Cultivate until flowers form. Borer, grub and fungal disease susceptible.

Companion Plants: Beans, cabbage, corn, eggplant, horseradish, and marigolds.

Maturity/Harvest: *Early:* 90–110 days. *Midseason:* 100–120 days. *Late:* 110–140 days. Harvest new potatoes when flowers begin to fade; mature potatoes, when foliage withers, digging carefully with a garden fork, 8–10 in. (20–25 cm) from stalk and working inward to the vine. Harvest promptly. Brush clinging soil from tubers.

Storage/Tips: Fresh, stored in a cool, dark, well-ventilated spot, for 6 months; avoid refrigeration. Use new potatoes immediately.

Pumpkins: Warm season. Vining plants, 5–20 ft. (1.5–6 m) long, bear large, gold, flute-shaped male and female flowers that set orange or white, round or oval, squashlike fruit with a thick, smooth rind scored with vertical grooves. Pumpkins range in size from tiny to huge, depending on cultivar. Grow them for their orange flesh, which can be baked or steamed, for seed to roast for eating, or as ornamental seasonal displays.

Yield: Allow 1–2 plants of each cultivar per household member.

Planting: In average climates in full sun in late spring when soil warms to 65–90°F (18–32°F); in hot, arid climates, in summer after heat has broken and 4 months of mild weather remain. Sow 5–6 seeds, 1 in. (25 mm) deep, 3–4 in. (75–100 mm) apart, thinning to 2–3 plants per mound, raised 6–10 in. (15–25 cm) high and 2 ft. (60 cm) wide, 6–8 ft. (1.8–2.4 m) apart, installing sturdy tripod supports at time of planting.

Growing Temperature: 50–90°F (10–32°C). Best in warm, dry climates.

Soil: Moist, well-drained soil. Fertility: Rich. 6.0–7.5 pH. Prepare soil at least 2 ft. (60 cm) deep.

Care: Easy. Keep evenly moist; avoid wetting foliage. Fertilize monthly with 5–10–10 formula until flowers form. For largest pumpkins, after 2–3 reach 2–3 in. (50–75 mm) wide, remove remaining female flowers with immature fruit beneath their blossoms and leave male, pollen-bearing flowers. Protect fruit from direct contact with soil. Aphid, cucumber beetle, vine borer, squash bug and fungal disease susceptible.

Companion Plants: Corn, squash, sunflowers.

Maturity/Harvest: 90–120 days. Cut pumpkins when full colored and desired size, rinds resist a fingernail's penetration, and the vines have withered; use sharp hand shears and leave 4 in. (10 cm) of stem on the fruit. Best flavor after first frost. Cure in garden after cutting for use as holiday decoration.

Storage/Tips: For best fresh storage, cure in garden in direct sun at 75–80°F (24–27°C) for 2 weeks after harvest. Stored in a cool, dry spot for 3 months; pureed and frozen, 6 months; cooked and canned, 1 year. Personalize children's pumpkins by scoring their soft, green rind before they reach full size; the scratches will harden into a white callus as they mature.

Radishes or Daikon: Cool season. Deeply toothed, rough-textured leaves rise from swollen, black, cream, purple, red, yellow, or multicolored roots with mostly white flesh and varying from carrotlike to globe shaped. Radishes range from zesty mild to very spicy, depending on cultivar. Table cultivars form seed when they mature, as do most annuals; Asian cultivars may overwinter and form seed the second season as biennials.

Yield: Allow 15–20 plants per household member.

Planting: In average climates, sow seed in full sun–partial shade in spring when soil warms to 45–85°F (7–29°C), or in autumn; in mild-winter climates, in late autumn–early winter. Sow 1 seed, ½ in. (12 mm) deep, 1 in. (25 mm) apart, thinning to 4 in. (10 cm) apart, in mounded rows raised 4–8 in. (10–20 cm) tall and 6 in. (15 cm) wide, 10–16 in. (25–40 cm) apart. Plant successions every 2 weeks.

Growing Temperature: 50–75°F (10–24°C). Zones 3–10. Shade plants in full sunlight at temperatures over 85°F (29°C).

Soil: Moist, well-drained, sandy loam. Fertility: Rich. 5.5–6.8 pH. Prepare soil at least 1 ft. (30 cm) deep. Rotate plantings to prevent accumulation of pest larvae in soil.

Care: Easy. Keep evenly moist; allow soil surface to dry between waterings. Fertilize only at time of planting with 5–10–10 formula or well-rotted manure. Root maggot susceptible.

Companion Plants: Cucumbers, lettuce, nasturtiums, peas, and peppers.

Maturity/Harvest: 22–70 days. Pull roots when full colored and 1 in. (25 mm) wide, rinsing and chilling after harvest; avoid removing tops. Harvest promptly; leaving radishes in ground past maturity causes hollowing, cracking, and pithy texture combined with a bitter flavor remniscent of earthy soil.

Storage/Tips: Fresh in vegetable keeper of refrigerator for 3–4 weeks. Use raw whole radishes as crudités, or slice them for use as a garnish in green salads; sliced fresh radishes also can be added to Asian stir-fried dishes.

Rhubarb: Cool-season perennial. Broad-leaved plants, to 3 ft. (90 cm) tall and wide, bear edible green, red, and red-tinged, fleshy stalks, 10–15 in. (25–38 cm) long. Rhubarb may require up to 4 years before it produces a full harvest. Often grown as a garden ornamental for its attractive foliage. Choose cultivars known to be successful in your region.

Yield: Allow 2–3 plants per household member, yielding 4–6 lbs. (1.8–2.7 kg) of rhubarb stalks.

Planting: In average climates, in full sun–partial shade in early spring when soil warms to 40–85°F (5–29°C); in mild-winter climates, in autumn after summer heat has broken and 3–4 months of mild weather remain. Set out root divisions 3–4 in. (75–100 mm) deep, 2–3 ft. (60–90 cm) apart, in mounded rows raised 6–8 in. (15–20 cm) tall and 18 in. (45 cm) wide, 4–6 ft. (1.2–1.8 m) apart.

Growing Temperature: 35–75°F (2–24°C). Best in mild, cool-summer climates. Shade plants in full sunlight at temperatures over 85°F (29°C).

Soil: Moist, well-drained loam. Fertility: Rich. 5.0–6.8 pH. Prepare soil at least 30 in. (75 cm) deep.

Care: Easy. Keep evenly moist. Fertilize at time of planting and after each harvest with 5–10–5 formula. Cultivate using care to avoid cutting the widespread, shallow roots. In cold-winter climates, cut remaining stems to the crown in autumn after frost, mulch with 1–2 ft. (30–60 cm) of straw, and cover with 1–2 in. (25–50 mm) of soil; uncover in spring when soil is workable. Replant with new stock or by dividing root crowns after 4 harvests. Pest and disease resistant.

Warning

Foliage of rhubarb is fatally toxic if ingested. Avoid planting in areas frequented by children and pets.

Companion Plants: Artichokes, asparagus, and cole vegetables.

Maturity/Harvest: Requires 2–4 years for first full harvest. Cut stalks when stems reach 2 ft. (60 cm) long, thinning outer stalks and leaving the central growth bud and 4–6 leaves to resprout. Cut and remove flower stalks as they appear.

Storage/Tips: Fresh in vegetable keeper of refrigerator for 2–4 weeks; cut, blanched, and frozen, 3–4 months; processed as sauce or pie fillings and frozen, 1 year; processed and canned, 3 years. Chop tart, stringy rhubarb stalks into pieces 1–2 in. (25–50 mm) long, cover with water, boil, and add sugar to taste to make tangy sauce for hotcakes, waffles, and ice cream.

Rutabagas or Swedish Turnips: Cool season. Smooth, waxy, oval leaves rise on long reddish stalks from swollen, red, white, and yellow, tough-skinned, globe-shaped roots, 3–5 lbs. (1.1–1.8 kg), Sweeter than turnips, a close relative; eat both the young leaves, as you would turnip greens, and the tasty, distinctively flavored roots.

Yield: Allow 4–8 plants per household member.

Planting: In average climates, sow seed in full sun in early summer when soil warms to 50–70°F (10–21°C); in mild-winter climates, in spring, then again in early autumn. Sow seed ½ in. (12 mm) deep, 4 in. (10 cm) apart, thinning to 10–16 in. (25–40 cm) apart, in rows 18–36 in. (45–90 cm) apart. Plant successions 3–4 weeks apart.

Growing Temperature: 40–75°F (4–24°C).

Soil: Moist, well-drained, sandy loam. Fertility: Rich. 5.5–6.8 pH. Prepare soil at least 2 ft. (60 cm) deep.

Care: Easy. Keep evenly moist; irregular watering may crack roots. Fertilize only at time of planting with 5–10–10 formula or well-rotted manure supplemented with gypsum. In cold-winter climates before the first hard freeze, mulch with 6–10 in. (15–25 cm) of straw covered with 4–6 in. (10–15 cm) of soil. Cultivate. Trim outermost foliage, and lodge plants when roots begin to swell. Pest and disease resistant.

Companion Plants: Beets, carrots, and turnips.

Maturity/Harvest: 85–100 days. Harvest when tops are 1 ft. (30 cm) tall and roots are 3–4 in. (75–100 mm) wide, digging carefully with a garden fork.

Storage/Tips: *Roots:* fresh, in ground at 24–80°F (- 4–27°C), for 4 months; in vegetable keeper of refrigerator, 2–4 months; diced, blanched, and frozen, 4–6 months. *Greens:* fresh in vegetable keeper of refrigerator for 5–7 days; steamed and frozen, 3–4 months.

Salsify: Cool-season biennial. Often termed "vegetable oyster" for its striking flavor, which depends on the root's age and growing conditions, salsify is narrow, long, and carrot-shaped. Young salsify is both tender and mild; with maturity, plants become strong flavored and stringy textured, with strap-shaped foliage, 2–4 ft. (60–120 cm) tall. Left to overwinter, it blooms with a ball-shaped, purple flower reminiscent of onion in its second season. Black salsify, a distant relative with black-skinned roots and white flesh, has similar culture, care, and uses.

Yield: Allow 10 plants per household member.

Planting: In average climates, sow seed in full sun in spring when soil warms to 40–60°F (4–16°C); in mild-winter climates, in early autumn. Sow seed ½ in. (12 mm) deep, ½ in. (12 mm) apart, thinning to 3–4 in. (75–100 mm) apart, in rows 20–30 in. (50–75 cm) apart. Plant successions every 3–4 weeks.

Growing Temperature: 45–85°F (7–29°C). Zones 3–10. If temperatures exceed 85°F (29°C) for extended periods, roots will develop slowly and plants may fail.

Soil: Moist, well-drained, sandy loam. Fertility: Rich. 6.0–6.8 pH. Prepare soil at least 2 ft. (60 cm) deep.

Care: Easy. Keep evenly moist. Fertilize only at time of planting with 5–10–5 formula. Mulch in hot-summer climates. Cultivate. Pest and disease resistant.

Companion Plants: Carrots, potatoes, rutabagas, sweet potatoes, and turnips.

Maturity/Harvest: 120–150 days. Harvest as needed when 6–12 in. (15–30 cm) long, digging carefully with a garden fork. In cold-winter climates before the first hard freeze, mulch with 1–2 ft. (30–60 cm) of straw and 1–2 in. (25–50 mm) of soil.

Storage/Tips: Fresh in ground for 3–4 months; in vegetable keeper of refrigerator, 3–4 weeks; diced, steamed, and frozen, 6 months. Substitute salsify for oyster whenever the shellfish's flavor is desired: eat raw slices as crudités; boiled and mashed on crackers as canapés; or battered with egg and cracker crumbs and fried in butter as mock oysters.

Shallots: Cool-season perennial. A close relative of onion with narrow, hollow leaves, to 2 ft. (60 cm) tall, and bunching habit with groups of pungent, swollen roots containing garliclike cloves, ¾–1½ in. (19–38 mm) wide, flavored between onion and garlic. Each clove is protected by a brown papery sheath. Shallots left in the ground from season to season eventually divide into multiple plants, called "shallot bunches."

Yield: Allow 4–6 plants per household member.

Planting: In average climates, plant starts in full sun–partial shade in spring when soil warms to 35–90°F (2–32°C); in mild-winter climates, in autumn when soil temperatures drop below 50°F (10°C) or in late winter. Plant individual cloves, broad end down, with ½ in. (12 mm) of soil to cover, 5–8 in. (13–20 cm) apart, in rows 2–4 ft. (60–120 cm) apart. Shallots require a 1-month dormant period after planting, with temperatures of 32–50°F (0–10°C).

Growing Temperature: 40–85°F (4–29°C). Zones 3–9. Best in cold-winter climates, requiring warmth to develop bulbs.

Soil: Moist, well-drained, sandy loam. Fertility: Rich. 5.0–6.8 pH. Avoid planting in sites previously used to grow garlic to prevent accumulation of pest organisms in soil.

Care: Easy. Keep evenly moist. Fertilize annually in spring with 5–10–10 formula. Mulch over bunches when sprouts emerge with organic compost in a layer 1–2 in. (25–50 mm) deep. Cultivate. Lodge stalks intended for harvest when 16–18 in. (40–45 cm) tall, 3–4 weeks before planned harvest date. Pest and disease susceptible; choose resistant cultivars.

Companion Plants: Beets, lettuce, strawberries, summer savory, and tomatoes.

Maturity/Harvest: 60–120 days. Harvest when tops wither, separating heads carefully from the bunch with a hand trowel or fork. Cure harvested bulbs for 2–3 weeks in a sunny, warm, dry area before use or storage.

Storage/Tips: Fresh, in a porous fabric bag in a dark, cool, dry spot, for 6 months; minced, packed into ice cube trays, frozen, and sealed in airtight containers, 1 year. Substitute shallots for onions in quiches, omelets, and delicately flavored dishes, or sauté with wine and butter to make sauces for red meat dishes. Chopped raw shallot greens can be used as a garnish, as for chives.

Spinach, Garden; Malabar; or New Zealand: Warm or cool season, depending on species: deep-green, cool-season annual; warm-season, bushy annual native to New Zealand; and warm-season, perennial vine native to India. Choose cultivars known to be successful in your region.

Yield: *New Zealand* and *Spinach:* Allow 15 plants per household member. *Malabar:* Allow 3 plants per household member.

Planting: *Spinach:* In average climates, sow seed in partial shade in spring when soil warms to 50–65°F (10–18°C); in mild-winter climates, in autumn. Sow seed ½ in. (12 mm) deep, 1 in. (25 mm) apart, thinning to 3–4 in. (75–100 mm) apart, in rows 1–2 ft. (30–60 cm) apart. Plant successions every 2–3 weeks. *New Zealand:* In average climates, sow seed in full sun in spring when soil warms to 60–85°F (16–29°C); in mild-winter climates, in autumn or early spring. Sow seed ½ in. (12 mm) deep, 1 in. (25 mm) apart, thinning to 3–4 in. (75–100 mm) apart, in rows 1–2 ft. (30–60 cm) apart. *Malabar:* In average climates, sow seed in full sun in spring when soil warms to 60–85°F (16–29°C); in mild-winter climates, in autumn or early spring. Soak seed before planting, then sow 2 seeds, ¾ in. (19 mm) deep, 4 in. (10 cm) apart, thinning to 1 ft. (30 cm) apart, in rows 3 ft. (90 cm) apart, installing trellises at time of planting.

Growing Temperature: *Spinach:* 60–70°F (16–21°C); bolts in temperatures over 75°F (24°C) and when daylight hours lengthen in summer. *New Zealand* and *Malabar:* 60–90°F (16–32°C).

Soil: Moist, well-drained, sandy soil. Fertility: Rich. 6.0–6.8 pH level. *Malabar:* ground hardy, zones 9–10. Prepare soil at least 1 ft. (30 cm) deep.

Care: Moderate–challenging. Keep evenly moist; avoid wetting foliage. Fertilize monthly with 10–5–5 formula. Cultivate. *Malabar:* pinch vine ends when 18–24 in. (45–60 cm) long to encourage branching, training vines on trellis supports. Disease resistant. Leaf miner susceptible.

Companion Plants: *Spinach:* Cole vegetables, lettuce. *New Zealand* and *Malabar:* husk tomatoes, strawberries.

Maturity/Harvest: *Spinach:* 40–50 days. Cut leaves when 4–7 in. (10–18 cm) long, thinning outer leaves and leaving the central growth bud to resprout; harvest heads by cutting the stem 3 in. (75 mm) above the soil, leaving the central growth bud to sprout additional leaves. Harvest promptly; leaves left on plants have gritty texture due to silica crystals in mature cell walls. *New Zealand* and *Malabar:* 50–75 days. Cut leaves when 3–5 in. (75–125 mm) long, every 5–7 days, until the first frost.

Storage/Tips: Fresh in vegetable keeper of refrigerator for 10–14 days; blanched, chilled, and frozen, 4–6 months.

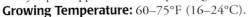

Squash, Summer: Warm season. Summer squash—crookneck, scallop, straightneck, and zucchini—are vining plants with large, hairy leaves bearing many black, orange, yellow, and multicolored, round, oval, gourdlike, tubular, scallop-edged, or crookneck-shaped squash.

Yield: Allow 1–2 plants of each cultivar per household member.

Planting: In average climates, in full sun in spring when soil warms to 60–85°F (16–29°C); in mild-winter climates, in late summer. Sow 4–5 seeds, 2–3 in. (50–75 mm) deep, 3–4 in. (75–100 mm) apart, thinning to 2 plants per drill, in hills raised 1 ft. (30 cm) high and 2 ft. (60 cm) wide, 6–8 ft. (1.8–2.4 m) apart, or in rows 3–5 ft. (90–150 cm) apart, installing sturdy tripod supports at time of planting.

Growing Temperature: 60–75°F (16–24°C).

Soil: Moist, well-drained soil. Fertility: Rich. 5.5–6.8 pH. Prepare soil at least 30 in. (75 cm) deep.

Care: Easy. Keep evenly moist; avoid wetting foliage or fruit. Fertilize monthly with 5–10–10 formula. Cultivate. Keep heavy fruits from direct soil contact by placing squash on boards. Aphid, vine borer, squash bug and fungal disease susceptible.

Companion Plants: Beans, nasturtiums, and bush peas.

Maturity/Harvest: 50–65 days. Cut squash when the rind is tender and before seeds mature.

Storage/Tips: Fresh in vegetable compartment of refrigerator for 2–3 weeks; cooked and frozen, 6–8 months. Eat summer squash whole or sliced: steamed, boiled, broiled, or buttered, wrapped in foil, and grilled or baked. Squash blossoms, dipped in batter and fried until golden and crunchy, are a delicacy and a sure means of limiting squash production.

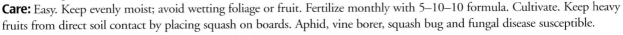

Squash, Winter: Warm season. Winter squash—acorn, banana, buttercup, Hubbard, spaghetti, and turban—are vining plants with large, hairy leaves bearing many black, orange, yellow, and multicolored, round, oval, club-shaped, or asymetrical squash with thick rinds and containing succulent flesh with varied textures and flavors, 4–30 in. (10–75 cm) long and wide.

Yield: Allow 1–2 plants of each cultivar per household member.

Planting: In average climates, in full sun in spring when soil warms to 65–85°F (18–29°C); in mild-winter climates, in spring and early autumn. Sow 4–5 seeds, 2–3 in. (50–75 mm) deep, 3–4 in. (75–100 mm) apart, thinning to 2 plants per drill, in hills raised 1 ft. (30 cm) high and 2 ft. (60 cm) wide, 6–8 ft. (1.8–2.4 m) apart, or in rows 3–6 ft. (90–180 cm) apart, installing sturdy tripod supports at time of planting.

Growing Temperature: 50–90°F (10–32°C). Flowers will drop at temperatures over 100°F (38°C).

Soil: Moist, well-drained soil. Fertility: Rich. 5.5–6.8 pH. Prepare soil at least 30 in. (75 cm) deep.

Care: Easy. Keep evenly moist; avoid wetting foliage or fruit. Fertilize monthly with 5–10–10 formula. Cultivate. Keep heavy fruits from direct soil contact by placing squash on boards. Aphid, vine borer, squash bug and fungal disease susceptible.

Companion Plants: Beans, nasturtiums, and bush peas.

Maturity/Harvest: 60–110 days. Cut when rinds are full colored—some acorn squash remain green, with semi-hard rinds—and stems become hard and dry, before frost; cut squash stems 2–4 in. (50–100 mm) from fruit with hand shears and wipe away any clinging soil. Avoid washing squash.

Storage/Tips: For best fresh storage, cure in garden in direct sun at 75–80°F (24–27°C) for 2 weeks after harvest. Fresh, stored in a cool, dry spot, for 3–4 months; cooked and frozen, 4–6 months; cooked and canned, 1 year. Exposure to frost concentrates sugars for better flavor and texture. Spaghetti squash, a novelty, is prepared by roasting whole, then splitting and scraping to yield spaghetti-like, stringy flesh for use in vegetarian dishes with cream sauces, butter, or olive oil.

Sunflowers: Warm season. An ornamental plant, usually 5–12 ft. (1.5–3.7 m) tall, though dwarf cultivars of small stature are available, bear broad, toothed leaves and golden yellow, many-rayed, composite flowers, 4–18 in. (10–45 cm) wide with a pithy, central bed containing up to several hundred tasty seed. Sunflowers attract pollinating bees to vegetable gardens.

Yield: Allow 2–4 plants per household member; large-flowered cultivars yield 1–2 lbs. (450–900 g) of dried seed per plant.

Planting: In all climates, in full sun in spring when soil warms to 65–85°F (18–29°C). Sow seed ½ in. (12 mm) deep, 8–12 in. (20–30 cm) apart, thinning to 18 in. (45 cm) apart, in rows 30–36 in. (75–90 cm) apart, or broadcast over an area and thin to 18 in. (45 cm) apart, installing stakes at time of planting in sites exposed to strong wind.

Growing Temperature: 60–105°F (16–41°C). Best in warm-summer climates.

Soil: Damp, well-drained soil. Fertility: Rich. 5.8–6.2 pH. Prepare soil at least 18 in. (45 cm) deep.

Care: Easy. Keep evenly damp; allow soil surface to dry between waterings. Fertilize monthly with acidic 5–10–10 formula or supplment with garden sulfur. Cultivate. Pest and disease resistant. Staggered rows of sunflowers provide shade, windbreaks for other plants.

Companion Plants: Beans, cucumbers, peas, Malabar spinach; use sunflowers as living stakes for pole and vining plants.

Maturity/Harvest: 70–80 days. Harvest heads when dry with hard seed loosely held in the mature flower head, cutting stalks 1 ft. (30 cm) below the flower and hanging heads upside down in a warm, dry spot for 4–6 weeks to completely dry the seed.

Storage/Tips: Remove seed from head. Fresh, stored a cool, dry spot, for 6 months; roasted, sealed in airtight bags, and frozen, 1 year. To roast seed, spread on a cookie sheet, bake at 250°F (120°C) for about 1 hour. Raw or roasted seed will also feed birds throughout the winter.

Sweet Potatoes or Yams: Warm-season tuber. Closely related to morning glory but unrelated to potato, tender tropical vining plants, to 3 ft. (90 cm) tall, bear pink and purple flowers with brown, red, or tan tubers reminiscent of elongated potatoes with firm gold or yellow flesh and sweet flavor.

Yield: Allow 5 plants per household member, yielding 20–25 sweet potatoes.

Planting: In average climates, sow tubers indoors in moist sand 6–8 weeks before soil is expected to warm to 60°F (16°C), maintaining a temperature of 80°F (27°C) for 3–4 weeks after planting, then reducing temperature to 70°F (21°C) when sprouts are 3–4 in. (75–100 mm) long, and hardening seedlings 10 days before transplanting; in mild-winter climates, in full sun in spring, when soil first warms to 60–70°F (16–21°C) and is less than 85°F (29°C). Set out seedlings 2–3 in. (50–75 mm) deep, 12–18 in. (30–45 cm) apart, in rows raised 1 ft. (30 cm) high and 18 in. (45 cm) wide, 3–4 ft. (90–120 cm) apart, installing lattice or trellises at time of planting.

Growing Temperature: 65–95°F (18–35°C). Very heat tolerant. Best in long-season, subtropical and arid climates.

Soil: Moist, well-drained, sandy soil. Fertility: Rich. 5.0–6.5 pH. Prepare soil at least 2 ft. (60 cm) deep.

Care: Moderate. Keep evenly moist. Fertilize monthly during growth with acidic 5–10–10 fertilizer or supplement with garden sulfur. Cultivate. Avoid pruning or pinching vines. Train vines onto lattice or trellises. Disease resistant. Nematode susceptible.

Companion Plants: Beets, parsnips, salsify, Malabar and New Zealand spinach, and turnips.

Maturity/Harvest: 110–150 days. Harvest after 4 months, when test digging reveals fully developed potatoes, carefully digging with a garden fork, 8–10 in. (20–25 cm) from the stem, then gently pulling potatoes from central growth bud. Harvest promptly whenever vines wither or turn yellow, or upon frost.

Storage/Tips: For best fresh storage, cure in garden in direct sun for 3–4 hours, then place in a humid spot at 80–85°F (27–29°C) for 10–15 days after harvest. Fresh, stored in a dry, cool spot, 2–5 months. Eat sweet potatoes and yams baked, boiled, steamed, or mashed; they are rich in vitamin A and C.

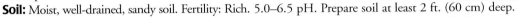

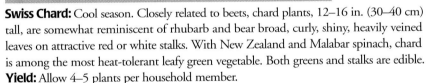

Swiss Chard: Cool season. Closely related to beets, chard plants, 12–16 in. (30–40 cm) tall, are somewhat reminiscent of rhubarb and bear broad, curly, shiny, heavily veined leaves on attractive red or white stalks. With New Zealand and Malabar spinach, chard is among the most heat-tolerant leafy green vegetable. Both greens and stalks are edible.

Yield: Allow 4–5 plants per household member.

Planting: In average climates, sow seed in full sun when soil warms to 50–85°F (10–29°C); in mild-winter climates, in autumn or late winter. Sow seed ½ in. (12 mm) deep, 1–2 in. (25–50 mm) apart, thinning to 8–12 in. (20–30 cm) apart, in rows 15–25 in. (38–63 cm) apart. Plant successions every 2–3 weeks.

Growing Temperature: 40–80°F (4–27°C). Bolts in sustained temperatures over 80°F (27°C). Shade plants in full sunlight at temperatures over 85°F (29°C) to prevent bitter flavor in leaves.

Soil: Moist, well-drained, sandy loam. Fertility: Rich. 6.0–6.8 pH. Prepare soil at least 2 ft. (30 cm) deep.

Care: Easy. Keep evenly moist; avoid wetting foliage. Fertilize every 4–6 weeks with 10–5–5 formula. Cultivate. Lodge or pinch flower stalk if plants begin to bolt. Inspect frequently for foliage damage due to chewing and sap-sucking insect pests, root damage by boring pests.

Companion Plants: Chicory, garlic, leeks, mustard, onions.

Maturity/Harvest: 45–55 days. Harvest beginning when plants are 6 in. (15 cm) tall, thinning outer leaves and leaving the central growth bud to resprout. In row plantings, harvest down the row over successive days; the first plants will recover as you reach the end of the row.

Storage/Tips: Fresh in vegetable keeper of refrigerator for 2–3 weeks; blanched, chilled, and frozen, 6 months. Eat chard greens fresh or steamed as for collards, spinach, and other greens; use diced chard stems to thicken and color soups and stews.

Tomatoes, Cherry or Miniature: Warm season. Smallest of the tomatoes at ¾–1½ in. (19–38 mm) in diameter, a perfect snack and salad food. They ripen in hues of gold, red, yellow, and even zebra-stripe green.

Yield: Allow 1 plant of each cultivar per household member, mixing early and late cultivars.

Planting: Sow seed indoors 10–14 weeks before soil is expected to warm to 55°F (13°C) and harden seedlings 7–10 days before transplanting. Set out seedlings in full sun when soil warms to 55–85°F (13–29°C), or plant in late summer in hot climates, after heat has broken and 3 months of warm weather remains. Sow 2–3 seeds ½ in. (12 mm) deep, 18 in. (45 cm) apart, thinning to 3 ft. (90 cm) apart. Plant seedlings 3 ft. (90 cm) apart, in rows 35–45 in. (90–115 cm) apart. For staking cultivars, thin to 24 in. (60 cm) apart, in rows 35–45 in. (90–115 cm) apart, installing stakes or cages at time of planting.

Growing Temperature: 65–90°F (18–32°C). Flowers may fail to set fruit at temperatures over 85°F (29°C). Shade plants in full sunlight at temperatures over 90°F (32°C).

Soil: Moist, well-drained soil. Fertility: Rich. 5.5–6.8 pH. Prepare soil at least 3 ft. (90 cm) deep.

Care: Easy. Keep evenly moist; avoid wetting foliage, fruit, or vines. Fertilize monthly with 5–10–10 formula until fruit begins to set; avoid high-nitrogen fertilizers. Mulch. For container plantings, choose pots at least 2 ft. (60 cm) deep with ample drainage. Inspect frequently for foliage damage or droppings due to tomato hornworm, a large, green moth larva, and other pests.

Companion Plants: Asparagus, carrots, chives, marigolds, nasturtiums, onions, and parsley.

Maturity/Harvest: 50–90 days. Pick when full colored and desired size for eating; when green for pickling. Ripe tomatoes dimple when their skins are pressed by a fingernail. Support vines while gently removing fruit.

Storage/Tips: Fresh at 60–70°F (16–21°C), for 7–10 days; pickled, to 2 years. Grow tomatoes in containers indoors for year-round fruit; in winter use ultraviolet plant lights to supplement sunlight, an equivalent of at least 6 hours' sunlight per day.

Tomatoes, Cooking: Warm season. Usually oblong or pear shaped, with meatier flesh and sweeter flavor than eating varieties. Many cultivars are determinate, ripening together and providing ample quantities to can.

Yield: Allow 3–6 plants of each cultivar, yielding 8–10 qts. (7.6–9.5 l).

Planting: Sow seed indoors 10–14 weeks before the soil is expected to warm to 60°F (16°C) and harden seedlings 7–10 days before transplanting. Set out seedlings in full sun when soil warms to 60–85°F (16–29°C). Sow 2–3 seeds ½ in. (12 mm) deep, 14 in. (36 cm) apart, thinning to 42 in. (1.1 m) apart. Plant seedlings 42 in. (1.1 m) apart, in rows 40–50 in. (1–1.2 m) apart. For staking cultivars, thin to 24 in. (60 cm) apart, in rows 36–48 in. (90–120 cm) apart, installing stakes or cages at time of planting. Plant successions of determinate cultivars every 2–3 weeks.

Growing Temperature: 65–90°F (18–32°C). Protect plants from temperatures below 40°F (4°C) Flowers may fail to set fruit at temperatures over 85°F (29°C). Shade plants in full sunlight at temperatures over 90°F (32°C).

Soil: Moist, well-drained soil. Fertility: Rich. 5.5–6.8 pH. Prepare soil at least 3 ft. (90 cm) deep.

Care: Easy. Keep evenly moist; avoid wetting foliage, fruit, or vines. Fertilize monthly with 5–10–10 formula until fruit begins to set; avoid high-nitrogen fertilizers. Mulch. Inspect frequently for foliage damage or droppings due to tomato hornworm, a large, green moth larva, and other pests. Cooking cultivars are prone to blossom-end rot, a growth disorder; prevent it by planting resistant varietals or by watering regularly and dusting soil with crushed oyster shell, gypsum, and other high-calcium supplements.

Companion Plants: Asparagus, carrots, chives, marigolds, nasturtiums, onions, and parsley.

Maturity/Harvest: 50–90 days. *Determinate varieties:* pick when full colored. *Indeterminate varieties:* pick when full colored, firm, and fragrant. Ripe tomatoes dimple when their skins are pressed by a fingernail. Support vines while gently removing fruit.

Storage/Tips: Fresh at 60–70°F (16–21°C) for 7–10 days; cut, packaged, and frozen, 3–4 months; canned, to 2 years; dried, to 1 year. Avoid refrigerating fresh tomatoes. Dry sliced tomatoes on drying trays or in a vegetable dehydrator. Freeze or use overripe fruit immediately for cooking; avoid canning due to loss of natural acids that increases hazard of botulism.

Tomatoes, Slicing or Eating: Warm season. Largest, juiciest, and most flavorful, eating tomatoes come in both early and midseason varieties; those with longer maturities have best taste and texture. Tomatoes produce a bountiful series of harvests in long-season regions while requiring the entire season to ripen in frost areas.

Yield: Allow 1–2 plants of each cultivar per household member, mixing early and late cultivars. For juicing, allow 3–6 plants of each cultivar, yielding 5–8 qts. (4.7–7.6 l).

Planting: Sow seed indoors 10–14 weeks before soil is expected to warm to 55°F (13°C) and harden seedlings 7–10 days before transplanting. Set out seedlings in full sun when soil warms to 55–85°F (13–29°C), or plant in late summer in hot climates, after heat has broken and 3 months of warm weather remains. Sow 2–3 seeds ½ in. (12 mm) deep, 18 in. (45 cm) apart, thinning to 42 in. (1.1 m) apart. Plant seedlings 42 in. (1.1 m) apart, in rows 40–50 in. (1–1.2 m) apart. For staking cultivars, thin to 24 in. (60 cm) apart, in rows 36–48 in. (90–120 cm) apart, installing stakes or cages at time of planting.

Growing Temperature: 65–90°F (18–32°C). Flowers may fail to set fruit at temperatures over 85°F (29°C). Shade plants in full sunlight at temperatures over 90°F (32°C).

Soil: Moist, well-drained soil. Fertility: Rich. 5.5–6.8 pH. Prepare soil at least 3 ft. (90 cm) deep.

Care: Easy. Keep evenly moist; avoid wetting foliage, fruit, or vines. Fertilize monthly with 5–10–10 formula until fruit begins to set; avoid high-nitrogen fertilizers. Mulch. Inspect frequently for foliage damage or droppings due to tomato hornworm, a large, green moth larva, and other pests.

Companion Plants: Asparagus, carrots, chives, marigolds, onions, and parsley.

Maturity/Harvest: 50–90 days. Pick when full colored and desired size for eating; when green for frying, pickling. Ripe tomatoes dimple when their skins are pressed by a fingernail. Support vines while gently removing fruit.

Storage/Tips: Fresh at 60–70°F (16–21°C), for 7–10 days; juiced and frozen, to 6 months; pickled, to 2 years. The tomato of choice for sandwiches, salads, and pizza, or picked green and pickled, or breaded and fried.

Turnips: Cool season. Plants produce salad greens and edible, bulbous roots with white interiors and crisp texture. Most are globe- or oval-shaped. To grow turnips for greens, either harvest before roots form or choose greens-only cultivars.

Yield: Allow 5–10 plants per household member.

Planting: Sow seed in full sun–partial shade in late summer for early autumn harvest, zones 3–7; in early spring for summer harvest when soil warms to 40–75°F (4–24°C), then again in early autumn for late autumn harvest, zones 8–9; or in late autumn for winter harvest, zones 10–11. Sow seed ½ in. (12 mm) deep, 1 in. (25 mm) apart, thinning to 4–6 in. (10–15 cm) apart, in rows 15–36 in. (38–90 cm) apart. Plant successions every 3–4 weeks.

Growing Temperature: 40–75°F (4–24°C). If temperatures exceed 75°F (24°C) for extended periods, roots will develop slowly and plants may fail.

Soil: Moist, well-drained soil. Fertility: Rich. 5.5–6.8 pH. Prepare soil 1 ft. (30 cm) deep.

Care: Easy. Keep evenly moist; avoid wetting foliage, fruit, or vines. Fertilize monthly with 5–10–10 formula. Mulch to avoid sunburn. Cultivate. Pest and disease resistant

Companion Plants: Bush beans, peas, and southern peas.

Maturity/Harvest: 30–60 days. *Greens:* pick greens when 1 ft. (30 cm) long, thinning outer foliage and leaving the central growth bud to resprout. *Roots:* harvest roots when 2–3 in. (50–75 mm) wide, digging carefully with a garden fork. Harvest promptly; leaving turnips in ground past maturity causes woody texture.

Storage/Tips: Fresh in vegetable keeper of refrigerator, 7–10 days for greens and 2–3 months for roots; cooked and frozen, 6 months. Immature roots store indefinitely in the ground at soil temperatures of 35–80°F (2–27°C). Turnip greens are generally rare in produce markets and prized for their delicate flavor, delicious if eaten raw in salads, or steamed. The turnip bulb, with its unique, sweet flavor, may be eaten raw, baked, or boiled and mashed.

USDA Plant Hardiness Around the World
North America

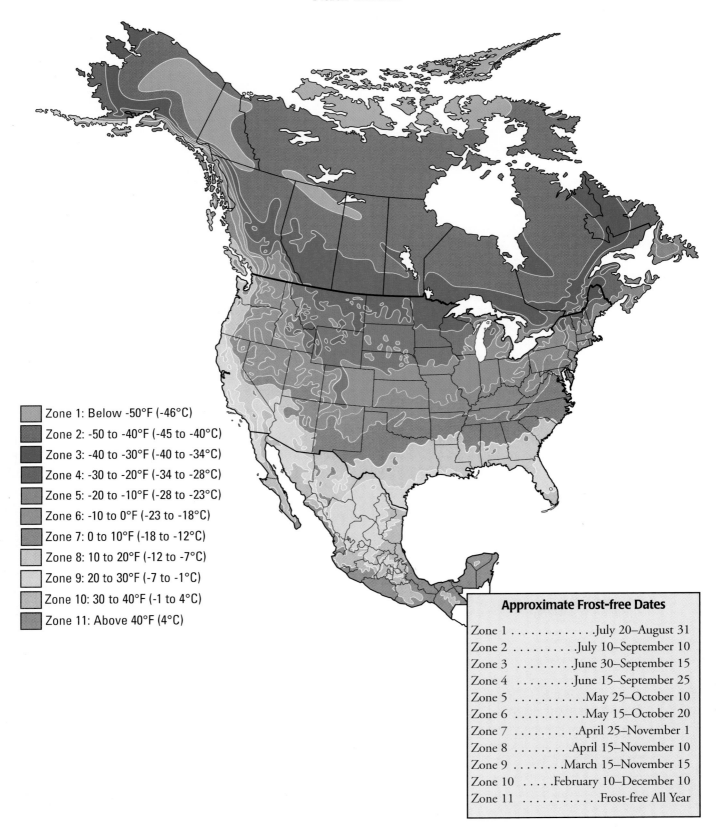

Zone 1: Below -50°F (-46°C)

Zone 2: -50 to -40°F (-45 to -40°C)

Zone 3: -40 to -30°F (-40 to -34°C)

Zone 4: -30 to -20°F (-34 to -28°C)

Zone 5: -20 to -10°F (-28 to -23°C)

Zone 6: -10 to 0°F (-23 to -18°C)

Zone 7: 0 to 10°F (-18 to -12°C)

Zone 8: 10 to 20°F (-12 to -7°C)

Zone 9: 20 to 30°F (-7 to -1°C)

Zone 10: 30 to 40°F (-1 to 4°C)

Zone 11: Above 40°F (4°C)

Approximate Frost-free Dates

Zone 1 . . . . .July 20–August 31

Zone 2 . . . . .July 10–September 10

Zone 3 . . . . .June 30–September 15

Zone 4 . . . . .June 15–September 25

Zone 5 . . . . .May 25–October 10

Zone 6 . . . . .May 15–October 20

Zone 7 . . . . .April 25–November 1

Zone 8 . . . . .April 15–November 10

Zone 9 . . . . . . .March 15–November 15

Zone 10 . . . . .February 10–December 10

Zone 11 . . . . .Frost-free All Year

USDA Plant Hardiness Around the World
Australia

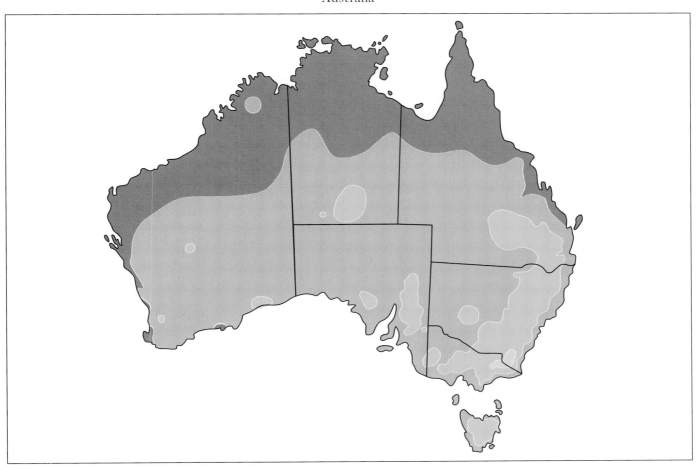

South Africa

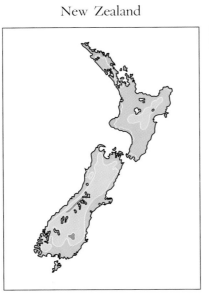

New Zealand

Europe

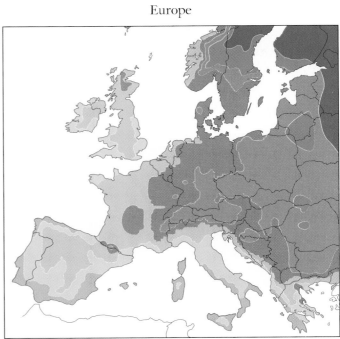

ON-LINE INDEX

(www.almanac.com/garden)
The Old Farmer's Almanac. Guidelines for planting, pruning.

(www.agr.ca/agriweb/ho.htm)
Agriculture Canada. Directory (French and English).

(www.backyardgardener.com)
Backyard Gardener. Seed germination database, forums.

(www.botany.com)
Botany.com. Easily searched plant encyclopedia.

(www.gardenguides.com)
Garden Guides. Vegetable and herb selection, links, forums.

(www.gardentimeonline.com/Vegetables)
Garden Time. Planting calendar, seed starting guide.

(www.gardenweb.com)
GardenWeb. Extensive forums, links, seed exhange.

(www.hgtv.com)
Home and Garden Television. Varied how-to gardening information and demonstration videos.

(horticulture.tamu.edu.7998/vegetable/)
Texas A&M University. Integrated Pest Management, pest photographs.

(www.mastercomposter.com)
Master Composter. Local, national, and international programs, products for composting, message board.

(www.reeusda.gov)
Cooperative State Research, Education, and Extension Services.

(www.usda.gov)
United States Department of Agriculture. Comprehensive agricultural statistics and resources.

(http://webgarden.osu.edu)
Ohio State University. Horticultural dictionary, plant directory.

INDEX

bacterial, 70
controlling, 57, 67, 70
fungal, 70
infected foliage disposal, 70
prevention of, 54, 58, 70
symptoms, causes, and cures, 71
viral, 70
Dominant bud, 64
Double digging, 24
Downy mildew, 70–71
Drainage, 21–22, 26–28, 58
Drip irrigation, 18, 34–35, 58–59
Drying, 76

E
Eggplants, 13, 32, 39, 42, 72, 74–76, 93
Endive, Belgian or French. See Chicory
Endive, curly, 13, 36, 42, 74, 93
Equipment, vegetable gardening, 18
Erosion, 58
Escarole, 93
Exposure, sun and wind, 11

F
False chamomile, 95
Fennel, 95
Fennel, Florence, 95
Fertility, garden soil, 21
Fertilizers, 18, 22, 24, 62, 71
application techniques, 62–63
bloodmeal, 62
fish emulsion, 62
foliar, 52, 62
guano, 62
liquid, 62
manure, 62
mineral phosphate, 62
organic, 62
selection, 25, 57
starter, 51
synthetic, 62
Freezing, preserving vegetables, 76–77
French endive, 91
French intensive gardening, 4
Frogs, 68
Frost, 11, 36, 39, 46, 48, 52, 74
Fungicides. See Chemicals, Garden
Furrows, watering, 31
Fusarium wilt, 70–71

G
Garlic, 64, 74–76, 94
Germination, 46, 48
Ginger, 95
Gourds, 12, 39, 54, 74, 76, 94
Grapes, 10
Gray mold. See Botrytis rot
Greenhouses, 36, 46
Grid diagrams. See Spacing, 13
Ground cherries, 97
Group planting, 12
Growing information, 40

Growth, controlling, 64–65
Gypsum, 24

H
Hardening, 39, 50
Hardiness zone maps, 11, 36, 116–117
Harvesting, 57, 73–75
Hazard Warnings,
hot peppers, 106
household bleach, 69
rhubarb, 109
Heat requirements, 42
Herbicides. See Chemicals, Garden
Herbs, 1–2, 95–96
Hills, 31, 34, 49
Horseradish, 74, 95
Horticultural oils, 68–69
Hot caps, 18, 46, 52
Hot peppers, 106
Husk tomatoes, 97
Hyssop, 95

I–J–K
Indeterminate plants, 74
Indoor planting, 46
Infected foliage, disposal of, 70
Information, resources, 19, 118
Insecticidal soap, 67
Insects, beneficial, 68
Integrated Pest Management, 68
Intensive gardening, 4, 12
IPM. See Integrated Pest Management
Iron phosphate, 69
Irrigation, 6, 11, 18, 31, 57, 59, 70
drip, 59
planning, 34
soaker hose, 59
systems for, 21, 35
timers, 34–35
Jerusalem artichokes, 97
Kale, 70, 98
Kelp extract, 57
Kohlrabi, 98

L
Landscape fabrics, 26–28
Lavender, 96
Leaf miners, 69
Leaf spot, 71
Leeks, 2, 39, 76, 99
Lemon balm, 96
Lemon verbena, 96
Lettuce, 2, 6, 12, 39, 42, 48, 58, 74, 76
bibb, 99
butterhead, 99
celtuce, 2, 100
cos, 101
crisphead, 100
iceberg, 100
Lettuce, asparagus. See Asparagus lettuce
looseleaf, 101
romaine, 101

Lime, garden, 24
Loam, composition of, 22
Lodging vegetables, 64, 74
Lovage, 96

M
Macronutrients, for vegetables, 22
Marigold, pot, 96
Marigolds, 3
Marjoram, 96
Materials, vegetable gardening, 18
Maturity intervals, vegetables, 43–45
Melons, 13, 32, 36, 39, 42, 54, 72, 76, 102
Microclimates, 9, 11
Micronutrients, 22, 57, 62
Milky spore, 69
Mint, 3, 96
Mirliton, 90
Mollusks, 66
Mosaic virus, 70–71
Mulch, 4, 18, 52–53, 62, 74
Mustard, 36, 39, 74

N–O
Nasturtium, 3
Nematodes, 69
Nitrate salts. See Fertilizer, 62
Nitrogen, 22, 62
Nutrient deficiencies, symptoms of, 62
Nutrients, 22, 24, 62
Oils, horticultural, 68
Okra, 12, 76, 103
Onion-family vegetables, 94, 99, 103, 110
Onions, 2, 13, 39, 42, 48, 58, 64, 74–76, 103
On-line resources, 118
Oregano, 2, 96
Organic gardening, 10, 68

P–Q
Pak choy, 87
Parasitic wasps, 69
Parsley, 2, 96
Parsnips, 42, 74, 104
Peanuts, 12, 104
Peas, 3, 12, 32, 39, 48, 74–77, 105–106
black-eyed, 105
English, 3, 76, 105
garden, 105
snap, 105
snow, 106
southern, 12, 42, 105
sugar, 106
sweet, 3
Peppers, 12–13, 36, 39, 42, 58, 74–76, 106–107
chili, 106
hot, 106
sweet, 107
Percolation, testing for, 22
Pesticides. See Chemicals, Garden
Pests, 12–13, 30, 60, 62, 68–69

I N D E X